Programming Logic and Design, Introductory,
Second Edition

Joyce Farrell

University of Wisconsin

Stevens Point

**COURSE
TECHNOLOGY**
—★—
™
THOMSON LEARNING

Australia • Canada • Mexico • Singapore • Spain • United Kingdom • United States

COURSE TECHNOLOGY
™
THOMSON LEARNING

Programming Logic and Design, Introductory, Second Edition
by Joyce Farrell

Product Manager: Tricia Coia	**Development Editor:** Lisa Ruffolo	**Cover Designer:** Betsy Young
Managing Editor: Jennifer Locke	**Editorial Assistant:** Janet Aras	**Compositor:** Gex Publishing Services
Senior Editor: Jennifer Muroff	**Production Editor:** Karen Jacot	**Manufacturing Coordinator:** Alexander Schall

BRIEF
Contents

PREFACE   ix

CHAPTER ONE
An Overview of Computers and Logic   1

CHAPTER TWO
Understanding Structure   29

CHAPTER THREE
Modules, Hierarchy Charts, and Documentation   61

CHAPTER FOUR
Writing a Complete Program   91

CHAPTER FIVE
Making Decisions   111

CHAPTER SIX
Looping   149

CHAPTER SEVEN
Control Breaks   177

CHAPTER EIGHT
Arrays   209

APPENDIX A   A-1

APPENDIX B   B-1

INDEX   I-1

TABLE OF
Contents

PREFACE   **ix**

CHAPTER ONE
An Overview of Computers and Logic   **1**

Understanding Computer Components and Operations   1
Understanding the Programming Process   5
    Understand the Problem   5
    Plan the Logic   6
    Code the Program   7
    Translate the Program into Machine Language   7
    Test the Program   8
    Put the Program into Production   9
Understanding the Data Hierarchy   9
Using Flowchart Symbols and Pseudocode Statements   11
Using and Naming Variables   15
Ending a Program by Using Sentinel Values   17
Using the Connector   19
Assigning Values to Variables   20
Understanding Data Types   22
Chapter Summary   23
Exercises   24

CHAPTER TWO
Understanding Structure   **29**

Understanding Unstructured Spaghetti Code   29
Understanding the Three Basic Structures   31
Using the Priming Read   38
Understanding the Reasons for Structure   42
Recognizing Structure   44
Two Special Structures—Case and Do Until   49
    The Case Structure   49
    The Do Until Loop   52
Chapter Summary   54
Exercises   55

CHAPTER THREE
Modules, Hierarchy Charts, and Documentation   61
Modules, Subroutines, Procedures, Functions, or Methods   61
    Modularization Provides Abstraction   62
    Modularization Allows Multiple Programmers to Work on a Problem   62
    Modularization Allows You to Reuse Your Work   63
    Modularization Makes It Easier to Identify Structures   63
Modularizing a Program   66
Modules Calling Other Modules   69
Declaring Variables   71
Creating Hierarchy Charts   73
Understanding Documentation   75
Output Documentation   75
Input Documentation   81
Completing the Documentation   85
Chapter Summary   86
Exercises   87

CHAPTER FOUR
Writing a Complete Program   91
Understanding the Mainline Logical Flow Through a Program   91
Housekeeping Tasks   94
    Declaring Variables   94
    Opening Files   99
    Printing Headings   100
    Reading the First Input Record   100
Writing the Main Loop   104
Performing End-Of-Job Tasks   107
Chapter Summary   107
Exercises   108

CHAPTER FIVE
Making Decisions   111
Evaluating Boolean Expressions to Make Comparisons   111
Using the Logical Comparison Operators   114
Understanding AND Logic   118
Writing AND Decisions for Efficiency   122
Combining Decisions in an AND Situation   124
Avoiding Common Errors in an AND Situation   125
Understanding OR Logic   127
Avoiding Common Errors in an OR Situation   129
Writing OR Decisions for Efficiency   130
Combining Decisions in an OR Situation   131
Using Selections within Ranges   132
Common Errors Using Range Checks   133
Using Decision Tables   135
Chapter Summary   142
Exercises   143

CHAPTER SIX
Looping   149
Using a While Loop with a Loop Control Variable   150
Using a Counter to Control Looping   152
Looping with a Variable Sentinel Value   156
Looping by Decrementing   158
Avoiding Common Loop Mistakes   159
Using the For Loop   161
Using the Do Until Loop   163
Recognizing the Characteristics Shared by All Loops   165
Nesting Loops   166
Using a Loop to Accumulate Totals   168
Chapter Summary   172
Exercises   173

CHAPTER SEVEN
Control Breaks   177
Understanding Control Break Logic   177
Performing Single-Level Control Breaks   178
Using Control Data Within the Control Break Module   184
Performing Control Breaks with Totals   189
Performing Multiple-Level Control Breaks   194
Performing Page Breaks   202
Chapter Summary   205
Exercises   206

CHAPTER EIGHT
Arrays   209
Understanding Arrays   209
How Arrays Occupy Computer Memory   210
Manipulating an Array to Replace Using Nested Decisions   211
Array Declaration and Initialization   221
Run-Time and Compile-Time Arrays   223
Loading an Array from a File   226
Searching for an Exact Match in an Array   228
Using Parallel Arrays   230
Remaining within Array Bounds   233
Improving Search Efficiency using an Early Exit   235
Searching an Array for a Range Match   237
Chapter Summary   240
Exercises   241

APPENDIX A   A-1

APPENDIX B   B-1

INDEX   I-1

Preface

Programming Logic and Design, Introductory, Second Edition, provides the beginning programmer with a guide to developing structured program logic. This textbook assumes that students have no programming language experience. The writing is nontechnical and emphasizes good programming practices. The examples are business examples; they do not assume mathematical background beyond high school business math. Additionally, the examples illustrate one or two major points; they do not contain so many features that students become lost following irrelevant and extraneous details.

The examples in *Programming Logic and Design*, Introductory, Second Edition, have been created to provide students with a sound background in logic no matter what programming languages they might eventually use to write programs. This book can be used in a standalone logic course that students take as a prerequisite to a programming course, or as a companion book to an introductory programming text using any programming language.

ORGANIZATION AND COVERAGE

Programming Logic and Design, Introductory, Second Edition, introduces students to programming concepts, enforcing good style and logical thinking. General programming concepts are introduced in Chapter 1. Chapter 2 discusses the key concepts of structure, including what structure is, how to recognize it, and, most importantly, the advantages to writing structured programs. Chapter 3 extends the information on structured programming to the area of modules. By Chapter 4 students can write complete, structured business programs. Chapters 5 and 6 explore the intricacies of decision making and looping. Students learn to develop sophisticated programs that use control breaks and arrays in Chapters 7 and 8.

Programming Logic and Design, Introductory, Second Edition, combines text explanation with flowcharts and pseudocode examples to provide students with alternative means of expressing structured logic. Numerous detailed, full-program exercises at the end of each section illustrate the concepts explained within the section, and reinforce students' understanding and retention of the material presented.

Programming Logic and Design, Introductory, Second Edition, distinguishes itself from other programming logic language books in the following ways:

- It is written and designed to be non-language specific. The logic used in this book can be applied to any programming language.

- The examples are everyday business examples; no special knowledge of mathematics, accounting, or other disciplines is assumed.

- The concept of structure is covered earlier than in many other texts. Students are exposed to structure naturally, so they will automatically create properly designed programs.

- Text explanation is interspersed with both flowcharts and pseudocode so students can become comfortable with both logic development tools and understand their interrelationship.

- Complex programs are built through the use of complete business examples. Students see how an application is built from start to finish instead of studying only segments of programs.

FEATURES

New to this edition of the text is the use of camel casing for naming variables and methods, and the addition of parentheses to method names. These improvements expose students to variable and method names that closely resemble those they will be most likely to use in introductory programming classes in C++, Java, Visual Basic, or Pascal. To improve students' comprehension of the decision-making process, endif has been added to the pseudocode in all decision examples. Additional end-of-chapter exercises are included so students have more opportunities to practice concepts as they learn them.

Programming Logic and Design is a superior textbook because it also includes the following features:

- **Objectives:** Each chapter begins with a list of objectives so the student knows the topics that will be presented in the chapter. In addition to providing a quick reference to topics covered, this feature provides a useful study aid.

- **Tips:** These notes provide additional information—for example, an alternative method of performing a procedure, another term for a concept, background information on a technique, or a common error to watch out for.

- **Summaries:** Following each section is a summary that recaps the programming concepts and techniques covered in the section. This feature provides a concise means for the student to recap and check understanding of each chapter's main points.

- **Exercises:** Each chapter section concludes with meaningful programming exercises that provide students with additional practice of the skills and concepts they learned in the lesson. These exercises increase in difficulty and are designed to allow students to explore logical programming concepts.

TEACHING TOOLS

The following supplemental materials are available when this book is used in a classroom setting. All of the teaching tools available with this book are provided to the instructor on a single CD-ROM.

Electronic Instructor's Manual. The Instructor's Manual that accompanies this textbook includes:

- Additional instructional material to assist in class preparation, including suggestions for lecture topics.
- Solutions to all end-of-chapter materials, including the Review Questions and Hands-on Projects.

ExamView®. This textbook is accompanied by ExamView, a powerful testing software package that allows instructors to create and administer printed, computer (LAN-based), and Internet exams. ExamView includes hundreds of questions that correspond to the topics covered in this text, enabling students to generate detailed study guides that include page references for further review. The computer-based and Internet testing components allow students to take exams at their computers, and also save the instructor time by grading each exam automatically.

PowerPoint Presentations. This book comes with Microsoft PowerPoint slides for each chapter. These are included as a teaching aid for classroom presentation, to make available to students on the network for chapter review, or to be printed for classroom distribution. Instructors can add their own slides for additional topics they introduce to the class.

Solution Files. Solutions to end-of-chapter review questions, exercises, and Hands-on Projects are provided on the Teaching Tools CD-ROM and may also be found on the Course Technology Web site at **www.course.com**. The solutions are password protected.

Distance Learning. Course Technology is proud to present online courses in WebCT and Blackboard, as well as at MyCourse.com, Course Technology's own course enhancement tool, to provide the most complete and dynamic learning experience possible. When you add online content to one of your courses, you're adding a lot: practice tests, topic reviews, projects, and, most of all, a gateway to the 21st century's most important information resource. We hope you will make the most of your course, both online and offline. For more information on how to bring distance learning to your course, contact your local Course Technology sales representative.

ACKNOWLEDGMENTS

I would like to thank all of the people who helped to make this book a reality, especially Lisa Ruffolo, Development Editor, whose hard work, attention to detail, and perceptive appreciation for the methodology required to teach this subject matter have made this a quality textbook. Thanks also to Kristen Duerr, Vice President and Publisher; Tricia Coia, Product Manager; Jennifer Locke, Managing Editor; Jennifer Muroff, Senior Editor; Margarita Donovan, Senior Product Manager; Karen Jacot, Production Editor; Janet Aras, Editorial Assistant; and Beverly Jackson, Quality Assurance Tester. I am grateful to be able to work with so many fine people who are dedicated to producing quality instructional materials.

I am grateful to the many reviewers who provided helpful and insightful comments during the development of this revision, including R. Scott Cost, University of Maryland at Catonsville; Bob Husson, Craven Community College; Cathleen Kennedy, College of San Mateo; Marilyn D. Moore, Morehead State University; George Novotny, Ferris State University; Steve Prettyman, Chattahoochee Technical Institute; and Pamela Silvers, Asheville-Buncombe Technical Community College.

Thanks, too, to my husband, Geoff, who acts as friend and advisor in the book writing process. This book, as was its previous edition, is dedicated to him and to my daughters, Andrea and Audrey.

Joyce Farrell

1

AN OVERVIEW OF COMPUTERS AND LOGIC

After studying Chapter 1, you should be able to:

♦ Understand computer components and operations
♦ Describe the steps involved in the programming process
♦ Describe the data hierarchy
♦ Understand how to use flowchart symbols and pseudocode statements
♦ Use and name variables
♦ Use a sentinel, or dummy value, to end a program
♦ Use a connector symbol
♦ Assign values to variables
♦ Recognize the proper format of assignment statements
♦ Describe data types

UNDERSTANDING COMPUTER COMPONENTS AND OPERATIONS

The two major components of any computer system are its hardware and its software. **Hardware** is the equipment, or the devices, associated with a computer. For a computer to be useful, however, it needs more than equipment; a computer needs to be given instructions. The instructions that tell the computer what to do are called **software**, or programs, and are written by programmers. This book focuses on the process of writing these instructions.

Together, computer hardware and software accomplish four major operations:

1. Input
2. Processing
3. Output
4. Storage

Hardware devices that perform input include keyboards and mice. Through these devices, **data**, or facts, enter the computer system. Processing data items may involve organizing them, checking them for accuracy, or performing mathematical operations on them. The piece of hardware that performs these sorts of tasks is the **Central Processing Unit,** or **CPU**. After data have been processed, the resulting information is sent to a printer, monitor, or some other output device. Often, you also want to store the output information on hardware, such as magnetic disks or tapes. Computer software consists of all the instructions that control how and when the data are input, how they are processed, and the form in which they are output or stored.

Computer hardware by itself is useless without a programmer's instructions or software, just as your stereo equipment doesn't do much until you provide music on a CD or tape. You can enter instructions into a computer system through any of the hardware devices you use for data: for example, a keyboard or disk drive.

You write computer instructions in a computer **programming language** such as Visual Basic, Pascal, COBOL, RPG, C#, C++, Java, or Fortran. Just as some humans speak English and others speak Japanese, programmers also write programs in different languages. Some programmers work exclusively in one language, while others know several and use the one that seems most appropriate for the task at hand.

No matter which programming language a computer programmer uses, the language has rules governing its word usage and punctuation. These rules are called the language's **syntax**. If you ask, "How the get to store do I?" in English, most people can figure out what you probably mean even though you have not used proper English syntax. However, computers are not nearly as smart as most humans; with a computer you might as well have asked, "Xpu mxv ot dodnm cadf B?" Unless the syntax is perfect, the computer cannot interpret the programming language instruction at all.

Every computer operates on circuitry that consists of millions of on-off switches. Each programming language uses a piece of software to translate the specific programming language into the computer's on-off circuitry language, or **machine language**. The language translation software is called a **compiler** or **interpreter**, and it tells you if you have used a programming language incorrectly. Therefore, syntax errors are relatively easy to locate and correct. If you write a computer program using a language such as C++, but spell one of its words incorrectly or reverse the proper order of two words, the translator lets you know it found a mistake as soon as you try to run the program.

 Although there are differences in how compilers and interpreters work, their basic function is the same—to translate your programming statements into code the computer can use.

For a program to work properly, you must give the instructions to the computer in a specific sequence, you must not leave any instructions out, and you must not add extraneous instructions. By doing this, you are developing the **logic** of the computer program. Suppose you instruct someone to make a cake as follows:

```
Stir
Add two eggs
Add a gallon of gasoline
Bake at 350 degrees for 45 minutes
Add three cups of flour
```

Even though you have used the English language syntax correctly, the instructions are out of sequence, some instructions are missing, and some instructions belong to procedures other than baking a cake. If you follow these instructions, you are not going to end up with an edible cake, and you may end up with a disaster. Logical errors are much more difficult to locate than syntax errors; it is easier for you to determine whether *eggs* is spelled incorrectly in a recipe than it is for you to tell if there are too many eggs or they are added too soon.

Just as baking directions can be given correctly in French, German, or Spanish, the same logic of a program can be expressed in any number of programming languages. This book is almost exclusively concerned with the logic development process. Because it is not concerned with any specific language, this book could have been written in Japanese, C++, or Java. The logic is the same in any language. For convenience, the book uses English!

Once instructions have been input to the computer and translated into machine language, a program can be **run** or **executed**. You can write a program that takes a number (an input step), doubles it (processing), and tells you the answer (output) in a programming language such as Pascal or C++, but if you were to write it in English, it would look like this:

```
Get inputNumber
Compute calculatedAnswer as inputNumber times 2
Print calculatedAnswer
```

The instruction to `Get inputNumber` is an example of an input operation. When the computer interprets this instruction, it knows to look to an input device to obtain a number. Computers often have several input devices, perhaps a keyboard, a mouse, a CD drive, and two or more disk drives. When you learn a specific programming language, you learn how to tell the computer which of those input devices to access for input. For now, however, it doesn't really matter which hardware device is used as long as the computer knows to look for a number. The logic of the input operation—that the computer must obtain a number for input, and that the computer must obtain it before multiplying it by two—remains the same regardless of any specific input hardware device.

 Many computer professionals categorize disk drives and CD drives as storage devices rather than input devices. Such devices actually can be used for input, storage, and output.

Processing is the step that occurs when the mathematics is performed to double the `inputNumber`; the statement Compute `calculatedAnswer` as `inputNumber` times 2 represents processing. Mathematical operations are not the only kind of processing, but they are very typical. After you write a program, the program can be used on computers of different brand names, sizes, and speeds. Whether you use an IBM, Macintosh, or UNIX operating system, and whether you use a personal computer that sits on your desk or a mainframe that costs hundreds of thousands of dollars and resides in a special building in a university, multiplying by two is the same process. The hardware is not important; the processing will be the same.

In the number doubling program, the Print `calculatedAnswer` statement represents output. Within a particular program, this statement could cause the output to appear on the monitor, which might be a flat panel screen or a cathode ray tube, or the output could go to a printer, which can be laser or inkjet. The logic of the process is the same no matter what hardware device you use.

Besides input, processing, and output, the fourth operation in any computer system is storage. Storage comes in two broad categories. All computers have **internal storage**, probably referred to more often as **memory**, **main memory**, or **primary memory**. This storage is inside the machine and is the type of storage most often discussed in this book. Computers also have **external storage**, which is permanent storage outside the main memory of the machine on a device such as a floppy disk, hard disk, or magnetic tape. In other words, external storage is outside of the main memory, not necessarily outside the computer. Both programs and data sometimes are stored on each of these kinds of media.

To use computer programs, you must first load them into memory. You might type a program into memory from the keyboard, or you might use a program that has already been written and stored on a disk. Either way, a copy of the instructions must be placed in memory before the program can be run.

A computer system needs both internal memory and external storage. Internal memory is needed to run the programs, but internal memory is **volatile**—that is, its contents are lost every time the computer loses power. Therefore, if you are going to use a program more than once, you must store it, or **save** it, on some nonvolatile medium. Otherwise, the program in main memory is lost forever when the computer is turned off. External storage (usually disks or tape) provides a nonvolatile medium.

 Even though a hard disk drive is located inside your computer, the hard disk is not main, internal memory. Internal memory is temporary and volatile; a hard drive is permanent, nonvolatile storage.

Once you have a copy of a program in main memory, you must also place any data that the program requires into memory. For example, after you place the following program into memory and start to run it, you need to provide an actual `inputNumber`—for example, 8—that you also place in main memory.

```
Get inputNumber
Compute calculatedAnswer as inputNumber times 2
Print calculatedAnswer
```

The `inputNumber` is placed in memory in a specific memory location that the program will call `inputNumber`. Then, and only then, can the `calculatedAnswer`, in this case 16, be calculated and printed.

 Computer memory consists of millions of numbered locations where data can be stored. The memory location of `inputNumber` has a specific numeric address, for example, 48604. Your program associates `inputNumber` with that address. Every time you refer to `inputNumber` within a program, the computer retrieves the value at the associated memory location.

UNDERSTANDING THE PROGRAMMING PROCESS

A programmer's job involves writing instructions (such as the three instructions in the doubling program in the preceding section), and can be broken down into six **programming steps**:

1. Understand the problem.

2. Plan the logic.

3. Code the program.

4. Translate the program into machine language.

5. Test the program.

6. Put the program into production.

Understand the Problem

Professional computer programmers write programs to satisfy the needs of others. For example: the Human Resources department that needs a printed list of all employees, the Billing department that wants a list of clients who are 30 or more days overdue in their payments, and the office manager who would like to be notified when specific supplies reach the reorder point. Because programmers are providing a service to these users, programmers must first understand what it is the users want.

Suppose the director of Human Resources says to a programmer, "Our department needs a list of all employees who have been here over five years because we want to invite them to a special thank-you dinner." On the surface this seems like a simple enough request. An experienced programmer, however, will know that he or she may not yet understand the whole problem. Does the director want a list of full-time employees only, or a list of full- and part-time employees together? Does she want people who have worked for the company on a month-to-month contractual basis over the past five years, or regular employees only? Do the listed employees need to be working for the organization for five years as of today, as of the date of the dinner, or is some other date to be used as a cutoff? What about an employee who worked three years, took a two-year leave of absence, and has been back for three years? Does he or she qualify? The programmer cannot make any of these decisions; the user is the one who must address these questions.

More decisions still might be required. For example, what does the user want the report of five-year employees to look like? Should it contain both first and last names? Social Security numbers? Phone numbers? Addresses? Is all this data available? Several pieces of documentation are often provided to help the programmer understand the problem. This documentation includes print layout charts and file specifications, which you will learn about in Chapter 3.

Really understanding the problem may be one of the most difficult aspects of programming. On any job, the description of what the user needs may be vague; worse yet, the user may not even really know what it is he or she wants. A good programmer is often part counselor, part detective!

Plan the Logic

The heart of the programming process lies in planning the program's logic. During this phase of the programming process, the programmer plans the steps to the program, deciding what steps to include and how to order them. You can plan the solution to a problem in many ways. The two most common tools are flowcharts and pseudocode. Both tools involve writing the steps of the program in English, much as you would plan a trip on paper before getting into the car or plan a party theme before going shopping for food and favors.

 You may hear programmers refer to planning a program as "developing an algorithm." An algorithm is the sequence of steps necessary to solve any problem.

 You will learn more about flowcharts and pseudocode later in this chapter.

The programmer doesn't worry about the syntax of any particular language at this point, just about figuring out what sequence of events will lead from the available input to the desired output. You will learn more about planning the logic later; in fact, this book focuses on this step almost exclusively.

Code the Program

Once the programmer has developed the logic of a program, only then can he or she write the program in one of more than 400 programming languages. Now the programmer can worry about each command being spelled correctly and all of the punctuation getting into the right spots—in other words, using the correct *syntax*.

Some very experienced programmers can successfully combine the logic planning and the actual instruction writing, or **coding** of the program, in one step. This may work for planning and writing a very simple program, just as you can plan and write a post-card to a friend using one step. A good term paper or a Hollywood screenplay, however, needs planning before writing, and so do most programs.

Which step is harder, planning the logic or coding the program? Right now, it may seem to you that writing in a programming language is a very difficult task, considering all the spelling and grammar rules you must learn. However, the planning step is actually more difficult. Which is more difficult, thinking up the twists and turns to the plot of a best-selling mystery novel or writing a translation of an already written novel from English to Spanish? And who do you think gets paid more, the writer or the translator?

Translate the Program into Machine Language

Even though there are many programming languages, each computer knows only one language, its machine language, which consists of many 1s and 0s. Computers under-stand machine language because computers themselves are made up of thousands of tiny electrical switches, each of which can be set in either the on or off state, which is rep-resented by a 1 or 0, respectively.

Languages like Java or Visual Basic are available for programmers to use because some-one has written a translator program (a compiler or interpreter) that changes the English-like **high-level language** in which the programmer writes into the **low-level machine language** that the computer understands. If you write a programming language statement incorrectly, (for example by misspelling a word, using a word that doesn't exist in the language, or using illegal grammar), the translator program doesn't know what to do and issues an error message. You receive the same response when you speak nonsense to a human language translator. Imagine trying to look up a list of words in a Spanish-English dictionary if some of the listed words are misspelled—you can't complete the task until the words are spelled correctly. Although making errors is never desirable, syntax errors are not a major concern to programmers because the compiler or translator catches every syntax error, and the computer will not execute a program that contains them.

If you could use an English compiler and submit the sentence `The grl go to school`, the compiler would point out two syntax errors to you. The second word, `grl`, is illegal because it is not part of the English language. Once you corrected the word `girl`, the compiler would find another syntax error on the third word, `go`, because it is the wrong verb form for the subject `girl`. This doesn't mean `go` is necessarily the wrong word.

Maybe `girl` is wrong; perhaps the subject should be `girls`, in which case `go` is right. Compilers don't always know exactly what you mean, nor do they know what the proper correction should be, but they do know when something is wrong with your syntax.

Test the Program

A program that is free of syntax errors is not necessarily free of **logical errors**. For example, the sentence `The girl goes to school`, although syntactically perfect, is not logically correct if the girl is a baby or a drop-out.

Once a program is free from syntax errors, the programmer can test it—that is, execute it with some sample data to see whether or not the results are logically correct. Recall the number doubling program:

```
Get inputNumber
Compute calculatedAnswer as inputNumber times 2
Print calculatedAnswer
```

If you provide the value 2 as input to the program and the answer 4 prints out, you have executed one successful test run of the program.

However, if the answer 40 prints out, maybe it's because the program contains a logical error. Maybe the second line of code was mistyped with an extra zero so that the program reads:

```
Get inputNumber
Compute calculatedAnswer as inputNumber times 20
Print calculatedAnswer
```

The error of placing 20 instead of 2 in the multiplication statement caused a logical error. Notice that nothing is syntactically wrong with this second program—it is just as reasonable to multiply a number by 20 as by 2—but if the programmer intends only to double the `inputNumber`, then a logical error has occurred.

Programs should be tested with many sets of data. For example, if you write the program to double a number and enter 2 and get an output value of 4, it doesn't mean you have a correct program. Perhaps you have typed this program by mistake:

```
Get inputNumber
Compute calculatedAnswer as inputNumber plus 2
Print calculatedAnswer
```

An input of 2 results in an answer of 4, but it doesn't mean your program doubles numbers—it actually only adds 2 to them. If you test your program with additional data—for example using a 3 and you get an answer of 5, you know there is a problem with your code.

Selecting test data is somewhat of an art in itself, and it should be done carefully. If the Human Resources department wants a list of the names of five-year employees, it would be a mistake to test the program with a small sample file of only long-term employees. If no new employees are part of the data being used for testing, you don't really know if the program would have eliminated them from the five-year list. Many companies don't know that their software has a problem until an unusual circumstance occurs; for example, the first time an employee has more than nine dependents, the first time a customer orders more than 999 items at a time, or when, in an example that has been well documented in the popular press, a new century begins.

Put the Program into Production

Once the program is tested adequately, it is ready for the organization to use. Putting the program into production might mean simply running the program once if it was written to satisfy a user's request for a special list. However, the process might take months if the program will be run on a regular basis, or if it is one of a large system of programs being developed. Perhaps data entry people must be trained to prepare the input for the new program, users must be trained to understand the output, or existing data in the company must be changed to an entirely new format to accommodate this program. **Conversion**, the entire set of actions an organization must take to switch over to using a new program or set of programs, can sometimes take months or years to accomplish.

You might consider maintaining programs as a seventh step in the programming process. After programs are put into production, making required changes is called maintenance. Maintenance is necessary for many reasons. For example, new tax rates are legislated, the format of an input file is altered, or the end user requires additional information not included in the original output specifications.

You might consider retiring the program as the eighth and final step in the programming process. A program is retired when it is no longer needed by an organization—usually when a new program is in the process of being put into production.

UNDERSTANDING THE DATA HIERARCHY

Some very simple programs require very simple data. For example, the number doubling program requires just one value as input. Most business programs, however, use much more data—inventory files list thousands of items, personnel and customer files list thousands of people. When data are stored for use on computer systems, they are often stored in what is known as a **data hierarchy**, where the smallest usable unit of data is the character. **Characters** are letters, numbers, and special symbols such as "A", "7", and "$". Anything you can type from the keyboard in one keystroke (including a space or a tab) is a character. Characters are made up of smaller elements called bits, but just as most humans can use a pencil without caring whether atoms are flying around inside it, most computer users can store characters without caring about these bits.

Computers also recognize characters you cannot enter from the keyboard, such as foreign alphabet characters like φ or Σ.

Characters are grouped together to form a field. A **field** is a single data item such as `lastName`, `streetAddress`, or `annualSalary`. For most of us, an "S", an "m", an "i", a "t", and an "h" don't have much meaning individually, but if the combination of characters makes up your last name, "Smith", then as a group the characters have useful meaning.

Related fields are often grouped together to form a record. **Records** are groups of fields that go together for some logical reason. A random name, address, and salary aren't very useful, but if they're your name, your address, and your salary, then that's your record. An inventory record might contain fields for item number, color, and price; a student record might contain ID number, grade point average, and major.

Related records in turn, are grouped together to form a file. **Files** are groups of records that go together for some logical reason. The individual records of each student in your class might go together in a file called CLASS. Records of each person at your company might be in a file called PERSONNEL. Items you sell might be in an INVENTORY file.

Some files can have just a few records; others, like the file of credit card holders for a major department store chain or policyholders of an insurance company, can have thousands or even millions of records.

Finally, many organizations use database software to organize many files. A **database** holds a group of files, often called **tables**, that together serve the information needs of an organization. This book will not discuss database management; instead, it will concentrate on programs that use files for both input and output.

In summary, you can picture the data hierarchy as shown in Figure 1-1.

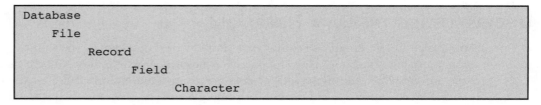

```
Database
    File
         Record
                Field
                      Character
```

Figure 1-1   The data hierarchy

A database contains many files. A file contains many records. Each record in a file has the same fields; each record's fields contain different data items that consists of one or more stored characters in each field.

As an example, you can picture a file as a set of index cards as shown in Figure 1-2. The stack of cards is the EMPLOYEE file, where each card represents one employee record. On each card, each line holds one field—`name`, `address`, or `salary`. Almost all the program examples in this book will use files that are organized in this way.

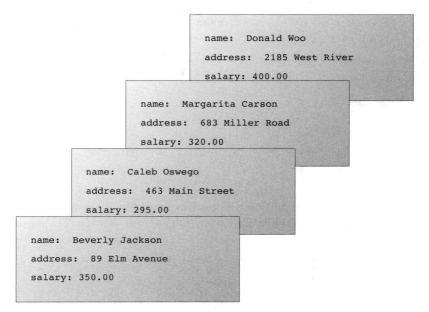

name: Donald Woo

address: 2185 West River

salary: 400.00

name: Margarita Carson

address: 683 Miller Road

salary: 320.00

name: Caleb Oswego

address: 463 Main Street

salary: 295.00

name: Beverly Jackson

address: 89 Elm Avenue

salary: 350.00

Figure 1-2   A file of employee records

USING FLOWCHART SYMBOLS AND PSEUDOCODE STATEMENTS

When programmers plan the logic for a solution to a programming problem, they often use one of two tools, **flowcharts** or **pseudocode** (pronounced "sue–dough–code"). A flowchart is a pictorial representation of the logical steps it takes to solve a problem. Pseudocode is an English-like representation of the same thing. *Pseudo* is a prefix that means false, and to *code* a program means to put it in a programming language; therefore *pseudocode* simply means "false code," or sentences that appear to have been written in a computer programming language but don't necessarily follow all the syntax rules of any specific language.

You have already seen pseudocode earlier in this chapter, and there is nothing mysterious about it. The following three statements constitute a pseudocode representation of a number doubling problem:

```
get inputNumber
compute calculatedAnswer as inputNumber times 2
print calculatedAnswer
```

Using pseudocode involves writing down all the steps you will use in a program. Some professional programmers prefer writing pseudocode to drawing flowcharts, because using pseudocode is more similar to writing the final statements in the programming language. Others prefer using flowcharts to represent the logical flow, because they can more easily visualize how the program statements will connect. Especially for beginning programmers, flowcharts are an excellent tool to help you visualize how the statements in a program are interrelated.

Almost every program involves the steps of input, processing, and output, as in the following program:

```
get inputNumber
compute calculatedAnswer as inputNumber times 2
print calculatedAnswer
```

Therefore, most flowcharts need some graphical way to separate these three steps. When you create a flowchart, you draw geometric shapes around the individual statements and connect them with arrows.

When you draw a flowchart, you use a parallelogram to represent an **input** operation. You write an input statement, in English, inside the parallelogram, as shown in Figure 1-3.

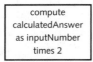

Figure 1-3   Input symbol

Arithmetic operation statements are examples of **processing**. In a flowchart you use a rectangle to represent a processing statement as shown in Figure 1-4.

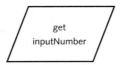

Figure 1-4   Processing symbol

To represent an **output** statement, you use the same symbol as you do for input statements—the parallelogram, as in Figure 1-5.

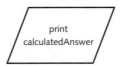

Figure 1-5   Output symbol

To show the correct sequence of these statements, you use arrows, or **flowlines**, to connect the steps. Whenever possible, most of a flowchart should read from top to bottom or from left to right on a page. That's the natural way we read English, so when flowcharts follow this convention, they are easier to understand.

To be complete, a flowchart should include two more elements: a **terminal** or start/stop symbol at each end. Often, you place a word like "start" or "begin" in the first terminal symbol and a word like "end" or "stop" in the other. The standard terminal symbol is shaped like a racetrack. Figure 1-6 shows a complete flowchart for the program that doubles a number, and the pseudocode for the same problem.

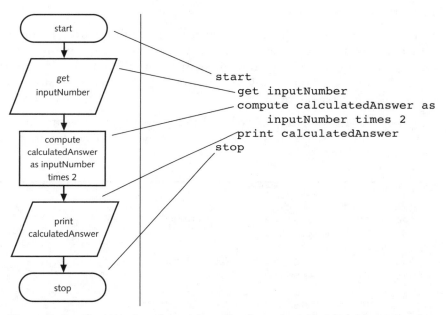

```
start
    get inputNumber
    compute calculatedAnswer as
        inputNumber times 2
    print calculatedAnswer
stop
```

Figure 1-6   Flowchart and pseudocode of program that doubles a number

In the pseudocode in Figure 1-6, the words start and stop are aligned in the left margin; the actual program statements are indented. This style is not required when you write pseudocode, but as you develop more complex programs, indenting the program statements within the start-stop pair will help you to see the beginning and ending points in program segments.

Programmers seldom create both pseudocode and a flowchart for the same problem. You usually use one or the other.

The logic for the program represented by the flowchart and pseudocode in Figure 1-6 is correct no matter what programming language the programmer eventually uses to write the corresponding code. After the flowchart or pseudocode has been developed, the programmer needs only to buy a computer, learn a language, code the program, compile it, test it, and put it into production.

"Whoa!" you are probably saying to yourself. "This is simply not worth it! All that work to create a flowchart, and *then* all those other steps? For five dollars I can buy a pocket calculator that will double any number for me!" You are absolutely right. If this were a real computer program, it simply would not be worth all the effort. Writing a computer program would be worth the effort only if you had many, let's say 10,000, numbers to find the double of in a limited amount of time, let's say the next two minutes. Then it would be worth your while to create a computer program.

Unfortunately, the number-doubling program represented in Figure 1-6 does not double 10,000 numbers; it doubles only one. You could execute the program 10,000 times, of course, but that would require you to sit at the computer telling it to run the program over and over again. You would be better off with a program that could process 10,000 numbers, one after the other.

One solution is to write the program as shown in Figure 1-7 and execute the same steps 10,000 times. Of course, writing this program would be very time consuming; you might as well buy the calculator.

```
start
    get inputNumber
    compute calculatedAnswer as inputNumber times 2
    print calculatedAnswer
    get inputNumber
    compute calculatedAnswer as inputNumber times 2
    print calculatedAnswer
    get inputNumber
    compute calculatedAnswer as inputNumber times 2
    print calculatedAnswer
    . . . and so on
```

Figure 1-7   Inefficient pseudocode for program that doubles 10,000 numbers

A better solution is to have the computer execute the same set of three instructions over and over again as shown in Figure 1-8. With this approach, the computer gets a number, doubles it, prints out the answer, and then starts over again with the first instruction. The same spot in memory, called `inputNumber`, is reused for the second number and for any subsequent numbers. The spot in memory named `calculatedAnswer` is reused each time to store the result of the multiplication operation.

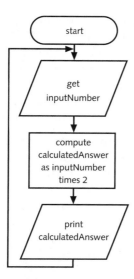

Figure 1-8   Flowchart of infinite number-doubling program

Using and Naming Variables

Programmers commonly refer to the locations in memory called `inputNumber` and `calculatedAnswer` as variables. **Variables** are memory locations, whose contents can vary or differ over time. Sometimes `inputNumber` can hold a 2 and `calculatedAnswer` will hold a 4; other times `inputNumber` can hold a 6 and `calculatedAnswer` will hold a 12. It is the ability of memory variables to change in value that makes computers and programming worthwhile. Because one memory location can be used over and over again with different values, you can write program instructions once and then use them for thousands of separate calculations. *One* set of payroll instructions at your company produces each individual's paycheck, and *one* set of instructions at your electric company produces each household's bill.

The number-doubling example requires two variables, `inputNumber` and `calculatedAnswer`. These can just as well be named `userEntry` and `programSolution`, or `inputValue` and `twiceTheValue`. As a programmer, you choose reasonable names for your variables. The language interpreter then associates the names you choose with specific memory addresses.

Every computer programming language has its own set of rules for naming variables. Most languages allow both letters and digits within variable names. Some languages allow hyphens in variable names, for example `hourly-wage`. Others allow underscores, as in `hourly_wage`. Still others allow neither. Some languages allow dollar signs or other special characters in variable names, for example `hourly$`; others allow foreign alphabet characters like π or Ω.

Different languages put different limits on the length of variable names, although in general, newer languages allow longer names. For example, in some very old versions of BASIC, a variable name could consist of only one or two letters and one or two digits. You could have some cryptic variable names like hw , a3 , or re02. In other languages, variable names can be very long. COBOL, for example, allows up to 30 characters in its variable names, so names like AMOUNT-OF-SALE and TOTAL-FOR-JANUARY are common. In addition, COBOL allows hyphens in its variable names for better readability.

Many modern languages, such as C++, C#, and Java, allow more than two hundred characters in a variable name. Variable names in these languages usually consist of lowercase letters, don't allow hyphens, but do allow underscores, so you can use a name like price_of_item. These languages are case sensitive, so HOURLYWAGE, hourlywage, and hourlyWage are considered three separate variable names, although the last example, in which the new word begins with an uppercase letter, is easiest to read. Most programmers who use the more modern languages employ the format in which multiple-word variable names are run together, and each new word within the variable name begins with an uppercase letter. This format is called **camel casing**, because such variable names, like hourlyWage, have a "hump" in the middle. The variable names in this text are shown using camel casing.

Even though every language has its own rules for naming variables, when designing the logic of a computer program, you should not concern yourself with the specific syntax of any particular computer language. The logic, after all, works with any language. The variable names used throughout this book follow only two rules:

1. *Variable names must be one word.* The name can contain letters, digits, hyphens, underscores, or any other characters you choose, with the exception of *spaces*. Therefore r is a legal variable name, as is rate, as is interestRate. The variable name interest rate is not allowed because of the space. No programming language allows spaces within a variable name. If you see a name such as interest rate in a flowchart or pseudocode, you should assume that the programmer is discussing two variables, interest and rate, each of which individually would be a fine variable name.

 When you write a program, your compiler may show variable names in a different color from the rest of the program. This visual aid helps your variable names stand out from words that are part of the programming language.

2. *Variable names should have some appropriate meaning.* This is not a rule of any programming language. When computing an interest rate in a program, the computer does not care if you call the variable g, u84, or fred. As long as the correct numeric result is placed in the variable, its actual name doesn't really matter. However, it's much easier to follow the logic of a program with a statement in it like compute finalBalance as equal to initialInvestment times interestRate than one with a statement

in it like `compute someBanana as equal to j89 times myFriendLinda`. You might think you will remember how you intended to use a cryptic variable name within a program, but six years later when a program requires changes, you, and other programmers working with you, will appreciate clear, descriptive, variable names.

Notice that the flowchart in Figure 1-8 follows these two rules for variables: both variable names, `inputNumber` and `calculatedAnswer`, are one word, and they have some appropriate meaning. Some programmers have fun with their variable names by naming them after friends or creating puns with them, but such behavior is unprofessional and marks those programmers as amateurs.

 Another general rule in all programming languages is that variable names may not begin with a digit, although usually they may contain digits. Thus in most languages budget2003 is a legal variable name, but 2013Budget is not.

ENDING A PROGRAM BY USING SENTINEL VALUES

Something is still wrong with the flowchart for doubling numbers shown in Figure 1-8. It never ends! If, for example, the input numbers are being entered at the keyboard, the program will keep accepting numbers and printing out doubles forever. Of course, the user could refuse to type in any more numbers. But the computer is very patient, and if you refuse to give it any more numbers, it will sit and wait forever. When you finally type in a number, the program doubles it, prints the result, and waits for another. The program cannot progress any farther while it is waiting for input; meanwhile, the program is occupying computer memory and tying up operating system resources. Refusing to enter any more numbers is not a practical solution. Another way to end the program is to simply turn the computer off! That'll fix it! But again, it's neither the best nor an elegant way to bring the program to an end.

A superior way to end the program is to set a predetermined value for `inputNumber` that means "Stop the program!" For example, the programmer and the user could agree that the user will never need to know the double of zero, so the user could enter a zero when he or she wants to stop. The program could then test any incoming value for `inputNumber` and, if it is a zero, stop the program. Testing a value is also called making a **decision**.

You represent a decision in a flowchart by drawing a **decision symbol** or a diamond. The diamond usually contains a question, the answer to which is either yes or no. All good computer questions have two mutually exclusive answers like yes and no or true and false. For example, "What day of the year is your birthday?" is not a good computer question because there are 366 possible answers. But "Is your birthday June 24?" *is* a good computer question because for everyone in the world, the answer is either yes or no.

The question to stop the doubling program should be "Is the `inputNumber` just entered equal to zero?" or "`inputNumber` = 0?" for short. The complete flowchart will now look like the one shown in Figure 1-9.

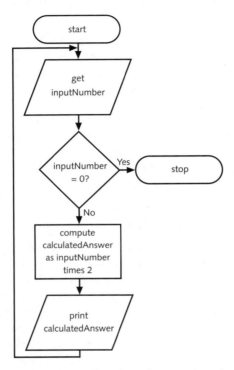

Figure 1-9   Flowchart for number-doubling program with sentinel value of zero

One drawback to using zero to stop a program, of course, is that it won't work if the user *does* need to find the double of zero. In that case, some other data entry value that the user never will need, such as 999 or −1 could be selected to signal that the program should end. A preselected value that stops the execution of a program is often called a **dummy value** because it does not represent real data, but just a signal to stop. Sometimes such a value is called a **sentinel value** because it represents an entry or exit point like a sentinel that guards a fortress.

Not all programs rely on user data entry from a keyboard; many read data from an input device such as a disk or tape drive. When organizations store data on a disk or tape, they do not commonly use a sentinel value to signal the end of the file. For one thing, an input record might have hundreds of fields, and if you store a dummy record in every file, you are wasting a large quantity of storage on "non-data." Additionally, it is often difficult to choose sentinel values for fields in a company's data files. Any `balanceDue`, even a zero or negative one, can be a legitimate value, and any `customerName`, even "ZZ" could be someone's name. Fortunately, programming languages can recognize the end of data in a file automatically, without a sentinel value, through a code that is stored at the end of the data. Many programming languages use the term **eof** (for "end of file") to talk about this marker. This book therefore uses **eof** to indicate the end of data, regardless of whether it is a special disk marker or a dummy value such as zero from the keyboard. Therefore, the flowchart now looks like the one in Figure 1-10.

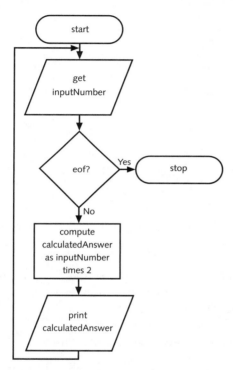

Figure 1-10   Flowchart using eof

USING THE CONNECTOR

By using just the input, processing, output, decision, and terminal symbols, you can represent the logic for many diverse applications. This book uses only one other symbol, the **connector**. A connector will be used when limited page size forces you to continue the flowchart on the following page. If a flowchart has six processing steps and a page provides room for only three, you might represent the logic as shown in Figure 1-11.

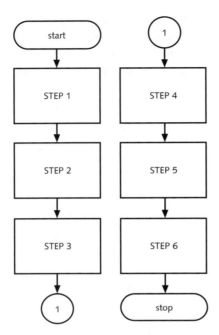

Figure 1-11   Flowchart using the connector

The circle at the bottom of the left column tells someone reading the flowchart that there is more to the flowchart. The circle should contain a number or letter that can then be matched to another number or letter somewhere else, in this case on the right. If a large flowchart needs more connectors, new numbers or letters would be assigned in sequence (1, 2, 3... or A, B, C...) to each successive pair of connectors.

When you are creating your own flowcharts, you should avoid using the connector if at all possible; flowcharts are more difficult to follow when they do not fit on a page. Your instructor or future programming supervisor may require that long flowcharts be redrawn so you don't need to use the connector. However, when continuing on a new page is unavoidable, the connector provides the means.

ASSIGNING VALUES TO VARIABLES

When you create a flowchart or pseudocode for a program that doubles numbers, you can include the statement `compute calculatedAnswer as inputNumber times 2`. This statement incorporates two actions. First, the computer computes the arithmetic value of `inputNumber` times 2. Second, the computed value is stored in the `calculatedAnswer` memory location. Most programming languages allow a shorthand expression for these **assignment statements** such as `compute calculatedAnswer as inputNumber times 2`. The shorthand takes the form `calculatedAnswer = inputNumber * 2`.

In Pascal, the same expression is `calculatedAnswer := inputNumber * 2`. You type a colon followed by an equal sign to create the assignment symbol. Java, C++, C#, Visual Basic, and COBOL all use the equal sign for assignment.

According to the rules of algebra, a statement like `calculatedAnswer = inputNumber * 2` should be exactly equivalent to the statement `inputNumber * 2 = calculatedAnswer`. To most programmers, however, `calculatedAnswer = inputNumber * 2` means "multiply `inputNumber` by 2 and store the result in the variable called `calculatedAnswer`." Whatever operation is performed to the right of the equal sign results in a value that is placed in the memory location to the left of the equal sign. Therefore, the statement `inputNumber * 2 = calculatedAnswer` means to take the value of `calculatedAnswer` and store it in a location called `inputNumber * 2`. A location called `inputNumber` is valid, but there can't be a location called `inputNumber * 2`. For one thing, `inputNumber * 2` can't be a variable because it has spaces in it. For another, a location can't be multiplied. Its contents can be multiplied, but the location itself cannot be. The statement `inputNumber * 2 = calculatedAnswer` contains a syntax error, no matter what programming language you use; a program with such a statement will not execute.

When you create an assignment statement, it may help to imagine the word "let" in front of the statement. Thus, you can read the statement `calculatedAnswer = inputNumber * 2` as "Let calculatedAnswer equal inputNumber times two." The BASIC programming language allows you to use the word "let" in such statements.

Computer memory is made up of millions of distinct locations, each of which has an address. Fifty years ago, programmers had to deal with these addresses and had to remember, for instance, that they had stored a salary in location 6428 of their computer. Today we are very fortunate that high-level computer languages allow us to pick a reasonable "English" name for a memory address and let the computer keep track of where it is. Just as it is easier for you to remember that the president lives in the White House than at 1600 Pennsylvania Avenue, Washington, D.C., it is also easier for you to remember that your salary is in a variable called `mySalary` than at memory location 6428.

Similarly, it does not usually make sense to perform mathematical operations on memory addresses, but it does make sense to perform mathematical operations on the *contents* of memory addresses. If you live in `blueSplitLevelOnTheCorner`, you can't add 1 to that, but you certainly can add 1 person to the number of people already in that house. For our purposes, then, the statement `calculatedAnswer = inputNumber * 2` means exactly the same thing as the statement `move inputNumber * 2 to calculatedAnswer`, which also means exactly the same thing as the statement `multiply inputNumber times 2 resulting in calculatedAnswer`. None of these statements, however, is equivalent to `inputNumber * 2 = calculatedAnswer`, which is an illegal statement.

Many programming languages allow you to create constants. A constant is a named memory location, similar to a variable, except its value never changes during a program. If you are working with a programming language that allows it, you might create a constant for a value like `pi = 3.14` or `countySalesTaxRate = .06`.

UNDERSTANDING DATA TYPES

Computers deal with two basic types of data—character and numeric. When you use a specific numeric value, like *43*, within a program, you write it using the digits and no quotation marks. A specific numeric value is often called a **numeric constant**, because it does not change—a 43 always has the value 43. When you use a specific character value, or **string** of characters, like "Chris," you enclose the string or **character constant** within quotation marks.

Some languages require single quotes surrounding character constants while others require double quotes. Many languages, like C++, C#, Java, and Pascal, reserve single quotes for a single character such as 'C', and double quotes for a character string such as "Chris".

Similarly, most computer languages allow at least two distinct types of variables. One type of variable can hold a number and is often called a **numeric variable**. In the statement `calculatedAnswer = inputNumber * 2` both `calculatedAnswer` and `inputNumber` are numeric variables; that is, their intended contents are numeric values such as 6 and 3, 150 and 75, or −18 and −9.

Most programming languages have a separate type of variable that can hold letters of the alphabet and other special characters such as punctuation marks. Depending on the language, these variables are called **character**, **text**, or **string variables**. If a working program contains the statement `lastName = "Lincoln"` then `lastName` is a character or string variable.

Programmers must distinguish between numeric and character variables because computers handle the two types of data differently. Therefore, means are provided within the syntax rules of computer programming languages to tell the computer which type of data to expect. How this is done is different in every language; some languages have different rules for naming the variables, but with others you must include a simple statement (called a **declaration**) telling the computer which type of data to expect.

Some languages allow for several types of numeric data. Languages like Pascal, C++, C#, and Java distinguish between **integer** or whole number numeric variables, and **floating-point** or fractional numeric variables that contain a decimal point. Thus, in some languages the numbers 4 and 4.3 would have to be stored in different types of variables.

Some programming languages allow even more specific variable types, but the character versus numeric distinction is universal. For the programs you develop in this book, assume each variable is one of the two broad types. If a variable called `taxRate` is supposed to hold a value of 2.5, assume that it is a numeric variable. If a variable called `inventoryItem` is supposed to hold a value of "monitor," assume that it is a character variable.

 Values like "monitor" and 2.5 are called constants or literal constants because they never change. A variable value *can* change. Thus, inventoryItem can hold "monitor" at one moment during the execution of a program, and later you can change its value to hold "modem".

By convention, this book encloses character data like "monitor" within quotation marks to distinguish the characters from yet another variable name. Also, by convention, numeric data is not enclosed within quotation marks. According to these conventions, then, `taxRate = 2.5` and `inventoryItem = "monitor"` are both valid statements. The statement `inventoryItem = monitor` is a valid statement only if monitor is also a character variable. In other words, if `monitor ="color"`, and subsequently `inventoryItem = monitor`, then the end result is that `inventoryItem = "color"`.

Every computer and every computer application handles text or character data differently from the way it handles numeric data. Every programming language requires that you distinguish variables as to their correct type and that you use each type of variable appropriately. (For example, you cannot perform arithmetic calculations with string data.) Identifying your variables correctly as numeric or character is one of the first steps you have to take when writing programs in any programming language.

CHAPTER SUMMARY

□ Together, computer hardware (equipment) and software (instructions) accomplish four major operations: input, processing, output, and storage. You write computer instructions in a computer programming language that requires specific syntax; the instructions are translated into machine language by a compiler or interpreter. When both the syntax and logic of a program are correct, you can run or execute the program to produce the desired results.

□ A programmer's job involves understanding the problem, planning the logic, coding the program, translating the program into machine language, testing the program, and putting the program into production.

□ When data are stored for use on computer systems, they are stored in a data hierarchy of character, field, record, and file.

□ When programmers plan the logic for a solution to a programming problem, they often use flowcharts or pseudocode. When you draw a flowchart, you use parallelograms to represent input and output operations and rectangles to represent processing.

□ Variables are named memory locations, the contents of which can vary. As a programmer, you choose reasonable names for your variables. Every computer programming language has its own set of rules for naming variables; however, all variable names must be written as one word without embedded spaces, and should have appropriate meaning.

❑ Testing a value involves making a decision. You represent a decision in a flowchart by drawing a diamond-shaped decision symbol which contains a question, the answer to which is either yes or no. You can stop a program's execution by testing a sentinel value with a decision.

❑ A circular connector symbol is used to continue a flowchart that does not fit on a single page.

❑ Most programming languages allow the equal sign to assign values to variables. Assignment always takes place from right to left.

❑ Programmers must distinguish between numeric and character variables because computers handle the two types of data differently. A variable declaration tells the computer which type of data to expect. By convention, character data is included within quotation marks.

EXERCISES

1. Match the definition with the appropriate term.

   1. Computer system equipment   a. compiler
   2. Another word for programs   b. syntax
   3. Language rules   c. logic
   4. Order of instructions   d. hardware
   5. Language translator   e. software

2. In your own words, describe the steps to writing a computer program.

3. Consider a student file that contains the following data:

LAST NAME	FIRST NAME	MAJOR	GRADE POINT AVERAGE
Andrews	David	Psychology	3.4
Broederdorf	Melissa	Computer Science	4.0
Brogan	Lindsey	Biology	3.8
Carson	Joshua	Computer Science	2.8
Eisfelder	Katie	Mathematics	3.5
Faris	Natalie	Biology	2.8
Fredricks	Zachary	Psychology	2.0
Gonzales	Eduardo	Biology	3.1

Would this set of data be suitable and sufficient to use to test each of the following programs? Explain why or why not.

a. A program that prints a list of Psychology majors

b. A program that prints a list of Art majors

c. A program that prints a list of students on academic probation—those with a grade point average under 2.0

d. A program that prints a list of students on the dean's list

e. A program that prints a list of students from Wisconsin

f. A program that prints a list of female students

4. Suggest a good set of test data to use for a program that gives an employee a $50 bonus check if the employee has produced more than 1,000 items in a week.

5. Suggest a good set of test data for a program that computes gross paychecks (that is, before any taxes or other deductions) based on hours worked and rate of pay. The program computes gross as hours times rate unless hours are over 40. Then the program computes gross as regular rate of pay for 40 hours, plus one and a half times the rate of pay for the hours over 40.

6. Suggest a good set of test data for a program that is intended to output a student's grade point average based on letter grades (A, B, C, D, or F) in five courses.

7. Suggest a good set of data for a program for an automobile insurance company that wants to increase its premiums by $50 a month for every ticket a driver receives in a three-year period.

8. Assume a grocery store keeps a file for inventory where each grocery item has its own record. Two fields within each record are the name of the manufacturer and the weight of the item. Name at least six more fields that might be stored for each record. Provide an example of the data for one record. For example, for one product the manufacturer is DelMonte, and the weight is twelve ounces.

9. Assume a library keeps a file with data about its collection, one record for each item the library loans out. Name at least eight fields that might be stored for each record. Provide an example of the data for one record.

10. Match the term with the appropriate shape.

    1. INPUT   a.

    2. PROCESSING   b.

    3. DECISION   c.

    4. TERMINAL   d.

    5. CONNECTOR   e.

11. Which of the following names seem like good variable names to you? If a name doesn't seem like a good variable name, explain why not.

    a. c

    b. cost

    c. costAmount

    d. cost amount

    e. cstofdngbsns

    f. costOfDoingBusinessThisFiscalYear

    g. cost2004

12. If myAge and yourRate are numeric variables, and departmentCode is a character variable, which of the following statements are valid assignments? If a statement is not valid, explain why not.

    a. myAge = 23

    b. myAge = yourRate

    c. myAge = departmentCode

    d. myAge = "departmentCode"

e. 42 = myAge

f. yourRate = 3.5

g. yourRate = myAge

h. yourRate = departmentCode

i. 6.91 = yourRate

j. departmentCode = Personnel

k. departmentCode = "Personnel"

l. departmentCode = 413

m. departmentCode = "413"

n. departmentCode = myAge

o. departmentCode = yourRate

p. 413 = departmentCode

q. "413" = departmentCode

13.   a. Draw a flowchart to represent the logic of a program that allows the user to enter a value. The program multiplies the value by 10 and prints out the result.

b. Write pseudocode for the same problem.

14.   a. Draw a flowchart to represent the logic of a program that allows the user to enter two values. The program prints the sum of the two values.

b. Write pseudocode for the same problem.

CHAPTER 2

UNDERSTANDING STRUCTURE

After studying Chapter 2, you should be able to:

♦ Describe the features of unstructured spaghetti code
♦ Describe the three basic structures of sequence, selection, and loop
♦ Use a priming read
♦ Appreciate the need for structure
♦ Recognize structure
♦ Describe two special structures—case and do until

UNDERSTANDING UNSTRUCTURED SPAGHETTI CODE

Professional computer programs usually get far more complicated than the number-doubling program from Chapter 1, shown in Figure 2-1.

```
get inputNumber
calculatedAnswer = inputNumber * 2
print calculatedAnswer
```

Figure 2-1 Number-doubling program

Imagine the number of instructions in the computer program that NASA uses to calculate the launch angle of a space shuttle, or in the program the IRS uses to audit your income tax return. Even the program that produces a paycheck for you on your job contains many, many instructions. Designing the logic for such a program can be a time-consuming task. When you add several thousand instructions to a program, including several hundred decisions, it is easy to create a complicated mess. The popular name for snarled program statements is **spaghetti code**. The reason for the name should be obvious—it's as confusing to follow as following one noodle through a plate of spaghetti.

For example, suppose you are in charge of admissions at a college, and you've decided you will admit prospective students based on the following criteria:

- You will admit students who score 90 or better on the admission test your college gives as long as they are in the upper 75 percent of their high school graduating class. (These are smart students who score well on the admissions test. Maybe they didn't do so well in high school because it was a tough school, or maybe they have matured.)

- You will admit students who score at least 80 on the admission test if they are in the upper 50 percent of their high school graduating class. (These students score fairly well on the test, and do fairly well in school.)

- You will admit students who score only 70 on your test if they are in the top 25 percent of their class. (Maybe these students don't take tests well, but obviously they are achievers.)

Figure 2-2 summarizes the admission requirements:

Test Score	High School Rank (%)
90–100	25–100
80–89	50–100
70–79	75–100

Figure 2-2   Admission requirements

The flowchart for this program could look like the one in Figure 2-3. This kind of flowchart is an example of spaghetti code. Many computer programs (especially older computer programs) bear a striking resemblance to the flowchart in Figure 2-3. Such programs might "work," that is, they might produce correct results, but they are very difficult to read and maintain, and their logic is difficult to follow.

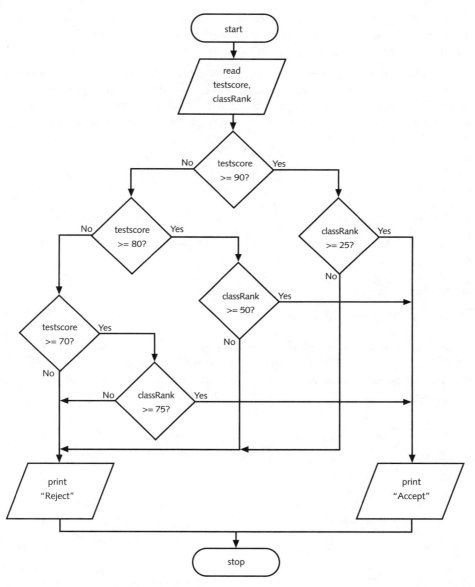

Figure 2-3   Spaghetti code example

UNDERSTANDING THE THREE BASIC STRUCTURES

In the mid–1960s, mathematicians proved that any program, no matter how complicated, can be constructed using only three sets of flowcharting shapes or structures. A **structure** is a basic unit of programming logic; each structure is a sequence, selection, or loop. With these three structures alone, you can diagram any event, from doubling a number to performing brain surgery.

The first of these structures is a sequence, as shown in Figure 2-4. With a **sequence**, you perform an action or event, and then you perform the next action in order. A sequence can contain any number of events, but there is no chance to branch off and skip any of the events. Once you start a series of events in a sequence, you must continue step-by-step until the sequence ends.

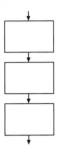

Figure 2-4   Sequence structure

The second structure is called a **selection**, or a **decision**, as shown in Figure 2-5. With this structure, you ask a question, and depending on the answer, you take one of two courses of action. Then, no matter which path you follow, you continue on with the next event.

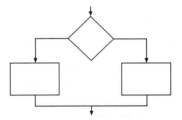

Figure 2-5   Selection structure

Some people call the selection structure an **if-then-else** because it fits the statement

```
if someCondition is true then
   do oneProcess
else
   do theOtherProcess
```

For example, while cooking you may decide

```
if we have brownSugar then
    use brownSugar
else
    use whiteSugar
```

Similarly, a payroll program might include a statement such as

```
if hoursWorked is more than 40 then
    calculate overtimePay
else
    calculate regularPay
```

Note that it is perfectly correct for one branch of the selection to be a "do nothing" branch. For example

```
if it is raining then
    take anUmbrella
```

or

```
if employee belongs to dentalPlan then
    deduct $40 from employeeGrossPay
```

The previous examples are **single-alternative ifs** and a diagram of their structure is shown in Figure 2-6. In these cases you don't take any special action if it is not raining or if the employee does not belong to the dental plan. The case where nothing is done is often called the **null case**.

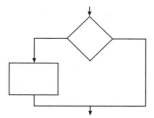

Figure 2-6   Single-alternative if structure

The third structure, shown in Figure 2-7, is a loop. You may hear programmers refer to looping as **repetition** or **iteration.** In a **loop**, you ask a question; if the answer requires an action, you perform the action and ask the original question again. If the question's answer requires that the action be taken again, you take the action and then ask the original question again. This continues until the answer to the question is such that the action is no longer required; then you exit the structure.

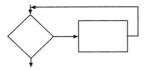

Figure 2-7   Loop structure

Some programmers call this structure a **do while** because it fits the statement

    while testCondition continues to be true, **do someProcess**

You encounter examples of looping every day, as in

    while you continue to beHungry

      take anotherBiteOfFood

or

    while unreadPages remain in the readingAssignment

      read another unreadPage

In a business program you can write

    while quantityInInventory remains low

      continue to orderItems

or

    while there are more retailPrices to be discounted

      compute a discount

All logic problems can be solved using only these three structures—sequence, selection, and looping. The three structures, of course, can be combined in an infinite number of ways. For example, there can be a sequence of steps followed by a selection or a loop followed by a sequence. Attaching structures end-to-end is called **stacking** structures. For example, Figure 2-8 shows a structured flowchart achieved by stacking structures and pseudocode that might follow that flowchart logic.

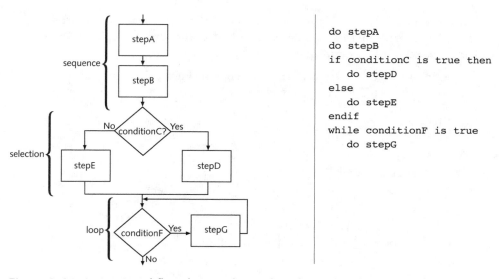

```
do stepA
do stepB
if conditionC is true then
    do stepD
else
    do stepE
endif
while conditionF is true
    do stepG
```

2

Figure 2-8   A structured flowchart and pseudocode

Additionally, you can replace any individual step in the preceding flowchart diagrams or pseudocode segments with another structure—any sequence, selection, or loop. For example, you can have a sequence of three steps on one side of a selection, as shown in Figure 2-9. Placing a structure within another structure is called **nesting** the structures. When you write the pseudocode for the logic shown in Figure 2-9, the convention is to indent all statements that depend on one branch of the decision as shown in the pseudocode. This shows that all three statements must execute if conditionA is not true.

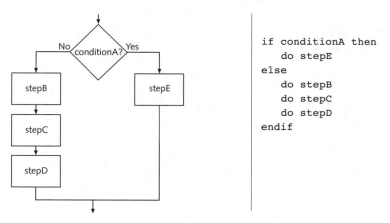

```
if conditionA then
    do stepE
else
    do stepB
    do stepC
    do stepD
endif
```

Figure 2-9   Flowchat and pseudocode for sequence within a selection

In the pseudocode in Figure 2-9, notice that the statements do stepB, do stepC, and do stepD align vertically and indent under the else. This shows that all three steps execute when conditionA is not true.

In place of one of the steps in the sequence in Figure 2-9, you can insert a selection. In Figure 2-10, stepC has been replaced with a selection structure that begins with a test of conditionF.

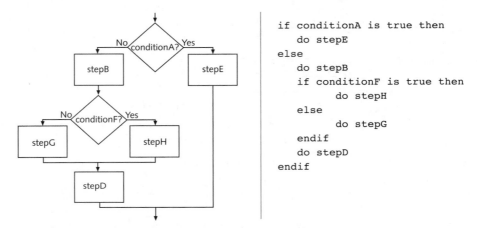

```
if conditionA is true then
    do stepE
else
    do stepB
    if conditionF is true then
            do stepH
    else
            do stepG
    endif
    do stepD
endif
```

Figure 2-10 Selection in a sequence within a selection

In the pseudocode shown in Figure 2-10, notice that do stepB, if conditionF then, else, and do stepD align vertically. This shows that they are all "on the same level." If you look at the same problem flowcharted in Figure 2-10, you see that you could draw a vertical line through the symbols with stepB, conditionF, and stepD. The flowchart and the pseudocode represent exactly the same logic. The stepH and stepG steps, on the other hand, are one level down; they are dependent on the answer to the conditionF question. Therefore, the do stepH and do stepG statements are indented one level further in the pseudocode.

Also notice that the pseudocode in Figure 2-10 has two endif statements. Each is aligned to correspond to an if. An endif always partners with the most recent if that does not already have an endif partner.

In place of do stepH on one side of the new selection in Figure 2-10, you can insert a loop. This loop, based on conditionI, appears inside the selection that is within the sequence that constitutes the "no" side of the original conditionA selection. See Figure 2-11.

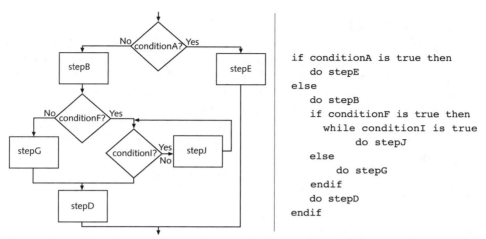

```
if conditionA is true then
   do stepE
else
   do stepB
   if conditionF is true then
      while conditionI is true
            do stepJ
   else
        do stepG
   endif
   do stepD
endif
```

Figure 2-11 Flowchart and pseudocode for loop within selection within sequence within selection

The combinations are endless, but each of a structured program's segments is a sequence, a selection, or a loop. Notice in Figure 2-12 that each structure has one entry and one exit point. One structure can attach to another only at one of these entry or exit points.

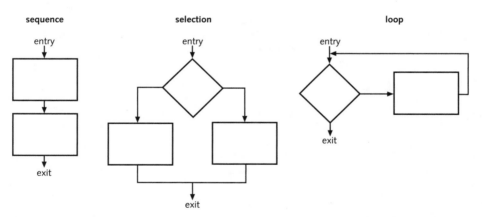

Figure 2-12   The three structures

In summary, a structured program has the following characteristics:

- A structured program includes only combinations of the three structures—sequence, selection, and loop.

- Structures connect to one another only at their entrance or exit points.

USING THE PRIMING READ

For a program to be structured and also work the way you want it to, sometimes you need to add extra steps. The priming read is one kind of added step. A **priming read** or **priming input** is the first read or data input statement in a program. If a program will read one hundred data records, you read the first data record in a statement separate from the other ninety-nine. You must do this to keep the program structured.

At the end of Chapter 1, you read about a program like the one in Figure 2-13. The program gets a number and checks for end of file. If it is not end of file, then the number is doubled, the answer is printed, and the next number is input.

Is the program represented by Figure 2-13 structured? At first, it might be hard to tell. The three allowed structures were illustrated in Figure 2-12.

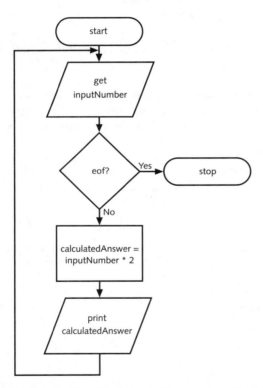

Figure 2-13   Flowchart of a number-doubling program

The flowchart in Figure 2-13 does not look exactly like any of the three shapes shown in Figure 2-12. However, because you may stack and nest structures while retaining overall structure, it might be difficult to determine whether the flowchart as a whole is structured. It's easiest to analyze the flowchart one step at a time. The beginning of the flowchart looks like Figure 2-14.

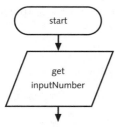

Figure 2-14 Beginning of a number-doubling flowchart

Is this portion of the flowchart structured? Yes, it's a sequence. The next part of the flow-chart looks like Figure 2-15.

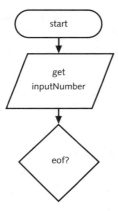

Figure 2-15 Number-doubling flowchart continued

The sequence is finished; either a selection or a loop is starting. You might not know which one, but you do know the sequence is not continuing because sequences can't have questions in them. With a sequence, each step must follow without any opportunity to branch away. Therefore, which type of structure starts with the question in Figure 2-15? Is it a selection or a loop?

With a selection structure, the logic goes in one of two directions after the question; then the flow comes back together. With a selection structure, the question is not asked a second time. In a loop, if the answer to the question results in the procedure execut-ing, then the logic returns to the question that started the loop; the question is always asked again.

In the doubling problem, if it is not eof (that is, if the end–of–file condition is not met), some math is done, an answer is printed, a new number is obtained, and the eof ques-tion is asked again. Therefore, the doubling problem contains a structure that is more like a loop than a selection.

The doubling problem *does* contain a loop, but it's not a structured loop. In a structured loop, the rules are:

1. You ask a question.

2. If the answer indicates you should perform a procedure, you do so.

3. If you perform the procedure, then you must go right back to repeat the question.

The flowchart in Figure 2-13 asks a question; if the answer is *no*, it performs more than one task: it does the arithmetic and it prints. Doing two things is acceptable because two steps constitute a sequence, and it is fine to nest a structure within another structure. However, when the sequence ends, the logic doesn't flow right back to the question. Instead, it goes *above* the question to get another number. For the loop in Figure 2-13 to be a structured loop, the logic must return to the eof question when the sequence ends.

The flowchart in Figure 2-16 shows the flow of logic returning to the eof immediately after the sequence. Figure 2-16 shows a structured flowchart, but the flowchart has one major flaw—it doesn't do the job of continuously doubling numbers.

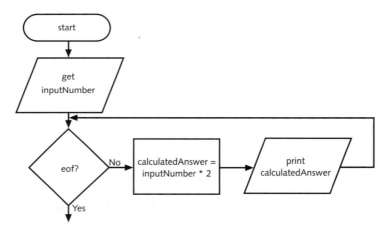

Figure 2-16   Structured, but nonfunctional, flowchart

Follow the flowchart in Figure 2-16 through a typical program run. Suppose when the program starts, the user enters a 9 for the value of inputNumber. That's not **eof**, so the number doubles, and 18 prints out as the **calculatedAnswer**. Then the question **eof?** is asked again. It can't be **eof** because the sentinel (ending) value can't be entered. The logic never returns to the **get inputNumber** step. Therefore, 9 doubles again and the answer, 18 prints again. It's still not eof, so the same steps are repeated. This goes on *forever*, with the answer 18 printing repeatedly. The program logic shown in Figure 2-16 is structured, but it doesn't work; the program in Figure 2-17 works, but it isn't structured!

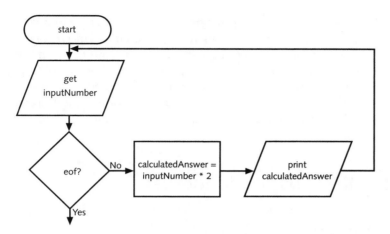

Figure 2-17 Functional, but nonstructured, flowchart

How can the number-doubling problem be both structured and work? Often, for a program to be structured, you must add something extra. In this case, it's an extra **get inputNumber** step. Consider the solution in Figure 2-18; it's structured, *and* it does what it's supposed to do! The program logic illustrated in Figure 2-18 contains a sequence and a loop. The loop contains another sequence.

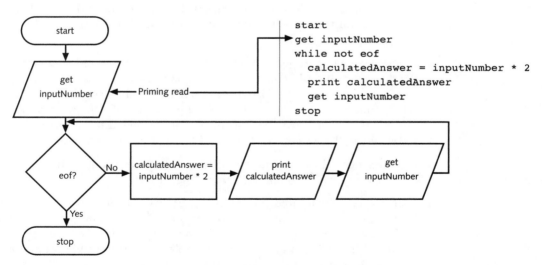

Figure 2-18 Functional, structured flowchart and pseudocode

The additional `get inputNumber` step is typical in structured programs. The first of the two input steps is the priming input, or priming read. The term *priming* comes from the fact that the read is first, or *primary* (what gets the process going, as in "priming the pump"). The purpose of the priming read step is to control the upcoming loop that begins with the eof question. The last element within the structured loop gets the next, and all subsequent input values. This is also typical in structured loops—the last step executed within the loop alters the condition tested in the question that begins the loop, which in this case is the `eof` question.

UNDERSTANDING THE REASONS FOR STRUCTURE

At this point you may very well be saying, "I liked the original doubling program just fine. I could follow it. Also, the first program had one less step in it, so it was less work. Who cares if a program is structured?"

Until you have some programming experience, it is difficult to appreciate the reasons for using nothing other than the three structures. However, staying with these three structures is better for the following reasons:

- Clarity—The doubling program is a small program. As programs get bigger, they get more confusing if they're not structured.

- Professionalism—All other programmers (and programming teachers you might encounter) expect your programs to be structured. It's the way things are done professionally.

- Efficiency—Most newer computer languages are structured languages with syntax that lets you deal efficiently with sequence, selection, and looping. Even programs written using older languages such as assembly languages, COBOL, and RPG, which were developed before the principles of structured programming, can be written in a structured form, and are expected to be written that way today. Newer languages like C++ and Java enforce structure by their syntax.

- Maintenance—In the future, you, as well as other programmers, will find it easier to modify and maintain structured programs.

- Modularity—Structured programs can be easily broken into routines that can be assigned to any number of programmers. The routines are then pieced back together like modular furniture at each routine's single entry or exit point. Additionally, often a module can be used in multiple programs, saving development time in the new project.

Most programs that you purchase are huge, consisting of thousands or millions of statements. If you've worked with a word processing program or spreadsheet, think of the number of menu options and keystroke combinations available to the user. Such programs are not the work of one programmer. The modular nature of structured programs means that work can be divided among many programmers; then the modules can be connected and a large program can be completed much more quickly. Money is often a motivating factor. The quicker you write a program and make it available for use, the sooner it begins making money for the developer.

Consider the college admission program from the beginning of the chapter. It has been rewritten in structured form in Figure 2-19. Not only is it easier to follow now, but also Figure 2-19 shows how you can simplify the main module even further by using a structured module that plugs into the main module in several locations. Figure 2-19 also shows structured pseudocode for the same problem.

 Don't be alarmed if it is difficult for you to follow the many nested ifs within the pseudocode in Figure 2-19. After you study the selection process in more detail, reading this type of pseudocode will become much easier for you.

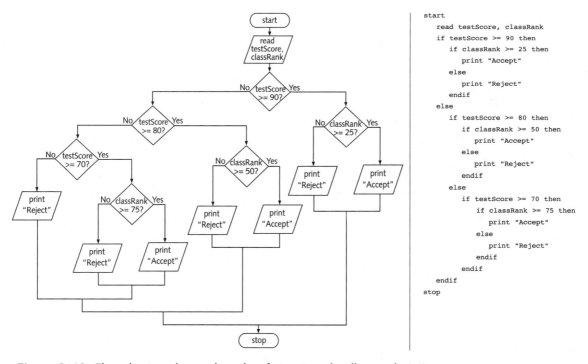

```
start
    read testScore, classRank
    if testScore >= 90 then
        if classRank >= 25 then
            print "Accept"
        else
            print "Reject"
        endif
    else
        if testScore >= 80 then
            if classRank >= 50 then
                print "Accept"
            else
                print "Reject"
            endif
        else
            if testScore >= 70 then
                if classRank >= 75 then
                    print "Accept"
                else
                    print "Reject"
                endif
            endif
        endif
    endif
stop
```

Figure 2-19: Flowchart and pseudocode of structured college admission program

RECOGNIZING STRUCTURE

When you are just learning about structured program design, it is difficult to detect whether a program's logic is structured or not. For example, is the flowchart segment in Figure 2-20 structured?

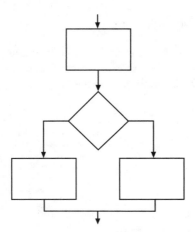

Figure 2-20   Example 1

Yes, it is. It has a sequence and a selection structure.

Is the flowchart segment in Figure 2-21 structured?

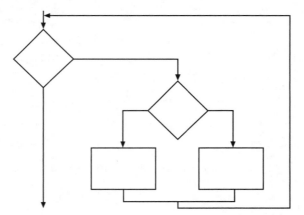

Figure 2-21   Example 2

Yes, it is. It has a loop, and within the loop is a selection.

Is the flowchart segment in Figure 2-22 structured? (The symbols are lettered so you can better follow the discussion.)

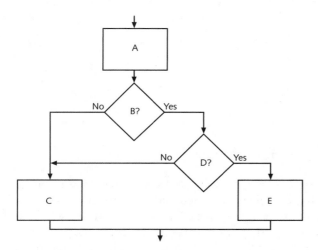

Figure 2-22   Example 3

No, it isn't; it is not constructed from the three basic structures. One way to straighten out a flowchart segment that isn't structured is to use what you can call the "spaghetti bowl" method; that is, picture the flowchart as a bowl of spaghetti that you must untangle. Imagine you can grab one piece of pasta at the top of the bowl, and start pulling. As you "pull" each symbol out of the tangled mess, you can untangle the separate paths until the entire segment is structured. For example, with the diagram in Figure 2-22, if you start pulling at the top, you encounter a procedure box, labeled A. (See Figure 2-23.)

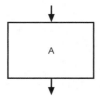

Figure 2-23   Untangling Example 3, first step

A single process like A is part of an acceptable structure—it constitutes at least the beginning of a sequence structure. Imagine you continue pulling symbols from the tangled segment. The next item in the flowchart is a question that tests a condition labeled B, as you can see in Figure 2-24.

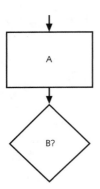

Figure 2-24   Untangling Example 3, second step

At this point, you know the sequence that was started with A has ended. Sequences never have decisions in them, so the sequence is finished; either a selection or a loop is beginning. A loop must return to the question at some later point. You can see from the original logic in Figure 2-22 that whether the answer to B is yes or no, the logic never returns to B. Therefore, B begins a selection structure, not a loop structure.

To continue detangling the logic, you pull up on the flowline that emerges from the left side (the "No" side) of Question B. You encounter C, as shown in Figure 2-25. When you continue beyond C, you reach the end of the flowchart.

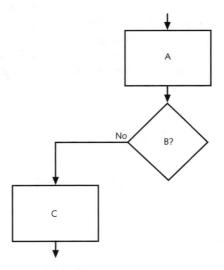

Figure 2-25   Untangling Example 3, third step

2

Now you can turn your attention to the *yes* side (the right side) of the condition tested in B. When you pull up on the right side, you encounter Question D. (See Figure 2-26.)

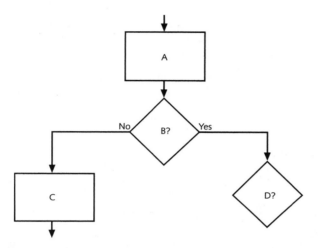

Figure 2-26 Untangling Example 3, fourth step

Follow the line on the left side of Question D. If the line is attached somewhere else, as it is (to Step C) in Figure 2-22, just untangle it by repeating the step that is tangled. (In this example you repeat Step C to untangle it from the other usage of C.) Continue pulling on the flowline that emerges from Step C, and you reach the end of the program segment, as shown in Figure 2-27.

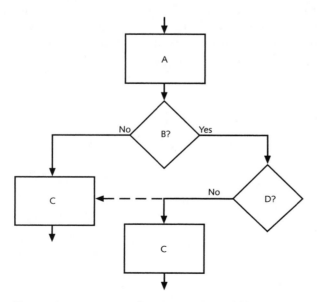

Figure 2-27 Untangling Example 3, fifth step

Now pull on the right side of Question D. Process E pops up, as shown in Figure 2-28; then you reach the end.

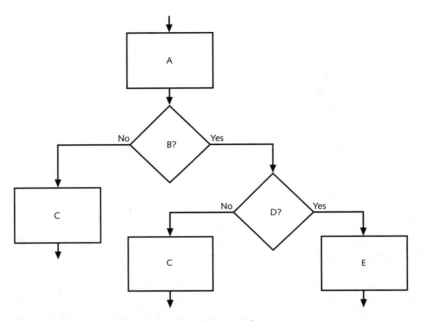

Figure 2-28   Untangling Example 3, sixth step

At this point the untangled flowchart has three loose ends. The loose ends of Question D can be brought together to form a selection structure, then the loose ends of Question B can be brought together to form another selection structure. The result is the flowchart shown in Figure 2-29. The entire flowchart segment is structured—it has a sequence (A) followed by a selection inside a selection.

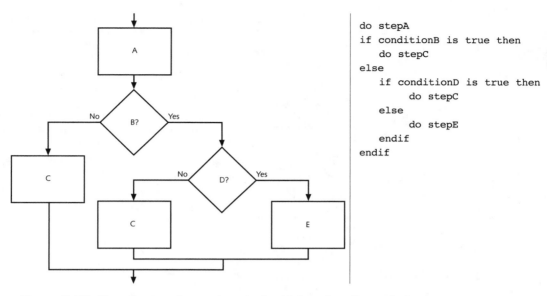

```
do stepA
if conditionB is true then
    do stepC
else
    if conditionD is true then
        do stepC
    else
        do stepE
    endif
endif
```

Figure 2-29 Flowchart and pseudocode for Untangling Example 3

If you would like to try structuring a very difficult example of an unstructured program, see Appendix A.

TWO SPECIAL STRUCTURES—CASE AND DO UNTIL

You can skip this section for now without any loss in continuity. Your instructor may prefer to discuss the case structure with the Decision chapter and the do until loop with the Looping chapter.

You can solve any logic problem you might encounter using only the three structures: sequence, selection, and loop. However, many programming languages allow two more structures: the case structure and the do until loop. These structures are never *needed* to solve a problem, but sometimes they are convenient. Programmers consider them both to be acceptable, legal structures.

The Case Structure

You use the **case structure** when there are several distinct possible values for a variable you are testing. Suppose you administer a school where tuition is $75, $50, $30, or $10 per credit hour, depending on whether a student is a freshman, sophomore, junior, or senior. The structured flowchart in Figure 2-30 shows a series of decisions that assign the correct tuition to a student.

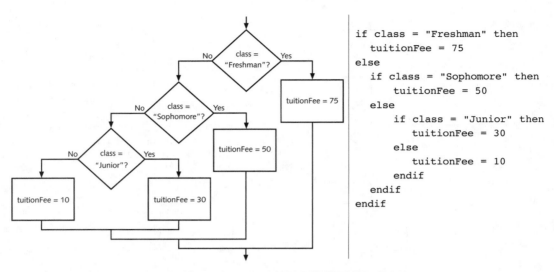

```
if class = "Freshman" then
   tuitionFee = 75
else
   if class = "Sophomore" then
      tuitionFee = 50
   else
      if class = "Junior" then
         tuitionFee = 30
      else
         tuitionFee = 10
      endif
   endif
endif
```

Figure 2-30 Flowchart and pseudocode of tuition decisions

This logic shown in Figure 2-30 is absolutely correct and completely structured. The `class="Junior"` selection structure is contained within the `class="Sophomore"` structure, which is contained within the `class="Freshman"` structure. Note that there is no need to ask if a student is a senior because if a student is not a freshman, sophomore, or junior, it is assumed the student is a senior.

Even though the program segments in Figure 2-30 are correct and structured, many programming languages permit a case structure as shown in Figure 2-31. When using the case structure, you test a variable against a series of values, taking appropriate action based on the variable's value. To many, these programs seem easier to read, and because you understand that the same results *could* be achieved with a series of structured selections (and thus be structured), the case structure is allowed. That is, if the first one is structured and the second one reflects the first one point by point, then the second one must be structured also.

Figure 2-31 Flowchart and pseudocode of case structure

The term default used in Figure 2-31 means "if none of the other cases were true." Each programming language you learn may use a different syntax for the default case.

Even though a programming language permits you to use the case structure, you should understand that the case structure is just a convenience that might make a flowchart, pseudocode, or actual program code easier to understand at first glance. When you write a series of decisions using the case structure, the computer still makes a series of individual decisions just as though you had used many if-then-else combinations. In other words, you might prefer looking at the diagram in Figure 2-31 to understand the tuition fees charged by a school, but a computer actually makes the decisions as shown in Figure 2-30—one at a time. When you write your own programs, it is always acceptable to express a complicated decision-making process as a series of individual selections.

The Do Until Loop

Recall that a structured loop (often called a do while) looks like Figure 2-32. A do until loop looks like Figure 2-33.

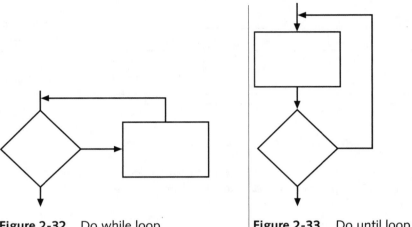

Figure 2-32   Do while loop   **Figure 2-33**   Do until loop

A difference exists between these two structures. In a do while loop, you ask a question and, depending on the answer, you might never enter the loop to execute the loop's procedure. Conversely, in a **do until loop** you ensure that the procedure executes at least once; then, depending on the answer to the controlling question, the loop may or may not execute additional times.

You can duplicate the same series of events generated by any do until loop by creating a sequence followed by a do while loop. Consider the flowcharts in Figures 2-34 and 2-35.

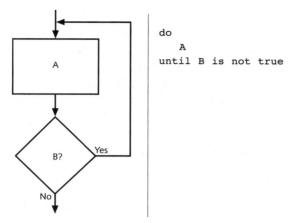

Figure 2-34 Flowchart and pseudocode for do until loop

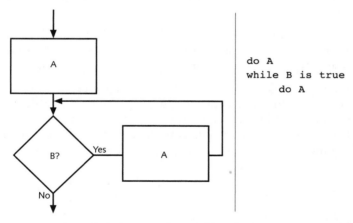

Figure 2-35 Flowchart and pseudocode for sequence followed by do while loop

In Figure 2–34, A is done, then B is asked. If B is yes, then A is done and B is asked again. In Figure 2-35, A is done, then B is asked. If B is yes, then A is done and B is asked again. Both flowcharts do exactly the same thing.

Because programmers understand that a do until can be expressed with a sequence followed by a do while, most languages allow the do until. Again, you are never required to use a do until; you can always accomplish the same events with a sequence followed by a do while.

CHAPTER SUMMARY

- The popular name for snarled program statements is spaghetti code.

- Clearer programs can be constructed using only three basic structures: sequence, selection, and loop. These three structures can be combined in an infinite number of ways by stacking and nesting them. Each structure has one entry and one exit point; one structure can attach to another only at one of these entry or exit points.

- A priming read or priming input is the first read or data input statement prior to beginning a structured loop. The last step within the loop gets the next, and all subsequent, input values.

- You use structured techniques to promote clarity, professionalism, efficiency, and modularity.

- One way to straighten a flowchart segment that isn't structured is to imagine the flowchart as a bowl of spaghetti that you must untangle.

- You can use a case structure when there are several distinct possible values for a variable you are testing. When you write a series of decisions using the case structure, the computer still makes a series of individual decisions.

- In a do while loop you ask a question and, depending on the answer, you might never enter the loop to execute the loop's procedure. In a do until loop, you ensure that the procedure executes at least once. You can duplicate the same series of events generated by any do until loop by creating a sequence followed by a do while loop.

EXERCISES

1. Match the term with the structure diagram. (Because the structures go by more than one name, there are more terms than diagrams.)

   1. sequence   5. decision
   2. selection   6. if-then-else
   3. loop   7. iteration
   4. do while

   a.

   b.

   c.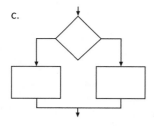

2. Match the term with the pseudocode segment. (Because the structures go by more than one name, there are more terms than pseudocode segments.)

   1. sequence   4. decision
   2. selection   5. if-then-else
   3. loop   6. iteration

   a. `while not eof`
      `   print theAnswer`

b. if inventoryQuantity > 0 then
       do fillOrderProcess
   else
       do backOrderNotification
   endif

c. do localTaxCalculation
   do stateTaxCalculation
   do federalTaxCalculation

3. Is each of the following segments structured or unstructured? If unstructured, redraw it so it does the same thing but is structured.

a.

b.

2

c.

d.

e.

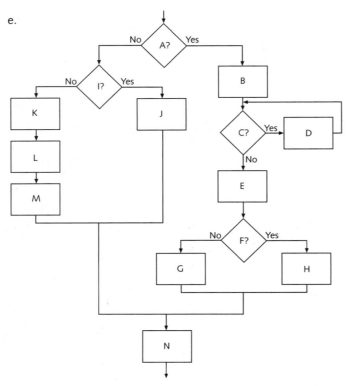

4. Write pseudocode for each example (a through e) in Exercise 3.

5. Assume you have created a mechanical arm that can hold a pen. The arm can perform the following tasks:

   ◻ lower the pen to a piece of paper

   ◻ raise the pen from the paper

   ◻ move the pen one inch along a straight line (If the pen is lowered, this action draws a one-inch line from left to right; if the pen is raised, this action just repositions the pen one inch to the right.)

   ◻ turn 90 degrees to the right

   ◻ draw a circle that is one inch in diameter

   Draw a structured flowchart or write pseudocode that would cause the arm to draw the following:

   a. a one-inch square

   b. a two-inch by one-inch rectangle

   c. a string of three beads

   Have a fellow student act as the mechanical arm and carry out your instructions.

2

6. Assume you have created a mechanical robot that can perform the following tasks:

   ◻ stand up

   ◻ sit down

   ◻ turn left 90 degrees

   ◻ turn right 90 degrees

   ◻ take a step

   Additionally, the robot can determine the answer to one test condition:

   ◻ Am I touching something?

   Place two chairs 20 feet apart, directly facing each other. Draw a structured flowchart or write pseudocode that would allow the robot to start from a sitting position in one chair, cross the room, and end up sitting in the other chair.

   Have a fellow student act as the robot and carry out your instructions.

7. Draw a structured flowchart of your preparation to go to work or school in the morning. Include at least two decisions and two loops.

8. Write structured pseudocode of your preparation to go to bed at night. Include at least two decisions and two loops.

3
MODULES, HIERARCHY CHARTS, AND DOCUMENTATION

After studying Chapter 3, you should be able to:

♦ Describe the advantages of modularization
♦ Modularize a program
♦ Understand how a module can call another module
♦ Explain how to declare variables
♦ Create hierarchy charts
♦ Understand documentation
♦ Create print charts
♦ Interpret file descriptions
♦ Understand the attributes of complete documentation

MODULES, SUBROUTINES, PROCEDURES, FUNCTIONS, OR METHODS

Programmers seldom write programs as one long series of steps. Instead, they break the programming problem down into reasonable units and tackle one small task at a time. These reasonable units are called **modules**. Programmers also refer to them as **subroutines**, **procedures**, **functions**, or **methods**.

 The name that programmers use for their modules usually reflects the programming language they use. COBOL, RPG, and BASIC programmers are most likely to use "subroutine." Pascal and Visual Basic programmers use "procedure" (or "subprocedure"). C and C++ programmers call their modules "functions," while C# and Java programmers are more likely to use "method."

You are never required to break a large program into modules, but there are at least four reasons for doing so:

- Modularization provides abstraction.

- Modularization allows multiple programmers to work on a problem.

- Modularization allows you to reuse your work.

- Modularization makes it easier to identify structures.

Modularization Provides Abstraction

One reason modularized programs are easier to understand is that they enable a programmer to see the big picture. **Abstraction** is the process of paying attention to important properties while ignoring nonessential details. Life would be tedious without abstraction. For example, you can create a list of things to accomplish today:

```
Do laundry
Call Aunt Nan
Start term paper
```

Without abstraction, the list of chores would begin:

```
Pick up laundry basket
Put laundry basket in car
Drive to laundromat
Get out of car with basket
Walk into laundromat
Set basket down
Find quarters for washing machine
...and so on.
```

You might list a dozen more steps before you finish the laundry and move on to the second chore on your original list. If you had to consider every small, **low-level** detail of every task in your day, you would probably never make it out of bed in the morning. Using a higher-level, more abstract list makes your day manageable.

Likewise, some level of abstraction occurs in every computer program. Fifty years ago, you had to understand the low-level circuitry instructions your computer used. But now, newer **high-level** programming languages allow you to use English-like vocabulary in which one broad statement corresponds to dozens of machine instructions. No matter which high-level programming language you use, if you display a message on the monitor, you are never required to understand how a monitor works to create each pixel on the screen. You write an instruction like `print message` and the details of the hardware operations are handled for you.

Modules or subroutines provide another way to achieve abstraction. For example, a payroll program can call a module named `computeFederalWithholdingTax`. You can write the mathematical details of the function later, someone else can write them, or you can purchase them from an outside source. When you plan your main payroll program, your only concern is that a federal withholding tax will have to be calculated; you save the details for later.

Modularization Allows Multiple Programmers to Work on a Problem

When you dissect any large task into modules, you gain the ability to divide the task among various people. Rarely does a single programmer write a commercial program that you buy off the shelf. Consider any word processing, spreadsheet, or database program you have used. Each program has so many options, and responds to user selections in so many possible ways, that it would take years for a single programmer to write all the instructions. Professional software developers can write new programs in weeks or months, instead of years, by dividing large programs into modules and assigning each module to an individual programmer or programming team.

Modularization Allows You to Reuse Your Work

If a subroutine or function is useful and well written, you may want to reuse it more than once within a program or in other programs. For example, a routine that checks the current month to make sure it is valid (not lower than 1 or higher than 12) is useful in many programs written for a business. A program that uses a personnel file containing each employee's birth date, hire date, last promotion date, and termination date can use the month-validation module four times with each employee record. Other programs in an organization can also use the module; these include programs that ship customer orders, plan employees' birthday parties, and calculate when loan payments should be made. If you write the month-checking instructions so they are entangled with other statements in a program, they are difficult to extract and reuse. On the other hand, if you place the instructions in their own module, the unit becomes easily used and portable to other applications.

You can find many real-world examples of **reusability**. When you build a house, you don't invent plumbing and heating systems; you incorporate systems with proven designs. This certainly reduces the time and effort it takes to build a house. Assuming the plumbing and electrical systems you choose are also in service in other houses, it also improves your house's **reliability**. Similarly, software that is reusable is more reliable, yet saves time and money. If you create the functional components of your programs as stand-alone modules and test them in your current programs, much of the work will already be done when you use the modules in future applications.

Modularization Makes It Easier to Identify Structures

When you combine several programming tasks into modules, it may be easier for you to identify structures. For example, you learned in Chapter 2 that the selection structure looks like Figure 3-1.

When you work with a program segment that looks like Figure 3-2, you may question whether it is structured. If you can modularize some of the statements and give them a more abstract group name, as in Figure 3-3, it is easier to see that the program involves a major selection and that the program segment is structured.

Figure 3-1   Selection structure

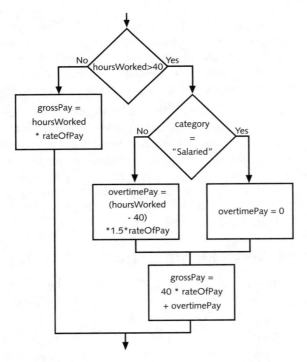

Figure 3-2   Section of logic from a payroll program

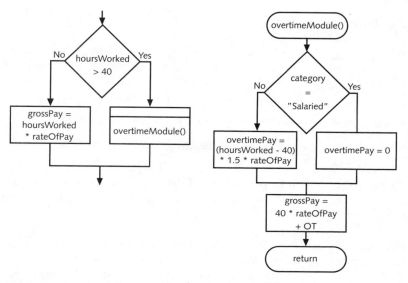

Figure 3-3   Modularized logic from a payroll program

The single program segment shown in Figure 3-2 accomplishes the same steps as the two program segments shown together in Figure 3-3; both programs are structured. The structure may be more obvious in the program segments in Figure 3-3 because you can see two distinct parts—a decision structure calls a subroutine that contains another decision structure, which is followed by a sequence. Neither of the program segments shown in Figures 3-2 and 3-3 is superior to the other in terms of functionality, but you may prefer to modularize to help you identify structures.

 As a professional programmer, you never modularize simply to *identify* whether a program is structured—you modularize for reasons of abstraction, ease of dividing the work, and reusability. However, as a beginning programmer, being able to see and identify structure is important.

MODULARIZING A PROGRAM

When you create a module or subroutine, you give the module a name. The rules for naming modules are different in every programming language, but they often are similar to the language's rules for variable names. In this text, module names will follow the same two rules used for variable names:

- Module names must be one word.

- Module names should have some meaning.

- Additionally, in this text module names will be followed by a set of parentheses. This will help you distinguish module names from variable names. This style corresponds to the way modules are named in many programming languages, such as Java, C++, C#, and Pascal.

 As you learn more about modules in specific programming languages, you will find that you sometimes place variable names within the parentheses of module names. For now, the parentheses we use at the end of module names will be empty.

 Most programming languages require that module names begin with an alphabetic character. This text will follow that convention.

When a program uses a module, you can refer to the main program as the **calling program**, because it "calls" the module's name when it wants to use the module. The flowchart symbol used to call a subroutine is a rectangle with a bar across the top. You place the name of the module you are calling inside the rectangle.

 Instead of placing only the name of the module you are calling in the flowchart, many programmers insert an appropriate verb such as "perform" or "do" before the module name.

You draw each module separately with its own sentinel symbols. The symbol that is the equivalent of the `start` symbol in a program contains the name of the module. This name must be identical to the name used in the calling program. The symbol that is the equivalent of the `end` symbol in a program does not contain "end"; after all, the program is not ending. Instead, the module ends with a "gentler," less final term such as `exit` or `return`. These words correctly indicate that when the module ends, the logical progression of statements will return to the calling program.

A flowchart and pseudocode for a program that calculates the arithmetic average of two numbers a user enters can look like Figure 3-4. Here the **main program**, or calling program, calls three modules.

The logic of the program in Figure 3-4 proceeds as follows:

1. The main program starts.

2. The main program calls the getInput() module.

3. Within the getInput()module, the prompt "Enter a number" displays.

4. Within the getInput() module, the program accepts a value into the firstNumber variable.

5. Within the getInput() module, the prompt "Enter another number" displays.

6. Within the getInput() module, the program accepts a value into the secondNumber variable.

7. The getInput() module ends, and control returns to the main calling program.

8. The main program calls the calculateAverage() module.

9. Within the calculateAverage() module, a value for the variable average is calculated.

10. The calculateAverage()module ends, and control returns to the main calling program.

11. The main program calls the printResult() module.

12. Within the printResult() module, the value of average displays.

13. Within the printResult() module, a thank-you message displays.

14. The printResult() module ends, and control returns to the main calling program.

15. The main program ends.

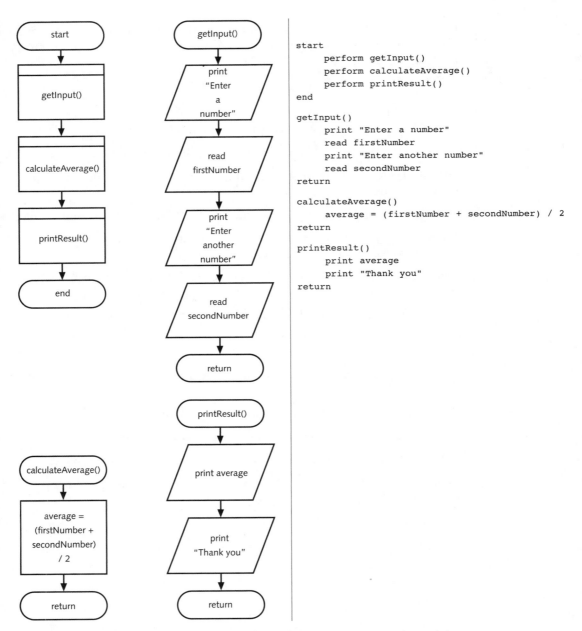

Figure 3-4 Flowchart and pseudocode for averaging program with modules

Whenever a main program calls a module, the logic transfers to the module. When the module ends, the logical flow transfers back to the main calling program and begins where it left off.

The computer keeps track of the correct memory address to which it should return after executing a module by recording the memory address in a location known as the *stack*.

MODULES CALLING OTHER MODULES

Just as a program can call a module or subroutine, any module can call another module. For example, the program illustrated in Figure 3-4 can be broken down further as shown in Figure 3-5.

After the program in Figure 3-5 begins:

1. The main program calls the `getInput()` module, and the logical flow transfers to that module.

2. From there, the `getInput()` module calls the `getFirstValue()` module, and the logical flow immediately transfers to the `getFirstValue()` module.

3. When `getFirstValue()` ends, control passes back to `getInput()` where `getSecondValue()` is called.

4. Control passes to `getSecondValue()`, and when this module ends control passes back to `getInput()`.

5. When `getInput()` ends, control returns to the main program.

6. Then `calculateAverage()` and `printResult()` execute as before.

Deciding whether to break down any particular module further into its own subroutines or submodules is an art. Programmers do follow some guidelines when deciding how far to break down subroutines or how much to put in them. Some companies may have arbitrary rules such as "a subroutine should never take more than a page," or "a module should never have more than 30 statements in it," or "never have a method or function with only one statement in it."

Rather than use such arbitrary rules, a better policy is to place together statements that contribute to one specific task. The more the statements contribute to the same job, the greater the **functional cohesion** of the module. A routine that checks the validity of a `month` variable's value, or one that prompts a user and allows the user to type in a value, would be considered cohesive. A routine that checks date validity, deducts insurance premiums, and computes federal withholding tax for an employee would be less cohesive.

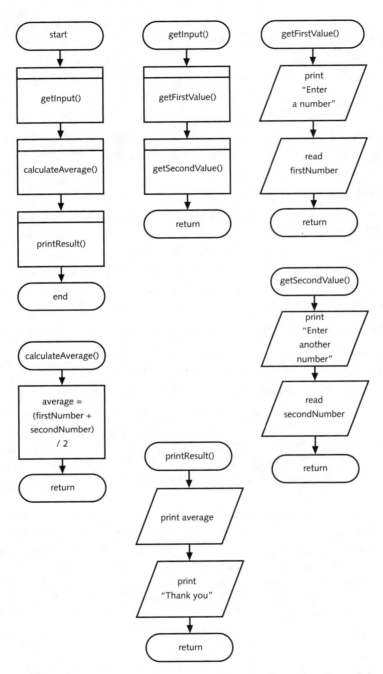

Figure 3-5   Flowchart for averaging program with submodules

DECLARING VARIABLES

The primary work of most modules in most programs you write is to manipulate data—for example, to calculate the figures needed for a paycheck, customer bill, or sales report. You store your program data in variables.

Many program languages require you to declare all variables before you use them. **Declaring a variable** involves providing a name for the memory location where the computer will store the variable value and notifying the computer what type of data to expect. Every programming language requires that you follow specific rules when declaring variables, but all the rules involve identifying at least two attributes for every variable:

- You must declare a data type.
- You must give the variable a name.

You learned in Chapter 1 that different programming languages provide different variable types, but all allow at least the distinction between character and numeric data. The rest of this book uses just two data types—`num` which will hold number values, and `char` which will hold all other values, including those that hold letters, and combinations of letters and numbers.

Remember, you also learned in Chapter 1 that variable names must not contain spaces, so this book uses statements such as `char lastName` and `num weeklySalary` to declare two variables of different types.

Some programming languages, like BASIC and RPG, do not require you to name any variable until the first time you use it. However, languages including COBOL, C++, C#, Java, and Pascal require that you declare variables with a name and a type. Some languages require that you declare all variables at the beginning of a program before you write any executable statements; others allow you to declare variables at any point, but require the declaration before you can use the variable. For our purposes, this book follows the convention of declaring all variables at the beginning of a program.

When you use many modern programming languages, variables typically are declared within each module that uses them. Such variables are known as **local variables**. As you continue your study of programming logic, you will learn how to use local variables and understand their advantages. For now, this text will use **global variables**—variables that are given a type and name once, and then used in all modules of the program.

For example, to complete the averaging program shown in Figure 3-5 so that its variables are declared, you can redraw the main program flowchart to look like Figure 3-6. Three variables are required, `firstNumber`, `secondNumber`, and `average`. The variables are declared as the first step in the program, before you use any of them, and each is correctly identified as numeric. They appear to the side of the "declare variables" step in an **annotation symbol** or **annotation box**, which is simply an attached box containing notes. You can use an annotation symbol any time you have more to write than conveniently fits within a flowchart symbol.

Many programming languages support more specific numeric types with names like int (for integers or whole numbers), float (for floating point or decimal-place values), and double (for double-precision floating point values, which means more memory space is reserved). Many languages distinguish even more precisely. For example, in addition to whole-number integers, C++, C#, and Java allow short integers and long integers, which require less and more memory, respectively.

Many programming languages support more specific character types. Often, programming languages provide a distinction between single character variables (like an initial or a grade in a class) and string variables, like a last name, which hold multiple characters.

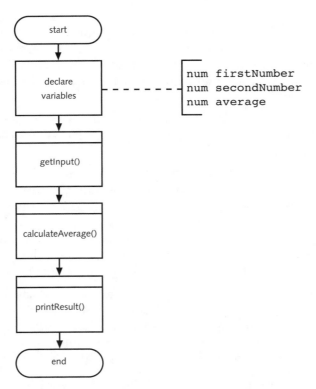

Figure 3-6   Averaging program with declared variables

Programmers sometimes create a **data dictionary**, which is a list of every variable name used in a program, along with its type, size, and description. When a data dictionary is created, it becomes part of the program documentation.

After you name a variable, you must use that exact name every time you refer to the variable within your program.

3

CREATING HIERARCHY CHARTS

When a program has several modules calling other modules, programmers often use a tool besides flowcharts or pseudocode to show the overall picture of how these modules are related to one another. You can use a **hierarchy chart** to illustrate modules' relationships. A hierarchy chart does not tell you what tasks are to be performed within a module; it doesn't tell you *when* or *how* a module executes. It tells you only which routines exist within a program and which routines call which other routines.

The hierarchy chart for the last version of the value-averaging program looks like Figure 3-7, and shows which modules call which others. You don't know *when* the modules are called or *why* they are called; that information is in the flowchart or pseudocode. A hierarchy chart just tells you which modules *are* called by other modules.

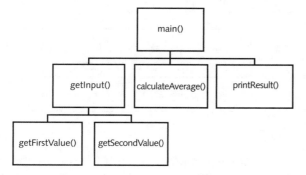

Figure 3-7   Hierarchy chart for value-averaging program

You may have seen hierarchy charts for organizations, such as the one in Figure 3-8. The chart shows who reports to whom, not when or how often they report. Program hierarchy charts operate in an identical manner.

Figure 3-8   An organizational hierarchy chart

Figure 3-9 shows an example of a hierarchy chart for the billing program of a mail order company. The hierarchy chart supplies module names only; it provides a general overview of the tasks to be performed without specifying any details.

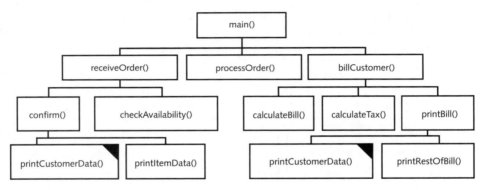

Figure 3-9   Billing program hierarchy chart

The hierarchy chart can be a useful tool when a program must be modified months or years after the original writing. For example, if a tax law changes, a programmer might be asked to rewrite the `calculateTax()` module in the billing program diagrammed in Figure 3-9. As the programmer changes the `calculateTax()` routine, the hierarchy chart shows what other dependent routines might be affected. A hierarchy chart is useful for "getting the big picture" in a complex program.

Because program modules are reusable, a specific module may be called from several locations within a program. For example, in the billing program hierarchy chart in Figure 3-9, you can see that the `printCustomerData()` module is used twice. By convention, you blacken a corner of each box representing the `printCustomerData()` module. This action alerts readers that any change to this module will affect more than one location.

Understanding Documentation

Documentation refers to all of the supporting material that goes with a program. Two broad categories of documentation are intended for the programmer and for the user. People who use computer programs are called **end users**, or **users** for short. Most likely you have been the end user of an application such as a word processing program or a game. When you purchase software that other programmers have written, you appreciate clearly written instructions on how to install and use the software. These instructions constitute user documentation. In a small organization, programmers may write user documentation, but in most organizations, systems analysts or technical writers produce end-user instructions. These instructions may take the form of a printed manual or may be presented online through a Web site or on a compact disc.

When programmers begin to plan the logic of a computer program, they require instructions known as **program documentation**. End users never see program documentation; rather, programmers use it when planning or modifying programs.

Program documentation falls into two categories: internal and external. **Internal program documentation** consists of **program comments**, or nonexecuting statements that programmers place within their code to explain program statements in English. The method for inserting comments within a program differs in each programming language, but every method provides a means for inserting illuminating comments that do not affect the running of a program. You will learn how to insert comments when you learn a specific programming language.

 In the BASIC programming language, program comments begin with the letters REM (for REMark). In C++, C#, and Java, comments can begin with two forward slashes (//). An RPG program indicates that a line is a comment if there is an asterisk (*) in the sixth typed position in the line.

External program documentation includes all the supporting paperwork that programmers develop before they write a program. Since most programs have input, processing, and output, usually there is documentation for all these functions.

Output Documentation

Output documentation is usually the first to be written. This may seem backwards, but if you're planning a trip, which do you decide first: how to get to your destination or where you're going?

Most requests for programs arise because a user needs particular information to be output, so the planning of program output is usually done in consultation with the person or persons who will be using the output. Only after the desired output is known can the programmer hope to plan the processes needed to produce the output.

Often the programmer does not design the output. Instead, the user who requests the output presents the programmer (or programming team) with an example or sketch of the desired result. Then the programmer might work with the user to refine the request, suggest improvements in the design, or clarify the user's needs. If you don't determine precisely what the user wants or needs at this point, you will write a program that the user soon wants redesigned and rewritten.

The most common type of output is a printed report. You can design a printed report on a **printer spacing chart**, which is also referred to as a **print chart** or a **print layout**. Figure 3-10 shows a printer spacing chart, which basically looks like graph paper. The chart has many boxes, and in each box the designer places one character that will be printed.

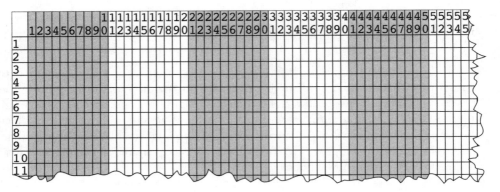

Figure 3-10   Printer spacing chart

    Besides using handwritten print charts, you can design report layouts on a computer using a word processing program or other design software.

For example, if you want to create a printed report with the title INVENTORY REPORT and you decide that the title looks best 11 spaces over from the left of the page and one line down, you would begin to create the printer spacing chart shown in Figure 3-11.

Figure 3-11   Printer spacing chart with first title

You might want to skip a line and print column headings ITEM NAME, PRICE, and QUANTITY IN STOCK, so the printer spacing chart would evolve into the one in Figure 3–12.

Figure 3-12   Printer spacing chart with title and column headings

The title and column headings will be **constant** on every page of the report, so they are written on the print chart literally. The exact spacing and use of upper- or lowercase make a difference. Notice that the constants used within a report do not need to follow the same rules as variable names. Within a report, constants like INVENTORY REPORT and ITEM NAME can contain spaces. These headings exist to help readers understand the information presented in the report—not for a computer to interpret.

A print layout typically shows how the variable data will appear on the report. Of course, the data will probably be different every time the report is run. Thus, instead of writing in actual item names and prices, the users and programmers usually use Xs to represent generic variable character data and 9s to represent generic variable numeric data. (Some programmers use Xs for both character and numeric data.) For example, Figure 3-13 shows how some data will look in the print chart.

Figure 3-13 Print chart with generic data

Each line with its Xs and 9s representing data is a **detail line**, because it contains the data details. Detail lines typically appear many times per page, as opposed to **heading lines**, which usually appear only once per page.

Even though an actual inventory report might eventually go on for hundreds or thousands of detail lines, writing two or three rows of Xs and 9s is sufficient to show how the data will appear. For example, if a report contains employee names and salaries, those data items will occupy the same print positions on output for line after line, whether the output eventually contains 10 employees or 10,000. A few rows of identically positioned Xs and 9s are sufficient to establish the pattern.

In any report layout, then, you write in constant data (like headings) that will be the same on every run of this report. You write Xs and 9s to represent the variable data (like the items, their prices, and their quantities) that will change from run to run.

In the inventory report layout shown in Figure 3-13, the headings truly are constant, but you should not assume that all headings are completely constant. Let's say that your user decides to include the date in the inventory report heading. The report might now have a layout like Figure 3-14. Notice that now there is variable data, the date, in the report heading.

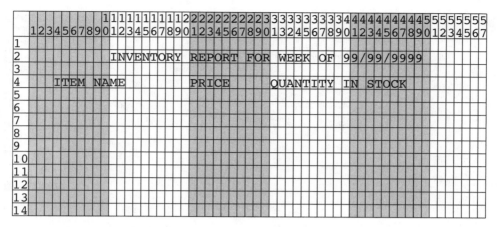

Figure 3-14   Variable data in report heading

For a long report that requires multiple pages, perhaps the user will also decide that the headings should appear at the top of every printed page, and that page numbers should also be added. Figure 3-15 shows how you might indicate page numbers.

Figure 3-15   Heading with page numbers

Just as variable data might appear in a heading, constants might appear in the detail lines. For example, if the company sells all of its inventory items by the dozen, then each number in the QUANTITY IN STOCK column actually represents the number of dozens of that item. The users might choose to see the word DOZEN with each detail line. The print chart in Figure 3-16 indicates that the word DOZEN would literally appear on each line.

```
         1111111111222222222233333333334444444444555555555
1234567890123456789012345678901234567890123456789012345678901234567
 1
 2               INVENTORY REPORT
 3
 4     ITEM NAME          PRICE       QUANTITY IN STOCK
 5
 6     XXXXXXXXXXXXXXXX   999.99           9999 DOZEN
 7     XXXXXXXXXXXXXXXX   999.99           9999 DOZEN
 8
 9
10
11
12
13
14
```

Figure 3-16   Print chart with literal in each detail line

Besides header lines and detail lines, reports often include special lines at the end of a report. These may have variable data only as in Figure 3–17, or constant data only as in Figure 3–18. Most often, however, reports will have both, as in Figure 3–19.

```
         1111111111222222222233333333334444444444555555555
1234567890123456789012345678901234567890123456789012345678901234567
 1
 2               INVENTORY REPORT
 3
 4     ITEM NAME          PRICE       QUANTITY IN STOCK
 5
 6     XXXXXXXXXXXXXXXX   999.99           9999
 7     XXXXXXXXXXXXXXXX   999.99           9999
 8
 9                                        99999
10
11
12
13
14
```

Figure 3-17   Report with variable data at end

```
            1111111111222222222233333333334444444444555555555
   123456789012345678901234567890123456789012345678901234567
1
2            INVENTORY REPORT
3
4    ITEM NAME            PRICE       QUANTITY IN STOCK
5
6    XXXXXXXXXXXXXXX      999.99            9999
7    XXXXXXXXXXXXXXX      999.99            9999
8
9    THANK YOU FOR USING THIS PROGRAM
10
11
12
13
14
```

Figure 3-18 Report with constant data at end

```
            1111111111222222222233333333334444444444555555555
   123456789012345678901234567890123456789012345678901234567
1
2            INVENTORY REPORT
3
4    ITEM NAME            PRICE       QUANTITY IN STOCK
5
6    XXXXXXXXXXXXXXX      999.99            9999
7    XXXXXXXXXXXXXXX      999.99            9999
8
9                        GRAND TOTAL:   999999
10
11
12
13
14
```

Figure 3-19 Report with combined constant and variable data at end

Even though lines at the end of a report don't always contain numeric totals, they are usually referred to generically as **total lines**.

INPUT DOCUMENTATION

Once you have planned the design of the output, you need to know what input is available to produce this output. If you are producing a report from stored data, you frequently will be provided with a **file description** that describes the data that are contained in a file. You usually find a file's description as part of an organization's information systems' documentation; physically, the description might be on paper in a binder in the Information Systems department, or it might be stored on a disk. If the file you will use comes from an outside source, the person requesting the report will have to provide you with a description of the data stored on the file. For example, Figure 3-20 shows an inventory file description for a file that could be used to produce the report described in Figure 3-13.

 Not all programs use previously stored input files. Some use interactive input data supplied by a user during the execution of a program.

 Some programs produce an output file that is stored directly on a storage device, such as a disk. If your program produces file output instead of printed report output, you will create a file description for your output. Other programs then may use your output file description as an input description for their programs.

```
INVENTORY FILE DESCRIPTION
File name: INVTRY
FIELD DESCRIPTION      POSITIONS     DATA TYPE     DECIMALS
Name of item           1—15          Character
Price of item          16—20         Numeric       2
Quantity in stock      21—24         Numeric       0
```

Figure 3-20   Inventory file description

The inventory file description in Figure 3-20 shows that each item's name occupies the first 15 characters of each record in the file. Some item names may require all 15 positions, for example "12 by 16 carpet", which contains exactly 15 characters including spaces. Other item names require fewer than the allotted 15 positions, for example "door mat". In such cases, the remaining allotted positions remain blank. Whether the item name requires all 15 positions or not, the price for each item begins in position 16 of each input record.

The price of any item in the inventory file is allowed five positions, 16 through 20. Two of the positions are reserved for decimal places. Typically, decimal points themselves are not stored in data files; they are **implied** or **assumed**. Also typically, numeric data are stored with leading zeros so that all allotted positions are occupied. Thus an item valued at $345.67 is stored as 34567, and an item valued at $1.23 is stored as 00123.

 Decimal points are implied in data files, but occupy positions on printed reports. Within data files, it is most efficient to save space. On printed reports, it is most important to represent information in a way that is easy for the reader to interpret.

Leading zeros fill numeric fields within files, but are not used on printed reports. Within data files, numeric fields must be totally numeric so spaces are not allowed within numeric fields. On printed reports, information must be easy for the reader to interpret; readers usually do not expect to see leading zeros in numeric data.

Typically, programmers create one program variable for each field that is part of the input file. In addition to the field descriptions contained in the input documentation, the programmer might be given specific variable names to use for each field, particularly if such variable names must agree with those other programmers working on the project are using. In many cases, however, programmers are allowed to choose their own variable names. Therefore, you can choose `itemName`, `nameOfItem`, `itemDescription`, or any other reasonable one-word variable name when you refer to the item name within your program. The variable names you use within your program need not match constants printed on the report. Thus, the variable `nameOfItem` might hold the characters that will print under the column heading NAME OF ITEM.

Recall the data hierarchy relationship introduced in Chapter 1:

- Database
- File
- Record
- Field
- Character

Whether the inventory file is part of a database or not, it will contain many records; each record will contain an item name, price, and quantity, which are fields. In turn, the field that holds the name of an item might contain up to 15 characters, for example "12 by 16 carpet", "blue miniblinds", or "diskette holder".

Organizations may use different forms to relay the information about records and fields, but the very least the programmer needs to know is:

- What is the name of the file?
- What data does it contain?
- How much room does the file and each of its fields take up?
- What type of data is each field—character or numeric?

The inventory file description in Figure 3-20 appears to contain all the information the programmer needs to create the output requested in Figure 3-13. The output lists each item's name, price, and quantity, and the input records clearly contain that data. Often, however, a file description more closely resembles the description in Figure 3-21.

```
INVENTORY FILE DESCRIPTION
File name: INVTRY
FIELD DESCRIPTION              POSITIONS    DATA TYPE      DECIMALS
Item number                   1—4          Numeric        0
Name of item                  5—19         Character
Size                          20           Numeric        0
Manufacturing cost of item    21—25        Numeric        2
Retail price of item          26—30        Numeric        2
Quantity in stock             31—34        Numeric        0
Reorder point                 35—38        Numeric        0
Sales rep                     39—48        Character
Sales last year               49—54        Numeric        0
```

Figure 3-21   Expanded inventory file description

The file description in Figure 3-21 contains nine fields. With this file description, it's harder to pinpoint the information needed for the report; but the necessary data fields are available, and you still can write the program. The input file contains more information than you need for the report you want to print, so you will ignore some of the input fields, such as item number and sales rep. These fields certainly may be used in other reports within the company. Typically, data input files contain more data than any one program requires.

However, if the input file description resembles Figure 3-22, then there is not enough data to produce the requested report.

```
INVENTORY FILE DESCRIPTION
File name: INVTRY
FIELD DESCRIPTION              POSITIONS    DATA TYPE      DECIMALS
Item number                   1—4          Numeric        0
Name of item                  5—19         Character
Size                          20           Numeric        0
Manufacturing cost of item    21—25        Numeric        2
Retail price of item          26—30        Numeric        2
Reorder point                 35—38        Numeric        0
Sales rep                     39—48        Character
Sales last year               49—54        Numeric        0
```

Figure 3-22   Insufficient inventory file description

In Figure 3-22, there is no indication that the input file contains a figure for quantity in stock. If the user really needs (or wants) the report as requested, it's out of the programmer's hands until the data can be collected from some source.

Each field printed on a report need not exist in the same format on the input file. Assume that a user requests a report in the format shown in Figure 3-23, and that the input file description is the one in Figure 3-22. In this case, it's difficult to determine whether you can create the requested report because the input file does not contain a profit field. However, since the input data includes the company's cost and the company's selling price for each item, you can calculate the profit within your program and produce the desired output.

```
                        1111111111222222222233333333334444444444555555555
          1234567890123456789012345678901234567890123456789012345 67
 1
 2                 PROFIT REPORT
 3
 4     ITEM NUMBER            PRICE       COST         PROFIT
 5
 6            9999            999.99     999.99       999.99
 7            9999            999.99     999.99       999.99
 8
 9
10
11
12
13
14
```

Figure 3-23   Requested profit report

COMPLETING THE DOCUMENTATION

When you have designed the output and confirmed that it is possible to produce it from the input, then you can plan the logic of the program, code the program, and test the program. The original output design, input description, flowchart or pseudocode, and program code all become part of the program documentation. These pieces of documentation typically are stored together in a binder within the programming department of an organization, where they can be studied later when program changes become necessary.

In addition to this program documentation, you typically must create user documentation. **User documentation** includes all the manuals or other instructional materials that nontechnical people use, as well as the operating instructions that computer operators and data-entry personnel need. It needs to be written clearly, in plain language, with reasonable expectations of the users' expertise. Within a small organization, the programmer may prepare the user documentation. In a large organization, user documentation is usually prepared by technical writers or systems analysts, who oversee programmers' work and coordinate programmers' efforts. These professionals consult with the programmer to ensure that the user documentation is complete and accurate.

The areas addressed in user documentation may include:

- How to prepare input for the program
- To whom the output should be distributed
- How to interpret the normal output

- How to interpret and react to any error message generated by the program
- How frequently the program needs to run

 Complete documentation also might include operations support documentation. This type of documentation provides backup and recovery information,
run-time instructions, and security considerations for computer center personnel who run large applications within data centers.

All these issues must be addressed before a program can be fully functional in an organization. When users throughout an organization can supply input data to computer programs and obtain the information they need in order to do their jobs well, then a skilled
programmer has provided a complete piece of work.

CHAPTER SUMMARY

- Programmers break programming problems down into smaller, reasonable units
  called modules, subroutines, procedures, functions, or methods. Modularization
  provides abstraction, allows multiple programmers to work on a problem, makes
  it easy to reuse your work, and allows you to identify structures more easily.

- When you create a module or subroutine, you give the module a name that a
  calling program uses when the module is about to execute. The flowchart symbol used to call a subroutine is a rectangle with a bar across the top; the name
  of the module that you are calling is inside the rectangle. You draw each module separately with its own sentinel symbols.

- A module can call other modules.

- Declaring a variable involves providing a name for the memory location where
  the computer will store the variable value and notifying the computer what
  type of data to expect.

- You can use a hierarchy chart to illustrate modules' relationships.

- Documentation refers to all of the supporting material that goes with a program.

- Output documentation is usually written first. You can design a printed report
  on a printer spacing chart to represent both constant and variable data.

- A file description lists the data that are contained in a file, including a description, size, and data type. Typically, numeric data are stored with leading zeros
  and without decimal points.

- In addition to program documentation, you typically must create user documentation, which includes the manuals or other instructional materials that
  nontechnical people use, as well as the operating instructions that computer
  operators and data-entry personnel may need.

EXERCISES

1. Redraw the following flowchart so that the compensation calculations are in a module.

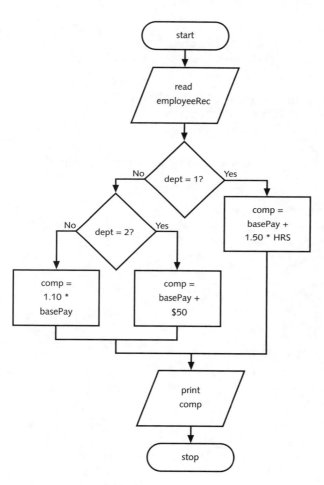

2. Rewrite the following pseudocode so the discount calculations are in a module.

```
start
   read customerRecord
   if quantityOrdered > 100 then
       discount = .20
   else
       if quantityOrdered > 12 then
           discount = .10
       endif
   endif
   total = priceEach * quantityOrdered
   total = total - discount * total
   print total
end
```

3. What are the final values of variables a, b, and c after the following program runs?

```
start
   a = 2
   b = 4
   c = 10
   while c > 6
       changeBAndC()
   if a = 2 then
       changeA()
   endif
   if c = 10 then
       changeA()
   else
       changeBAndC()
   endif
end

changeBAndC()
   b = b + 1
   c = c - 1
return

changeA()
   a = a + 1
   b = b - 1
return
```

4. Draw a typical hierarchy chart for a paycheck-producing program. Try to think of at least 10 separate modules that might be included.

5. Design a print chart for a payroll roster that is intended to list the following items for every employee: employee's first name, last name, and salary.

6. Design a print chart for a payroll roster that is intended to list the following items for every employee: employee's first name, last name, hours worked, rate per hour, gross pay, federal withholding tax, state withholding tax, union dues, and net pay.

7. Given the following input file description, determine if there is enough information provided to produce each of the requested reports:

```
INSURANCE PREMIUM LIST
File name: INSPREM
FIELD DESCRIPTION        POSITIONS      DATA TYPE      DECIMALS
Name of insured
    driver               1-40           Character
Birth date               41-46          Numeric           0
Gender                   47             Character
Make of car              48-57          Character
Year of car              58-61          Numeric           0
Miles driven
    per year             62-67          Numeric           0
Number of
     traffic tickets     68-69          Numeric           0
```

a. A list of the names of all insured drivers

b. A list of very high-risk insured drivers, defined as male, under 25 years old, with more than two tickets

c. A list of low-risk insured drivers, defined as those with no tickets in the last three years, and over 30 years old

d. A list of insured drivers to contact about a special premium offer for those with a passenger car who drive under 10,000 miles per year

8. Given the INSPREM file description in Exercise 7, design a print chart to satisfy each of the following requests:

a. A list of every driver's name and make of car

b. A list of the names of all insured drivers who drive more than 20,000 miles per year

c. A list of the name, gender, make of car, and year of car for all drivers who have more than two tickets

d. A report that summarizes the number of tickets held by drivers who were born in 1940 or before, from 1941–1960, from 1961–1980, and from 1981 on

e. A report that summarizes the number of tickets held by drivers in the four birth-date categories listed in Part d, grouped by gender

4

WRITING A
COMPLETE PROGRAM

After studying Chapter 4, you should be able to:
♦ Plan the mainline logic for a complete program.
♦ Describe typical housekeeping tasks.
♦ Describe tasks typically performed in the main loop of a program.
♦ Describe tasks performed in the end-of-job module.

UNDERSTANDING THE MAINLINE LOGICAL FLOW THROUGH A PROGRAM

You're ready to plan the logic for your first complete computer program. The output is an inventory report, as shown in Figure 4-1. The report lists inventory items along with the price, cost, and profit of each item.

```
         1111111111222222222233333333334444444444555555555566
1234567890123456789012345678901234567890123456789012345678901
1
2                       INVENTORY REPORT
3
4     ITEM              RETAIL PRICE   MANUFACTURING   PROFIT PER
5     DESCRIPTION       EACH           COST EACH       ITEM
6
7     XXXXXXXXXXXXXXX   999.99         999.99          999.99
8     XXXXXXXXXXXXXXX   999.99         999.99          999.99
9
10
11
12
13
14
```

Figure 4-1   Print chart for inventory report

Figure 4-2 shows the input INVENTORY file description.

```
INVENTORY FILE DESCRIPTION
File name: INVENTORY
FIELD DESCRIPTION        POSITIONS       DATA TYPE       DECIMALS
Item name                1-15            Character
Price                    16-20           Numeric             2
Cost                     21-25           Numeric             2
Quantity in stock        26-29           Numeric             0
```

Figure 4-2   Inventory file description

 In some systems, filenames are limited to eight characters, so INVENTORY might be an unacceptable filename.

Examine the print chart and the input file description. Your first task is to determine whether you have all the data you need to produce the report. The output requires the item name, price, and cost, and you can see that all three are data items on the input file. The output also requires a profit figure for each item; you can determine the profit by subtracting an item's cost from its selling price. The input record contains an additional field, "Quantity in stock." Input records often contain more data than an application needs, so you will ignore this field in your program. You have all the necessary data so you can begin to plan the program.

Where should you begin? It's wise to try to understand the big picture first. You can write a program that reads records from an input file and produces a printed report as a **procedural program**—that is, a program in which one procedure follows another from beginning until the end. You write the entire set of instructions for a procedural program, and when the program executes, each instruction takes place one at a time following your program's logic. The overall or **mainline logic** of almost every procedural computer program can follow a general structure that consists of three distinct parts:

1. Performing housekeeping, or initialization tasks. **Housekeeping** includes steps you must perform at the beginning of a program to get ready for the rest of the program.

2. Performing the main loop within the program. The **main loop** contains the steps that are repeated for every record.

3. Performing the end-of-job routine. The **end-of-job routine** holds the steps you take at the end of the program to finish the application.

 Not all programs are procedural; some are object-oriented. A distinguishing feature of many object-oriented programs is that the user determines the timing of events in the main loop of the program by using an input device such as a mouse. As you advance in your knowledge of programming, you will learn more about object-oriented techniques.

You can write any procedural program as one long series of program language statements, but most programmers prefer to break their programs into at least three parts. The main program can call the three major modules as shown in the flowchart and pseudocode in Figure 4-3. The module or subroutine names, of course, are entirely up to the programmer.

Figure 4-4 shows the hierarchy chart for this program.

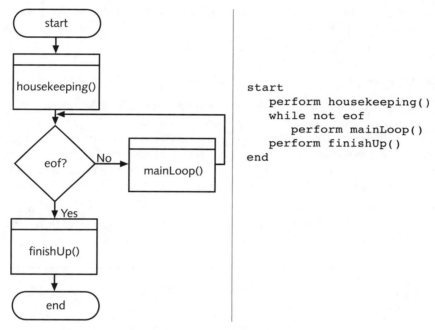

```
start
    perform housekeeping()
    while not eof
        perform mainLoop()
    perform finishUp()
end
```

Figure 4-3   Flowchart and pseudocode of mainline logic

Figure 4-4   Hierarchy chart for inventory report program

Breaking down a big program into three basic procedures helps keep the job manageable, allowing you to tackle a large job one step at a time. Dividing the work into routines allows you to assign the three major procedures to three different programmers if you choose. It also helps you keep the program structured.

HOUSEKEEPING TASKS

Housekeeping tasks include all the steps that must take place at the beginning of a program. Very often, this includes four major tasks:

- You declare variables.
- You open files.
- You perform any one-time-only tasks, such as printing headings at the beginning of a report.
- You read the first input record.

Declaring Variables

Your first task in writing any program is to **declare variables**. When you declare variables, you assign reasonable names to memory locations so you can store and retrieve data there. Declaring a variable involves selecting a name and a type. When you declare a variable in program code, the operating system will reserve space in memory to hold the contents of the variable. It will use the type (`num` or `char`) to determine how to store the information; it stores numeric and character values in different formats.

For example, within the inventory report program you need to supply variable names for the data fields that appear in each input record. You might decide on the variable names and types shown in Figure 4-5.

```
char    invItemName
num     invPrice
num     invCost
num     invQuantity
```

Figure 4-5   Variable declarations for the inventory file

 Some languages require that you provide storage size in addition to a type and name for each variable. Other languages provide a predetermined amount of storage based on the variable type; for example, four bytes for an integer or one byte for a character. Also, many languages require you to provide a length for strings of characters.

You can provide any names you choose for your variables. When you write another program that uses the same input file, you are free to choose completely new variable names. Similarly, other programmers can write programs that use the same file and choose their own variable names. The variable names just represent memory positions and are internal to your program. The files do not contain the variable names; files contain only data. When you read the characters "Cotton shirt" from an input file, it doesn't matter whether you store those characters at a memory location named `invItemName`, `nameOfItem`, `productDescription`, or any other one-word variable name.

Each of the four variable declarations in Figure 4-5 contains a type (character or numeric) and a name. You can choose any one-word names for the variables, but a typical practice involves beginning similar variables with a common **prefix**, for example, `inv`. In a large program in which you eventually declare dozens of variables, the `inv` prefix will help you immediately identify a variable as part of the inventory file.

Creating the inventory report shown in Figure 4-1 involves using the `invItemName`, `invPrice`, and `invCost` fields, but you do not need to use the `invQuantity` field in this program. However, the information regarding quantity does take room on the input file. If you imagine the surface of a disk as pictured in Figure 4-6, you can envision how the data fields follow one another in the file.

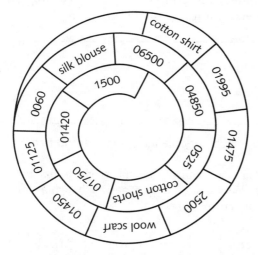

Figure 4-6 Representation of typical data for INVENTORY file

When you ask the program to read in an inventory record, four "chunks" of data will be transferred from the input device to the computer's main memory: name, price, cost, and quantity. When you declare the variables that represent the input data, you must provide a memory position for each of the four pieces of data, whether or not they all are used within this program.

In COBOL you can use the generic name FILLER for all unused data positions. This frees you from the task of creating variable names for items you do not intend to use.

Considering that dozens of programs within the organization might access the INVENTORY file, some organizations create the data file descriptions for you. This system is efficient because the description of variable names and types is stored in one location, and each programmer who uses the file simply imports the data file description into his or her own program. Of course, the organization must provide the programmer with documentation specifying the chosen names.

In most programming languages you can give a group of associated variables a **group name**. Just as it is easier to refer to "The Andersons" than it is to list "Nancy, Bud, Jim, Tom, Julie, Jane, Kate, and John," the benefit of using a group name is the ability to reference several variables with one all-encompassing name. For example, writing `read invRecord` is simpler than writing `read invItemName, invPrice, invCost, and invQuantity`. How you assign a group name to several variables differs in each programming language. This book follows the convention of underlining any group name and indenting the group members beneath, as shown in Figure 4-7.

```
invRecord
      char      invItemName
      num       invPrice
      num       invCost
      num       invQuantity
```

Figure 4-7   Variable declarations for the inventory file including a group name

A group of variables is often called a *data structure*, or more simply, a *structure*. Some object-oriented languages refer to a group as a *class*, although a class often contains methods as well as variables.

In addition to declaring variables, sometimes you want to provide a variable with an initial value. Providing a variable with a value when you create it is known as **initialization** or **defining the variable**. For example, for the inventory report shown in Figure 4-1, you might want to create a variable named `mainHeading` and store the value "INVENTORY REPORT" in that variable. The declaration is `char mainHeading = "INVENTORY REPORT"`. This indicates that `mainHeading` is a character variable, and that the character contents are the words "INVENTORY REPORT".

Declaring a variable provides it with a name and type. *Defining* a variable provides it with a value.

In some programming languages you can declare a variable such as `mainHeading` to be constant, or never changing. Even though `invItemName`, `invPrice`, and the other fields in the input file will hold a variety of values when a program executes, the `mainHeading` will never change.

In most programming languages, if you do not provide an initial value when declaring a variable, then the value is unknown or **garbage**. Some programming languages do provide you with an automatic starting value; for example in BASIC or RPG, all numeric variables automatically begin with the value zero. However, in C++, C#, Java, Pascal, and COBOL, variables do not receive any initial value unless you provide one. No matter which programming language you use, it is always clearest to provide a value for those variables that require them.

 Be especially careful to make sure all variables you use in calculations have initial values. If you perform arithmetic with garbage values, the result also will contain garbage.

When you declare the variables `invItemName`, `invPrice`, `invCost`, and `invQuantity`, you do not provide them with any initial value. The values for these variables will be assigned when the first file record is read into memory. It would be *legal* to assign a value to input file record variables—for example, `invItemName = "Cotton shirt"`, but it would be a waste of time and might mislead others who read your program. The first `invItemName` will come from an input device and may or may not be "Cotton shirt".

The report illustrated in Figure 4-1 contains three individual heading lines. The most common practice is to declare one variable or constant for each of these lines. The three declarations are as follows:

```
char mainHeading = "INVENTORY REPORT"
char columnHead1 = "ITEM            RETAIL PRICE
     MANUFACTURING        PROFIT PER"
char columnHead2 = "DESCRIPTION   EACH
     COST EACH            ITEM"
```

Within the program, when it is time to write the heading lines to an output device, you will code:

```
print mainHeading
print columnHead1
print columnHead2
```

You are not required to create variables for your headings. Your program can contain the following statements in which you use literal strings of characters instead of variable names. The printed results are the same either way.

```
print "INVENTORY REPORT"
print "ITEM            RETAIL PRICE MANUFACTURING PROFIT PER"
print "DESCRIPTION   EACH           COST EACH     ITEM"
```

Using variable names, as in `print mainHeading`, is usually more convenient than spelling out the heading's contents, especially if you will use the headings in multiple locations within your program.

When you write a program, you type spaces between the words within column headings so the spacing matches the print chart you created for the program. For convenience, some languages provide you with a tab character. The goal is to provide well-spaced output in readable columns.

Dividing the headings into three lines is not required either, but it is a common practice. In most programming languages you could write all the headings in one statement, using a code that indicates a new line at every appropriate position. Alternatively, most programming languages let you produce a character for output without advancing to a new line. You could write out the headings one character at a time, advancing to a new one only after all the line's characters had been individually printed, although this approach seems painstakingly detailed. Storing and writing one complete line at a time is a reasonable compromise.

Every programming language provides you with a means to physically advance printer paper to the top of a page when you print the first heading. Similarly, every language provides you with a means for producing double- and triple-spaced lines of text. Because the methods differ from language to language, examples in this book assume that if a print chart shows a heading that prints at the top of the page and then skips a line, when you create a corresponding variable like `mainHeading`, it also will print in this manner. You can add the appropriate language-specific codes to implement the `mainHeading` spacing when you write the actual computer program. Similarly, if you create a print chart that shows detail lines as double-spaced, assume your detail lines will double-space when you execute the step to write them.

Often you must create dozens of variables when you write a computer program. If you are using a flowchart to diagram the logic, it is physically impossible to fit the variables in one flowchart box. Therefore, you might want to use an annotation symbol. Similarly, when writing pseudocode, it is often more convenient to place variable names off to the side. The beginning of a flowchart for the `housekeeping()` module of the inventory report program is shown in Figure 4-8.

You learned about the annotation symbol in Chapter 3.

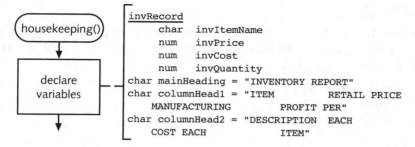

Figure 4-8   Beginning of flowchart for housekeeping() module for the inventory report program

Notice that the three heading variables defined in Figure 4-8 are not indented under `invRecord` like the `invRecord` fields are. This shows that although `invItemName`, `invPrice`, `invCost`, and `invQuantity` are part of the `invRecord` group, `mainHeading`, `columnHead1`, and `columnHead2` are not.

Opening Files

If a program will use input files, you must tell the computer where the input is coming from—for example, a specific disk drive, CD, or tape drive. This process is known as **opening a file**. Since a disk can have many files stored on it, the program also needs to know the name of the file being opened. In many languages if no input file is opened, input is accepted from a default or **standard input device**, most often the keyboard.

If a program will have output, you must also open a file for output. Perhaps the output file will be sent to a disk or tape. Although you might not think of a printed report as a file, computers treat a printer as just another output device, and if output will go to a printer, then you must open the printer output device as well. Again, if no file is opened, a default or **standard output device**, usually the monitor, is used.

When you flowchart, you usually write the command to open the files within a parallelogram. You use the parallelogram because it is the input/output symbol, and you are opening the input and output devices. You can use an annotation box to list the files that you open, as shown in Figure 4-9.

Figure 4-9   Specifying files that you open

Printing Headings

A common housekeeping task involves printing headings at the top of a report. In the inventory report example, three lines of headings appear at the beginning of the report. In this example, printing the heading lines is straightforward:

```
print mainHeading
print columnHead1
print columnHead2
```

Reading the First Input Record

The last task you execute in the `housekeeping()` module of most computer programs is to read the first data record in memory. When you read the four data fields for the inventory file data, you can write `read invItemName, invPrice, invCost, invQuantity,` but if you have declared a group name such as `invRecord`, it is simpler to write `read invRecord`. Using the group name is a shortcut to writing each field name.

When the last task within `housekeeping()` reads the first `invRecord`, the first task following `housekeeping()` is to check for `eof` on the file that contains the inventory records. An input device recognizes it has reached the end of a file when it attempts to read a record and finds no records available. Recall the mainline logic of the inventory report program from Figure 4-3—`eof` is tested immediately after `housekeeping()` ends.

If the input file has no records, when you read the first record the computer will recognize the end-of-file condition and proceed to the `finishUp()` module, never executing `mainLoop()`. More commonly, an input file does have records, and after the first `read` the computer will determine that the `eof` condition is false, and the logic will proceed to the mainLoop().

Immediately after reading from a file, the next step always should determine whether `eof` was encountered. Notice in Figure 4-3 that the `eof` question always follows both the `housekeeping()` module and the `mainLoop()` module. When the last instruction in each of these modules reads a record, then the `eof` question correctly follows each `read` instruction immediately.

Not reading the first record within the `housekeeping()` module is a mistake. If `housekeeping()` does not include a step to read a record from the input file, you must read a record as the first step in the `mainLoop()` as shown on the left side of Figure 4-10. In this program a record is read, a profit is calculated, and a line is printed. Then, if it is not `eof`, another record is read, a profit calculated, and a line printed. The program works well, reading records, calculating profits, and printing information until reaching a `read` command where the computer encounters the `eof` condition. When this last read occurs, the next steps involve computing a profit and writing a line—but there isn't any data to process. Depending on the programming language you use, either garbage data will calculate and print, or a repeat of the data from the last record before `eof` will print.

The figure on the right side of Figure 4–10 shows correct record-reading logic. The appropriate place for the priming record **read** is at the end of the preliminary housekeeping steps, and the appropriate place for all subsequent reads is at the end of the main processing loop.

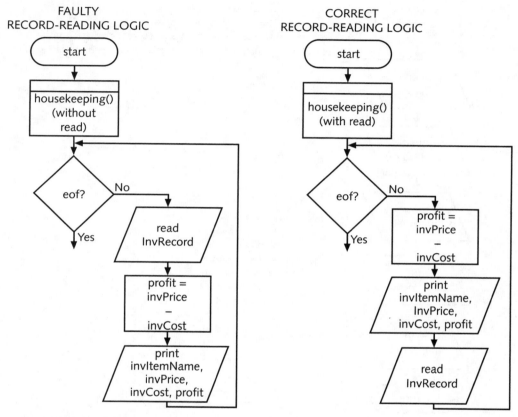

Figure 4-10 Comparing faulty and correct record-reading logic

 Reading an input record in the `housekeeping()` section is an example of a priming read. You learned about the priming read in Chapter 2.

 In some modern programming languages, such as Visual Basic, `read` commands can look ahead to determine if the *next* record is empty. With these languages, the priming read is no longer necessary. Because most languages do not currently have this type of read statement, this book will use the conventional priming read.

Figure 4–11 shows a completed `housekeeping()` routine for the inventory program in both flowchart and pseudocode versions.

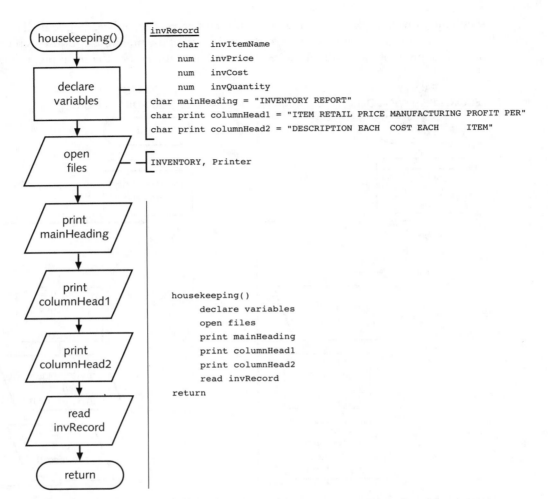

Figure 4-11   Flowchart and pseudocode for housekeeping() routine in inventory report program

As an alternative to including `print mainHeading`, `print columnHead1`, and `print columnHead2` within the `housekeeping()` module, you can place the three heading line statements in their own subroutine. In this case, the flowchart and pseudocode for `housekeeping()` will look like Figure 4-12, with the steps in the newly created `headings()` module appearing in Figure 4-13. Either approach is fine; the logic of the program is the same whether or not the heading line statements are segregated into their own routine. The programmer can decide on the program organization that makes the most sense.

4

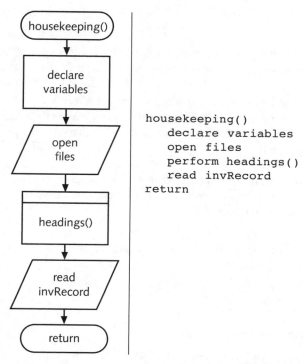

```
housekeeping()
    declare variables
    open files
    perform headings()
    read invRecord
return
```

Figure 4-12   Flowchart and pseudocode for housekeeping() with headings() module

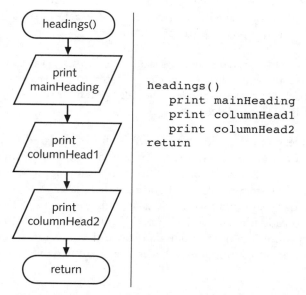

```
headings()
    print mainHeading
    print columnHead1
    print columnHead2
return
```

Figure 4-13   Flowchart and pseudocode for headings() module

WRITING THE MAIN LOOP

After you declare the variables for a program and perform the housekeeping tasks, the "real work" of the program begins. The inventory report described at the beginning of this chapter and depicted in Figure 4-1 needs just one set of variables and one set of headings, yet there might be hundreds or thousands of inventory items to process. The **main loop** of a program, controlled by the `eof` decision, is the program's "workhorse." Each data record will pass once through the main loop where calculations are performed with the data and the results printed.

 If the inventory report contains more records than fit on a page of output, you probably will want to print a new set of headings at the top of each page. You will learn how to do this in Chapter 7.

For the inventory report program to work, the `mainLoop()` module must include three steps:

1. Calculate the profit for an item.

2. Print the item information on the report.

3. Read the next inventory record.

At the end of `housekeeping()`, you read one data record into the computer's memory. As the first step in the `mainLoop()`, you can calculate an item's profit by subtracting its manufacturing cost from its retail price: `profit = invPrice - invCost`. The name `profit` is the programmer-created variable name for a new spot in computer memory where the value of the profit is stored.

 Recall that the standard way to express mathematical statements is to assign values from the right side of an equal sign to the left. That is, `profit = invPrice - invCost` assigns a value to `profit`. The statement `invPrice - invCost = profit` is an illegal statement.

Because you have a new variable, you must add `profit` to the list of declared variables at the beginning of the program. Programmers often work back and forth between the variable list and the logical steps during the creation of a program, listing some of the variables they will need as soon as they start to plan and adding others later as they think of them. Since `profit` will hold the result of a mathematical calculation, you should declare it as a numeric variable when you add it to the variable list as shown in Figure 4-14. Notice that like the headings, `profit` is not indented under `invRecord`. You want to show that `profit` is not part of the `invRecord` group; instead, it is a separate variable that you are declaring to store a calculated value.

You can declare `mainHeading`, `columnHead1`, `columnHead2`, and `profit` in any order. The important point is that none of these four variables are part of the `invRecord` group.

```
invRecord
        char    invItemName
        num     invPrice
        num     invCost
        num     invQuantity
char mainHeading = "INVENTORY REPORT"
char columnHead1 = "ITEM              RETAIL PRICE  MANUFACTURING    PROFIT PER"
char columnHead2 = "DESCRIPTION       EACH          COST EACH        ITEM"
num profit
```

Figure 4-14   Variable list for inventory report program, including profit

Although you can give a variable any legal name, you probably do not want to begin the name for the variable that holds the profit value with the `inv` prefix, because `profit` is not part of the INVENTORY input file. Beginning `profit` with the `inv` prefix might mislead those who read your program.

After you determine an item's profit, you can write a detail line of information on the inventory report: `print invItemName, invPrice, invCost, profit`.

The last step in the `mainLoop()` module of the inventory report program involves reading in the next `invRecord`. Figure 4-15 shows the flowchart and pseudocode for `mainLoop()`.

Just as headings are printed one full line at a time, detail lines are also printed one line at a time. You can print each field separately, as in the following code, but it is clearer and most efficient to write one full line at a time.

```
print invItemName
print invPrice
print invCost
print profit
```

In most programming languages you also have the option of calculating the profit and printing it in one statement, as in the following:

```
print invItemName, invPrice, invCost, invPrice - invCost
```

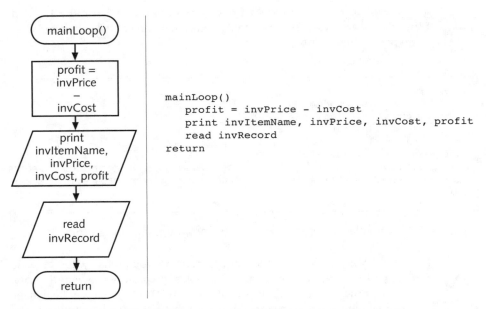

```
mainLoop()
    profit = invPrice - invCost
    print invItemName, invPrice, invCost, profit
    read invRecord
return
```

Figure 4-15   Flowchart and pseudocode for mainLoop() of inventory report program

If the language you use allows this type of statement in which a calculation takes place within the output statement, it is up to you to decide which format to use. Performing the arithmetic as part of the **print** statement allows you to avoid declaring a **profit** variable. However, if you need the **profit** figure for further calculations, then it makes sense to compute the profit and store it in a **profit** field. Using a separate **work variable** or **work field** such as **profit** to temporarily hold a calculation is never wrong, and often it's the clearest course of action.

After the detail line has been written, the last step you take before leaving the **mainLoop()** module is to read the next record from the input file into memory. When you exit the **mainLoop()**, the logic flows back to the **eof** question in the mainline logic. If it is not **eof**—that is, if an additional data record exists—then you enter the **mainLoop()** again, compute profit on the second record, print the detail line, and read the third record.

Eventually, during an execution of the **mainLoop()**, the program will read a new record and encounter the end of the file. Then when you ask the **eof** question in the main line of the program, the answer will be *yes*, and the program will not enter the **mainLoop()** again. Instead, the program logic will enter the **finishUp()** routine.

PERFORMING END-OF-JOB TASKS

Within any program, the end-of-job routine holds the steps you must take at the end of the program after all input records are processed. Some end-of-job modules print summaries or grand totals at the end of a report. Others might print a message such as "End of Report" so readers can be confident that they have received all the information that should be included. Very often, end-of-job modules must close any open files.

The end-of-job module for the inventory report program is very simple. The print chart does not indicate that any special messages, such as "Thank you for reading this report", print after the detail lines end. Likewise, there are no required summary or total lines; nothing special happens. Only one task needs to be performed in the end-of-job routine that this program calls finishUp(). In housekeeping() you opened files; in finishUp() you close them. The complete finishUp() module is flowcharted and written in pseudocode in Figure 4-16.

Figure 4-16 Flowchart and pseudocode of finishUp() module

Many programmers wouldn't bother with a subroutine for just one statement, but as you create more complicated programs, your end-of-job routines will get bigger and it will make more sense to see the necessary job-finishing tasks together in a module.

CHAPTER SUMMARY

◻ When you write a complete program, you first determine whether you have all the necessary data to produce the report. Then you plan the mainline logic, which usually includes modules to perform housekeeping, a main loop that contains the steps which repeat for every record, and an end-of-job routine.

◻ Housekeeping tasks include all steps that must take place at the beginning of a program. These tasks include declaring variables, opening files, performing any one-time-only tasks, such as printing headings at the beginning of a report, and reading the first input record.

❏ The main loop of a program is controlled by the `eof` decision. Each data record will pass once through the main loop where calculations are performed with the data and results are printed.

❏ Within any program, the end-of-job module holds the steps you must take at the end of the program after all the input records have been processed. Typical tasks include printing summaries, grand totals, or final messages at the end of a report, and closing all open files.

EXERCISES

1. A pet store owner needs a weekly sales report. The output consists of a printed report titled PET SALES. Fields printed on output are: type of animal and price. The input file description is shown below.

   File name: PETS

FIELD DESCRIPTION	POSITIONS	DATA TYPE	DECIMALS
Type of Animal	1–20	Character	
Price of Animal	21–26	Numeric	2

   a. Design the print chart, draw the hierarchy chart, and draw the flowchart for this program.

   b. Design the print chart, draw the hierarchy chart, and write the pseudocode for this program.

2. An employer wants to produce a personnel report. The output consists of a printed report entitled ACTIVE PERSONNEL. Fields printed on output are: last name of employee, first name of employee, and current salary. The input file description is shown below.

   File name: PERSONNEL

FIELD DESCRIPTION	POSITIONS	DATA TYPE	DECIMALS
Last Name	1–15	Character	
First Name	16–30	Character	
Soc. Sec. Number	31–39	Numeric	0
Department	40–41	Numeric	0
Current Salary	42–47	Numeric	2

   a. Design the print chart, draw the hierarchy chart, and draw the flowchart for this program.

   b. Design the print chart, draw the hierarchy chart, and write the pseudocode for this program.

3. An employer wants to produce a personnel report that shows the end result if she gives everyone a 10 percent raise in salary. The output consists of a printed report entitled PROJECTED RAISES. Fields printed on output are: last name of

employee, first name of employee, current salary, and projected salary. The input
file description is shown below.

File name: PERSONNEL

FIELD DESCRIPTION	POSITIONS	DATA TYPE	DECIMALS
Last Name	1–15	Character	
First Name	16–30	Character	
Soc. Sec. Number	31–39	Numeric	0
Department	40–41	Numeric	0
Current Salary	42–47	Numeric	2

4

a. Design the print chart, draw the hierarchy chart, and draw the flowchart for
this program.

b. Design the print chart, draw the hierarchy chart, and write the pseudocode for
this program.

4. A furniture store maintains an inventory file that includes data about every item it
sells. The manager wants a report that lists each stock number, description, and
profit, which is the retail price minus the wholesale price. The fields include a
stock number, description, wholesale price, and retail price. The input file description is shown below.

File name: FURNITURE

FIELD DESCRIPTION	POSITIONS	DATA TYPE	DECIMALS
Stock Number	1–4	Numeric	0
Description	5–29	Character	
Wholesale Price	30–35	Numeric	2
Retail Price	36–41	Numeric	2

a. Design the print chart, draw the hierarchy chart, and draw the flowchart for
this program.

b. Design the print chart, draw the hierarchy chart, and write the pseudocode for
this program.

5. A summer camp keeps a record for every camper including first name, last name,
birth date, and skill scores that range from 1 to 10 in four areas: swimming, tennis,
horsemanship, and crafts. The camp wants a printed report listing each camper's
data, plus a total score that is the sum of the camper's four skill scores.

a. Design the print chart, draw the hierarchy chart, and draw the flowchart for
this program.

b. Design the print chart, draw the hierarchy chart, and write the pseudocode for
this program.

6. An employer needs to determine how much tax to withhold for each employee.
This withholding amount computes as 20 percent of each employee's weekly pay.
The output consists of a printed report entitled WITHHOLDING FOR EACH
EMPLOYEE. Fields printed on output are: last name of employee, first name of

employee, hourly pay, weekly pay based on a 40-hour work week, and withholding amount per week. The input file description is shown below.

```
File name: EMPLOYEES
FIELD DESCRIPTION    POSITIONS    DATA TYPE    DECIMALS
Company ID           1—5          Numeric      0
First Name           6—17         Character
Last Name            18—29        Character
Hourly Rate          30—34        Numeric      2
```

a. Design the print chart, draw the hierarchy chart, and draw the flowchart for this program.

b. Design the print chart, draw the hierarchy chart, and write the pseudocode for this program.

7. A baseball team manager wants a report showing her players' batting statistics. A batting average is computed as hits divided by at-bats and is usually expressed to three decimal positions, for example .235. The output consists of a printed report entitled TEAM STATISTICS. Fields printed on output are: player number, first name, last name, and batting average. The input file description is shown below.

```
File name: BASEBALL
FIELD DESCRIPTION    POSITIONS    DATA TYPE    DECIMALS
Player Number        1—2          Numeric      0
First Name           3—18         Character
Last Name            19—35        Character
At-bats              36—38        Numeric      0
Hits                 39—41        Numeric      0
```

a. Design the print chart, draw the hierarchy chart, and draw the flowchart for this program.

b. Design the print chart, draw the hierarchy chart, and write the pseudocode for this program.

5

MAKING DECISIONS

After studying Chapter 5, you should be able to:
- ◆ Evaluate Boolean expressions to make comparisons
- ◆ Use the logical comparison operators
- ◆ Understand AND logic
- ◆ Write AND decisions for efficiency
- ◆ Combine decisions in an AND situation
- ◆ Avoid common errors in an AND situation
- ◆ Understand OR logic
- ◆ Avoid common errors in an OR situation
- ◆ Write OR decisions for efficiency
- ◆ Combine decisions in an OR situation
- ◆ Use selections within ranges
- ◆ Understand common errors using range checks
- ◆ Use decision tables

EVALUATING BOOLEAN EXPRESSIONS TO MAKE COMPARISONS

The reason people think computers are smart lies in the computer program's ability to make decisions. A medical diagnosis program that can decide if your symptoms fit various disease profiles seems quite intelligent, as does a program that can offer you different potential vacation routes based on your destination.

The selection structure (sometimes called a decision structure) involved in such programs is not new to you—it's one of the basic structures of structured programming. See Figures 5-1 and 5-2.

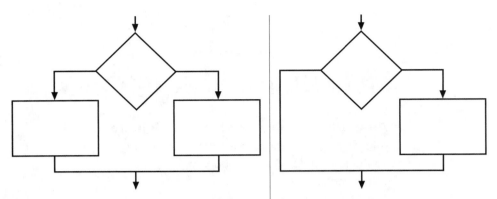

Figure 5-1   The dual-alternative selection structure

Figure 5-2   The single-alternative selection structure

You can refer to the structure in Figure 5-1 as a **dual-alternative** or **binary** selection because there are two possible outcomes: depending on the answer to the question represented by the diamond, the logical flow proceeds either to the left branch of the structure or to the right. The choices are mutually exclusive; that is, the logic can flow only to one of the two alternatives, never both. This selection structure also is called an **if-then-else** structure because it fits the statement:

```
if the answer to the question is yes, then
     do something
else
     do somethingElse
endif
```

The flowchart segment in Figure 5-2 represents a **single-alternative** or **unary** selection where action is required for only one outcome of the question. You call this form of the if-then-else structure an **if-then**, because no "else" action is necessary.

 You can call a single-alternative decision (or selection) a *single-sided decision.* Similarly, a dual-alternative decision is a *double-sided decision* (or selection).

For example, Figure 5-3 shows the flowchart and pseudocode for a typical if-then-else decision in a business program. Many organizations pay employees time-and-a-half (one and one half times their usual hourly rate) for hours in excess of 40 per week. The logic segments in the figure show this decision.

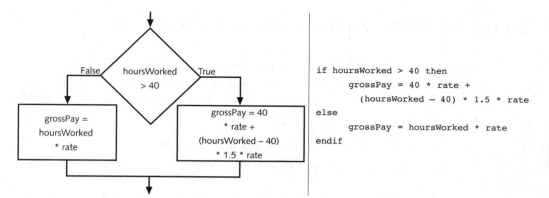

```
if hoursWorked > 40 then
        grossPay = 40 * rate +
            (hoursWorked - 40) * 1.5 * rate
else
        grossPay = hoursWorked * rate
endif
```

5

Figure 5-3 Flowchart and pseudocode for overtime decision

The typical if–then decision in Figure 5-4 shows the employee's paycheck being reduced if the employee participates in the dental plan. No action is taken if the employee is not in the dental plan.

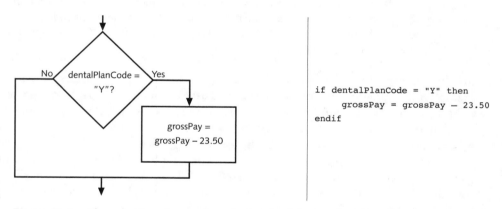

```
if dentalPlanCode = "Y" then
        grossPay = grossPay - 23.50
endif
```

Figure 5-4 Flowchart and pseudocode for dental plan decision

The expressions `hoursWorked > 40` and `dentalPlanCode = "Y"` that appear in Figures 5-3 and 5-4 are Boolean expressions. A **Boolean expression** is one that represents only one of two states, usually expressed as true or false. Every decision you make in a computer program involves evaluating a Boolean expression. True/false evaluation is "natural" from a computer's standpoint because computer circuitry consists of two-state, on-off switches, often represented by 1 or 0, so every computer decision yields a true-or-false, yes-or-no, 1-or-0 result.

 George Boole was a mathematician who lived from 1815 to 1864. He approached logic more simply than his predecessors did by expressing logical selections with common algebraic symbols. He is considered the founder of symbolic logic, and Boolean (true/false) expressions are named for him.

USING THE LOGICAL COMPARISON OPERATORS

Usually, you can compare only values that are of the same type; that is, you can compare numeric values to other numeric values and character values to other characters. You can ask every programming question by using only three types of comparisons (Boolean expressions). For any two values that are the same type, you can decide whether:

- The two values are equal.
- The first value is greater than the second value.
- The first value is less than the second value.

 Usually, character variables are not considered to be equal unless they are identical, including the spacing and whether or not they appear in upper- or lowercase. For example, "black pen" is *not* equal to "blackpen", "BLACK PEN", or "Black Pen".

 Some programming languages allow you to compare a character to a number. If this is the case, then a single character's numeric code value is used in the comparison. For example, most microcomputers use the ASCII coding system in which an uppercase "A" is represented numerically as a 65, an uppercase "B" is a 66, and so on.

In any Boolean expression, the two values used can be either variables or constants. For example, the expression `currentTotal = 100?` compares a variable, `currentTotal`, to a constant, 100. Depending on the `currentTotal` value, the expression is true or false. In the expression `currentTotal = previousTotal?`, both values are variables, and the result is also true or false depending on the values stored in each of the two variables. Although it's legal to do this, you would never use expressions in which you compare two constants, for example `20 = 20?` or `30 = 40?`. Such expressions are considered **trivial** because each always results in the same value: true for the first expression and false for the second.

Each programming language supports its own set of **logical comparison operators**, or comparison symbols, that express these Boolean tests. For example, many languages use the equal sign (=) to express testing for equivalency, so `balanceDue = 0?` compares `balanceDue` to zero. COBOL programmers can use the equal sign, but they also can spell out the expression as in `balanceDue equal to 0?`. C#, C++, and Java programmers use two equal signs to test for equivalency, so they write `balanceDue == 0?` to compare the two values.

 The reason some languages use two equal signs for comparisons is to avoid confusion with assignment statements like `balanceDue = 0`. In C++ or Java, this statement only assigns the value 0 to `balanceDue`; it does not compare `balanceDue` to zero.

Whenever you use a comparison operator, you must provide a value on each side of the operator. Comparison operators are sometimes called *binary operators* because of this requirement.

Most languages allow you to use the algebraic signs for greater than (>) and less than (<) to make the corresponding comparisons. Additionally, COBOL, which is very similar to English, allows you to spell out the comparisons in expressions like `daysPastDue is greater than 30` or `packageWeight is less than maximumWeightAllowed`. When you create a flowchart or pseudocode, you can use any form of notation you want to express "greater than" and "less than". It's simplest to use the symbols > and < if you are comfortable with their meaning.

In addition to the three basic comparisons you can make, most programming languages provide three others. For any two values that are the same type, you can decide whether:

- The first is greater than or equal to the second.
- The first is less than or equal to the second.
- The two are not equal.

Most programming languages allow you to express "greater than or equal to" by typing a greater-than sign immediately followed by an equal sign (>=). When you are drawing a flowchart or writing pseudocode, you might prefer a greater-than sign with a line under it ($\geq$) because mathematicians use that symbol to mean "greater than or equal to." However, when you write a program, you type >= as two separate characters because no single key on the keyboard expresses this concept. Similarly, "less than or equal to" is written with two symbols, < followed by =.

The operators >= and <= are always treated as a single unit; no spaces separate the two parts of the operator. Also, the equal sign always appears second. No programming language allows => or =< as comparison operators.

Any logical situation can be expressed using just three types of comparisons: equal, greater than, and less than. You never need the three additional comparisons (greater than or equal, less than or equal, or not equal), but using them often makes decisions more convenient. For example, assume you need to issue a 10% discount to any customer whose age is 65 or greater and charge full price to other customers. You can use the greater-than-or-equal-to symbol to write the logic as follows:

```
if customerAge >= 65 then
        discount = .10
else
        discount = 0
endif
```

As an alternative, if you want to use only the three basic comparisons (=, >, and <) you can express the same logic by writing:

```
if customerAge < 65 then
        discount = 0
else
        discount = .10
endif
```

In any decision for which a >= b is true, then a < b is false. Conversely, if a >= b is false, then a < b is true. By rephrasing the question and swapping the actions taken based on the outcome, you can make the same decision in multiple ways. Asking a question so the positive or true outcome results in the unusual action is often the clearest route. When your company policy is to "provide a discount for those who are 65 and older," the phrase greater than or equal to comes to mind, so it is the most natural to use. Conversely, if your policy is to "provide no discount for those under 65," then it is more natural to use the less than syntax. Either way, the same people receive a discount.

Comparing two amounts to decide if they are *not* equal to each other is the most confusing of all the comparisons. Using "not equal to" in decisions involves thinking in double negatives and makes you prone to include logical errors in your programs. For example, consider the flowchart segment in Figure 5-5.

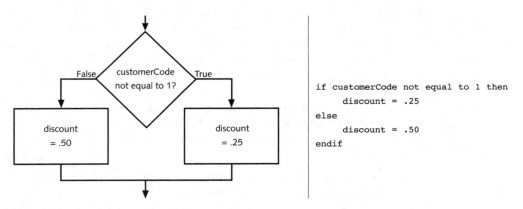

Figure 5-5   Using a negative comparison

In Figure 5-5, if the value of **customerCode** *is* equal to 1, the logical flow follows the false branch of the selection. If **customerCode** not equal to 1 is true, the **discount** is .25; if **customerCode** not equal to 1 is not true, it means the **customerCode** *is* 1, and the **discount** is .50. Even using the phrase "**customerCode not equal to 1 is not true**" is awkward.

Figure 5-6 shows the same decision, this time asked in the positive. Making the decision **if customerCode** *is* **1 then discount = .50** is clearer than trying to determine what **customerCode** is *not*.

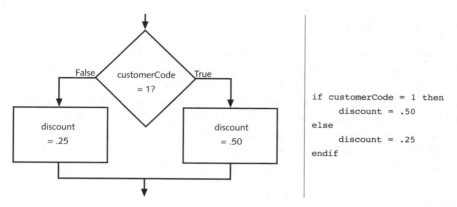

Figure 5-6 Using the positive equivalent of the negative comparison in Figure 5-5

Besides being awkward to use, the not equal to comparison operator is the one most likely to be different in the various programming languages you may use. COBOL allows you to write "not equal to"; Pascal uses a less-than sign followed immediately by a greater-than sign (<>); C#, C++, C, and Java use an exclamation point followed by an equal sign (!=). In a flowchart or in pseudocode, you can use the symbol that mathematicians use to mean "not equal," an equal sign with a slash through it (≠). When you program, you will not be able to use this symbol because no single key on the keyboard produces it.

Although NOT comparisons can be awkward to use, there are times when your meaning is clearest if you use one. For example, the mainline logic of many programs, including those you have worked with in this book, includes a statement like `while not eof, perform mainLoop()`.

Figure 5-7 summarizes the six comparisons and contrasts trivial (both true and false) and typical examples of their use.

Comparison	Trivial True Example	Trivial False Example	Typical Example
Equal to	7 = 7?	7 = 4?	amtOrdered = 12?
Greater than	12 > 3?	4 > 9?	hoursWorked > 40?
Less than	1 < 8?	13 < 10?	hourlyWage < 5.65?
Greater than or equal to	5 >= 5?	3 >= 9?	customerAge >= 65?
Less than or equal to	4 <= 4?	8 <= 2?	daysOverdue <= 60?
Not equal to	16 <> 3?	18 <> 18?	customerBalance <> 0?

Figure 5-7 Logical comparisons

UNDERSTANDING AND LOGIC

Often you need more than one selection structure to determine whether an action should take place. For example, suppose that your employer wants a report that lists workers who have registered for both insurance plans offered by the company: the medical plan and the dental plan. This type of situation is known as an **AND** situation because the employee's record must pass two tests—participation in the medical plan *and* participation in the dental plan—before you write that employee's information on the report. An AND situation requires a **nested decision** or a **nested if**; that is, a decision "inside of" another decision. The logic looks like Figure 5-8.

You first learned about nesting structures in Chapter 2.

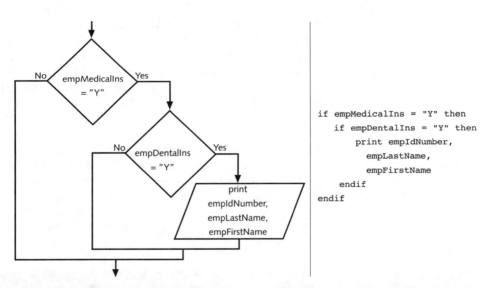

Figure 5-8   Flowchart and pseudocode of an AND decision

The AND decision shown in Figure 5-8 is part of a much larger program. To help you develop this program, suppose your employer provides you with the employee data file description shown in Figure 5-9, and you learn that the medical and dental insurance fields contain a single character, "Y" or "N", indicating each employee's participation status. With your employer's approval, you develop the print chart shown in Figure 5-10.

```
EMPLOYEE FILE DESCRIPTION
File Name: EMPFILE
FIELD DESCRIPTION    POSITIONS    DATA TYPE    DECIMALS    EXAMPLE
ID Number            1—4          Numeric      0           1234
Last Name            5—20         Character                Kroening
First Name           21—35        Character                Ginny
Department           36           Numeric      0           3
Hourly Rate          37—40        Numeric      2           17.50
Medical Plan         41           Character                Y
Dental Plan          42           Character                N
Number of            43—44        Numeric      0           2
 Dependents
```

Figure 5-9   Employee file description

Figure 5-10   Print chart for employees participating in both insurance plans

The mainline logic and `housekeeping()` routines for this program are diagrammed in Figures 5-11 and 5-12.

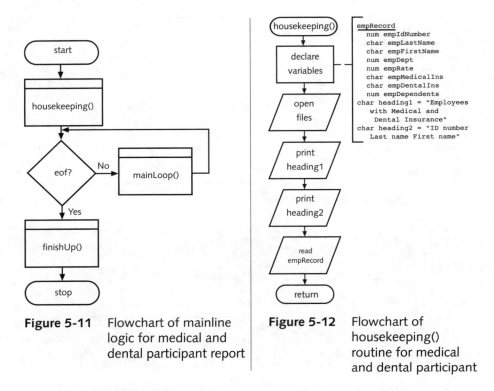

Figure 5-11   Flowchart of mainline logic for medical and dental participant report

Figure 5-12   Flowchart of housekeeping() routine for medical and dental participant

At the end of the **housekeeping( )** routine, the first employee record is read into computer memory. Assuming that the **eof** condition is not yet met, the logical flow proceeds to the **mainLoop( )**. Within the **mainLoop( )** module of this program, you ask the questions that determine whether the current employee's record will print; if so, then you print the employee's data. Whether or not the employee meets the medical and dental insurance requirements for printing, the last thing you do in the **mainLoop( )** is to read the next input record. Figure 5-13 shows the **mainLoop( )** module.

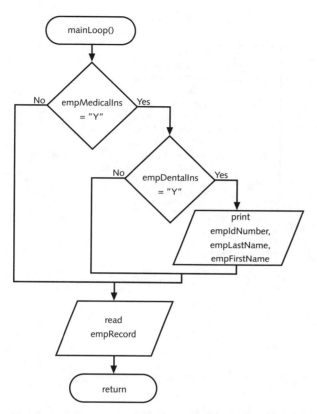

Figure 5-13   mainLoop( ) of program that lists medical and dental participants

The `mainLoop()` module works like this: If the employee has medical insurance, *then* and *only then,* test to see if the employee has dental insurance. If so, *then* and *only then,* print the employee's data. The dental insurance question is nested entirely within half of the medical insurance question structure. If an employee does not carry medical insurance, there is no need to ask about the dental insurance; the employee is already disqualified from the report. Pseudocode for the entire program is shown in Figure 5-14. Notice how the second (dental insurance) decision within the `mainLoop()` is indented within the first (medical insurance) decision. This technique shows the second question is asked only when the result of the first comparison is true.

```
start
    perform houskeeping()
    while not eof
            perform mainLoop()
    perform finishUp()
stop

housekeeping()
    declare variables ── ── ──┐
    open files
    print heading1
    print heading2
    read empRecord
return

mainLoop()
    if empMedicalIns = "Y" then
        if empDentalIns = "Y" then
            print empIdNumber, empLastName, empFirstName
        endif
    endif
    read empRecord
return

finishUp()
    close files
return
```

```
empRecord
    num empIdNumber
    char empLastName
    char empFirstName
    num empDept
    num empRate
    char empMedicalIns
    char empDentalIns
    num empDependents
char heading1 = "Employees with Medical
                 and Dental Insurance"
char heading2 = "ID number    Last name
                 First name"
```

Figure 5-14   Pseudocode of medical and dental participants report program

WRITING AND DECISIONS FOR EFFICIENCY

When you nest decisions because the resulting action requires that two conditions be true, you must decide which of the two decisions to make first. Logically, either selection in an AND situation can come first. However, when there are two selections, you often can improve your program's performance by making an appropriate choice as to which selection to make first.

For example, the nested decision structure in the `mainLoop()` logic of the program that produces a report of employees who participate in both the medical and dental insurance plans is written as in Figure 5-15.

```
if empMedicalIns = "Y" then
    if empDentalIns = "Y" then
        print empIdNumber, empLastName, empFirstName
    endif
endif
```

Figure 5-15   Finding medical and dental plan participants

Alternatively, you can write the decision as in Figure 5-16.

```
if empDentalIns = "Y" then
    if empMedicalIns = "Y" then
        print empIdNumber, empLastName, empFirstName
    endif
endif
```

Figure 5-16   Finding dental and medical plan participants

Examine the decision statements in the preceding figures. If you want to print employees who participate in the medical AND dental plans, you can ask about the medical plan first, eliminate those employees who do not participate, and ask about the dental plan only for those employees who "pass" the medical insurance test. Or you could ask about the dental plan first, eliminate those who do not participate, and ask about the medical plan only for those employees who "pass" the dental insurance test. Either way, the final list contains only those employees who have both kinds of insurance.

Does it make a difference which question is asked first? As far as the output goes, no. Either way, the same employee names appear on the report—those with both types of insurance. As far as program efficiency goes, however, it *might* make a difference which question is asked first.

Assume you know that out of 1,000 employees in your company, about 90%, or 900, participate in the medical insurance plan. Assume you also know that out of 1,000 employees, only about half, or 500, participate in the dental plan.

Using the logic in Figure 5-15, the program asks the first question `empMedicalIns = "Y"`? 1,000 times. For approximately 90% of the employees, or 900 of the records, the answer is `true`, thus the `empMedicalIns` field contains the character "Y". So 100 employees are eliminated, and 900 proceed to the next question about dental insurance. Only about half of the employees participate in the dental plan, so 450 out of the 900 will appear on the printed report.

Using the alternative logic in Figure 5-16, the program asks the first question `empDentalIns = "Y"`? 1,000 times. Because only about half of the company's employees participate, only 500 will "pass" this test and proceed to the medical insurance question. Then about 90% of the 500, or 450 employees, will appear on the report. Whether you use the logic in Figure 5-15 or 5-16, the same 450 employees who have both types of insurance appear on the report.

The difference lies in the fact that when using the logic in Figure 5-15, the program must ask 1,900 questions to produce the report—the medical insurance question tests all 1,000 employee records, and 900 continue to the dental insurance question. If you use the logic in Figure 5-16 to produce the report, the program asks only 1,500 questions—all 1,000 records are tested for dental insurance, but only 500 proceed to the medical insurance question. By asking about the dental insurance first, you "save" 400 decisions.

The 400-question difference between the first set of decisions and the second set really doesn't take much time on most computers. But it will take some time, and if there are hundreds of thousands of employees instead of only 1,000, or if many such decisions have to be made within a program, performance time can be significantly improved by asking questions in the proper order.

In many AND situations, the programmer has no idea which of two events is more likely to occur; in that case, you can legitimately ask either question first. In addition, even though you know the probability of each of two conditions, the two events might not be mutually exclusive; that is, one might depend on the other. For example, if employees with dental insurance are significantly more likely to carry medical insurance than those who don't carry dental insurance, the order in which to ask the questions might matter less or not matter at all. However, if you do know the probabilities of the conditions, or can make a reasonable guess, the general rule is: *In an AND situation, first ask the question that is less likely to be true.* This eliminates as many records as possible from having to go through the second decision and speeds up processing time.

COMBINING DECISIONS IN AN **AND** SITUATION

Most programming languages allow you to ask two or more questions in a single comparison by using a **logical AND operator**. For example, if you want to select employees who carry both medical and dental insurance, you can use nested `if`s, or you can include both decisions in a single statement by writing `empDentalIns = "Y" AND empMedicalIns = "Y"`? If the programming language you use allows an AND operator, you still must realize that the question you place first is the question that will be asked first, and cases that are eliminated based on the first question will not proceed to the second question. The computer can ask only one question at a time; even though you draw the flowchart segment in Figure 5-17, the computer will execute the logic in the flowchart in Figure 5-18.

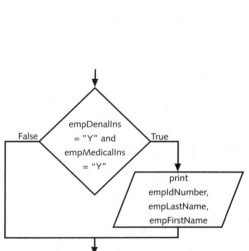

Figure 5-17 Flowchart of AND decision using an AND operator

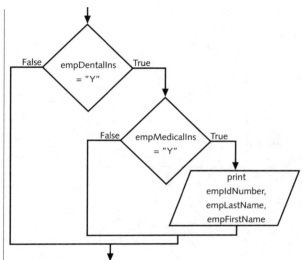

Figure 5-18 Computer logic of program containing an AND decision using an AND operator

5

AVOIDING COMMON ERRORS IN AN AND SITUATION

When you must satisfy two or more criteria to initiate an event in a program, you must make sure that the second decision is made entirely within the first decision. For example, if a program's objective is to print those employees who carry both medical and dental insurance, then the program segment shown in Figure 5-19 contains three different types of logic errors.

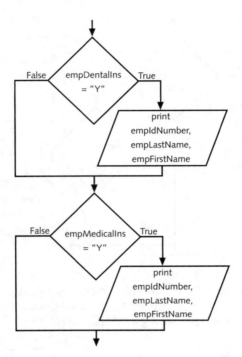

Figure 5-19   Incorrect logic to produce report with medical and dental participants

 C#, C++, C, and Java use the symbol && to represent the logical AND.

The diagram shows that the program asks the dental insurance question first. However, if an employee participates in the dental program, the employee prints immediately. The employee should not print, because the employee might not have the medical insurance. In addition, the program should eliminate an employee without dental insurance from the next selection, but every employee's record proceeds to the medical insurance question, where it might print whether the employee has dental insurance or not. Additionally, any employee who has both medical and dental insurance, having passed each test successfully, will appear twice on this report. For many reasons, the logic shown in Figure 5-19 is *not* correct for this problem.

Beginning programmers often make another type of error when they must make two comparisons on the same field while using a logical AND operator. For example, suppose you want to list employees who make between $10.00 and $11.99 per hour inclusive. You want to select employees whose `empRate` is greater than or equal to 10.00 AND whose `empRate` is less than 12.00; therefore, you need to make two comparisons on the same field. Without the logical AND operator, the comparison is:

```
if empRate >= 10.00 then
    if empRate < 12.00 then
        print empIdNumber, empLastName, empFirstName
    endif
endif
```

To check for `empRate` values that are 10.00 and greater, you can use either expression `empRate > 9.99?` or `empRate >= 10.00?`. To check for `empRate` values under 12.00, you can write `empRate <= 11.99?` or `empRate < 12.00?`.

The correct way to make this comparison with the AND operator is as follows:

```
if empRate >= 10.00 AND empRate < 12.00 then
    print empIdNumber, empLastName, empFirstName
endif
```

You substitute the AND operator for the `then if`. However, some programmers try to make the comparison as follows:

```
if empRate >= 10.00 AND < 12.00 then
    print empIdNumber, empLastName, empFirstName
endif
```

In most languages, the phrase `empRate >= 10.00 AND < 12.00` is incorrect. When you use a logical AND, you must use a complete Boolean expression on both sides of the AND. The expression to the right of the AND, `< 12.00`, is not a complete Boolean expression; you must indicate *what* is being compared to 12.00.

In COBOL and RPG you can write the equivalent of `empRate >= 10.00 AND < 12.00?` and the `empRate` variable is implied for both comparisons. Still, it is clearer and therefore preferable to use the two full expressions, `empRate >= 10.00 AND empRate < 12.00?`.

UNDERSTANDING OR LOGIC

Sometimes you want to take action when one *or* the other of two conditions is true. This is called an **OR** situation because either one condition must be met *or* some other condition must be met in order for an event to take place.

For example, suppose your employer wants a list of all employees who participate in either the medical or dental plan. Assuming you are using the same input file described in Figure 5-9, the mainline logic and `housekeeping()` module for this program are identical to those used in Figures 5-11 and 5-12. You need only to change the heading on the print chart (Figure 5-10) and change the `heading1` variable in Figure 5-12 from `heading1 = "Employees with Medical *and* Dental Insurance"` to `heading1 = "Employees with Medical *or* Dental Insurance"`. The substantial changes to the program occur in the `mainLoop()` module.

Figure 5-20 shows the possible logic for `mainLoop()` in this OR situation. As each record enters the `mainLoop()`, you ask the question `empMedicalIns = "Y"?`, and if the result is true, you print the employee data. Because the employee needs to participate in only one of the two insurance plans to be selected for printing, there is no need for further questioning. If the employee does not participate in the medical insurance plan, only then do you need to ask if `empDentalIns = "Y"?`. If the employee does not have medical insurance, but does have dental, you want this employee to print on the report.

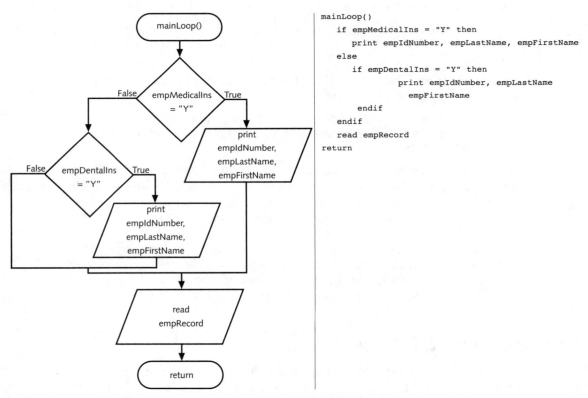

```
mainLoop()
    if empMedicalIns = "Y" then
        print empIdNumber, empLastName, empFirstName
    else
        if empDentalIns = "Y" then
            print empIdNumber, empLastName
                empFirstName
        endif
    endif
    read empRecord
return
```

Figure 5-20   Flowchart and pseudocode for mainLoop() that prints employees who have medical or dental insurance

AVOIDING COMMON ERRORS IN AN OR SITUATION

You might have noticed that the statement `print empIdNumber, empLastName, empFirstName` appears twice in the flowchart and in the pseudocode shown in Figure 5-20. The temptation is to redraw the flowchart in Figure 5-20 to look like Figure 5-21. Logically, you can argue that the flowchart in Figure 5-21 is correct because the correct employees print. However, this flowchart is not allowed because it is not structured.

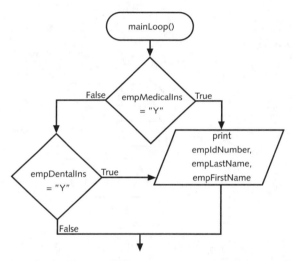

Figure 5-21   Incorrect flowchart for mainLoop() module

If you do not see that Figure 5-21 is not structured, go back and review Chapter 2. In particular, review the example that begins at Figure 2-22.

An additional source of error that is specific to the OR situation stems from a problem with language and the way people use it too casually. When your boss needs a report of all employees who carry medical or dental insurance, she is likely to say, "I need a report of all the people who have medical insurance and all those who have dental insurance." The request contains the word "and," and the report contains people who have one type of insurance "and" people who have another. However, the records you want to print are those from employees who have medical insurance OR dental insurance OR both. The logical situation is an OR situation. As a programmer it is up to you to clarify what really is being requested, and determine that often a request for A and B means a request for A or B.

WRITING OR DECISIONS FOR EFFICIENCY

You can write a program that creates a report containing all employees who take either the medical or dental insurance by using the `mainLoop()` in either Figure 5-22 or Figure 5-23.

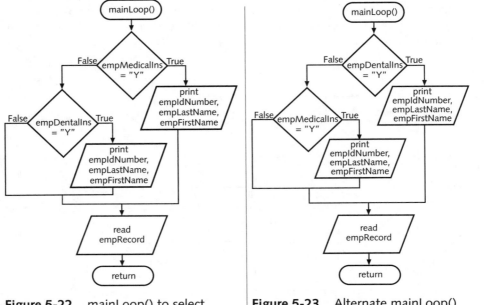

Figure 5-22   mainLoop() to select employees with medical or dental insurance

Figure 5-23   Alternate mainLoop() to select employees with medical or dental insurance

You might have guessed that one of these selections is superior to the other if you have some background information about the relative likelihood of each condition you are testing. For example, once again assume you know that out of 1,000 employees in your company, about 90%, or 900, participate in the medical insurance plan, and about half, or 500, participate in the dental plan.

When you use the logic shown in Figure 5-22 to select employees who participate in either insurance plan, you first ask about medical insurance. For 900 employees the answer is true; you print these employee records. Only about 100 records continue to the next question regarding dental insurance, where about half, or 50, fulfill the requirements to print. In the end, you print about 950 employees.

If you use Figure 5-23, you ask `empDentalIns = "Y"?`. The result is true for 50%, or 500 employees, whose names then print. Five hundred employee records then progress to the medical insurance question after which 90% or 450 of them print.

Using either scenario, 950 employee records appear on the list, but the logic used in Figure 5-22 requires 1,100 decisions while the logic used in Figure 5-23 requires 1,500 decisions. The general rule is: *In an OR situation, first ask the question that is more likely to be true.* Because a record qualifies for printing as soon as it passes one test, asking the more likely question first eliminates as many records as possible from having to go through the second decision. The time it takes to execute the program is decreased.

COMBINING DECISIONS IN AN OR SITUATION

When you need to take action when either one or the other of two conditions is met, you can use two separate, nested selection structures as in the previous examples. However, most programming languages allow you to ask two or more questions in a single comparison by using a **logical OR operator**—for example, `empDentalIns = "Y" OR empMedicalIns = "Y"`. When you use the logical OR operator, only one of the listed conditions must be met for the resulting action to take place. If the programming language you use allows this construct, you still must realize that the question you place first is the question that will be asked first, and cases that you eliminate based on the first question will not proceed to the second question. The computer can ask only one question at a time; even though you draw the flowchart in Figure 5-24, the computer will execute the logic in the flowchart in Figure 5-25.

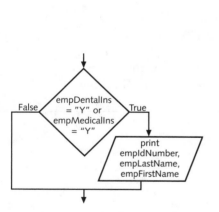

Figure 5-24 Flowchart of OR decision using an OR operator

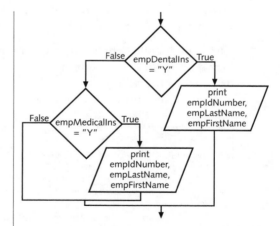

Figure 5-25 Computer logic of program containing an OR decision using an OR operator

 C#, C++, C, and Java use the symbol || to represent the logical OR.

USING SELECTIONS WITHIN RANGES

Business programs often need to make selections based on a variable falling within a range of values. For example, suppose you want to print a list of all employees and the names of their supervisors. An employee's supervisor is assigned based on the employee's department number, as shown in Figure 5-26:

```
DEPARTMENT NUMBER        SUPERVISOR
1-3                      Dykeman
4-7                      Erhardt
8-9                      Jackson
```

Figure 5-26   Supervisors by department

When you write the program that reads each employee's record, you could make nine decisions before printing the supervisor's name, such as `empDept = 1?`, `empDept = 2?`, and so on. However, it is more convenient to find the supervisor by using a range check.

To perform a **range check**, make comparisons using either the lowest or highest value in each range of values you are using to make selections. For example, to find each employee's supervisor as listed in Figure 5-26, use either the values 1, 4, and 8, which represent the low ends of each supervisor's department range, or use the values 3, 7, and 9, which represent the high ends.

The pseudocode representing the logic for choosing a supervisor name by using the high-end range values appears in Figure 5-27. You test the `empDept` value for less than or equal to the high end of the lowest range group. If the comparison evaluates as true, you know the `supervisorName`. If not, you continue checking.

```
if empDept <= 3 then
      supervisorName = "Dykeman"
else
      if empDept <= 7 then
            supervisorName = "Erhardt"
      else
            supervisorName = "Jackson"
      endif
endif
```

Figure 5-27   Using high-end values for a range check

In Figure 5-27, notice how each `else` aligns vertically with its corresponding `if`.

The flowchart for choosing a supervisor name using the reverse of this method, by seeking the low-end range values, appears in Figure 5-28. You compare `empDept` to the low end of the highest range first; if the `empDept` falls in the range, the `supervisorName` is known; otherwise you check the next lower group.

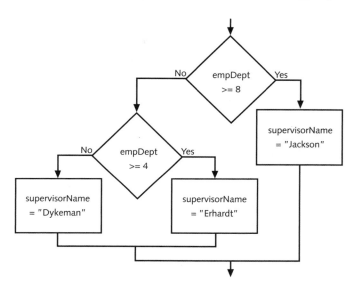

Figure 5-28   Using low-end values for a range check

COMMON ERRORS USING RANGE CHECKS

Two common errors that occur when programmers perform range checks both entail doing more work than is necessary. Figure 5-29 shows a range check in which the programmer has asked one question too many. If you know that all `empDept` values are positive numbers, then if the `empDept` is not greater than or equal to eight, and it is also not greater than or equal to four, then by default it must be greater than or equal to one. Asking whether `empDept` is greater than or equal to one is a waste of time; no employee record can ever travel the logical path on the far left.

Similarly, Figure 5-30 shows the beginning of an inefficient range selection. If `empDept` is greater than or equal to eight, "Jackson" is the supervisor. If the `empDept` is not greater than or equal to eight, the next question does not have to check for less than eight. The computer will never get to the second question unless the `empDept` is already less than eight, so you are wasting computer time asking a question that has previously been answered.

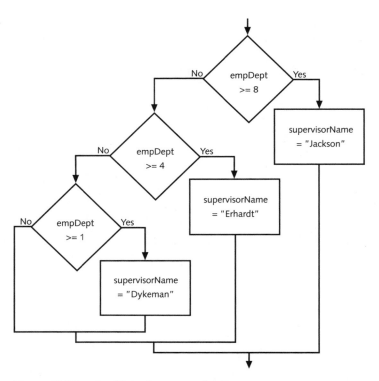

Figure 5-29   Inefficient range selection

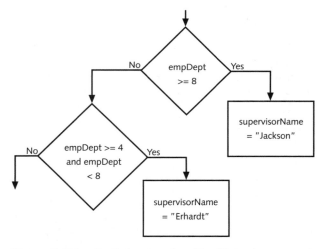

Figure 5-30   Partial example of inefficient range selection

USING DECISION TABLES

Some programs require multiple decisions to produce the correct output. Managing all possible outcomes of multiple decisions can be a difficult task, so programmers sometimes use a tool called a decision table to help organize the possible decision outcome combinations.

A **decision table** is a problem-analysis tool that consists of four parts:

- Conditions
- Possible combinations of Boolean values for the conditions
- Possible actions based on the conditions
- The actions that correspond to each Boolean value of each condition

For example, suppose a college collects input data like that shown in Figure 5-31. Each student's data record includes the student's age and a variable that indicates whether the student has requested a residence hall that enforces quiet study hours.

```
STUDENT FILE DESCRIPTION
File Name: STURESFILE
FIELD DESCRIPTION      POSITIONS     DATA TYPE      DECIMALS      EXAMPLE
ID Number              1-4           Numeric        0             5377
Last Name              5-20          Character                    Bowers
First Name             21-35         Character                    Laurel
Age                    36-37         Numeric        0             19
Request for Hall       38            Character                    Y
  with Quiet Hours
```

Figure 5-31   Student file description

Assume the residence hall director makes residence hall assignments based on the following rules:

- Students who are under 21 years old and who request a residence hall with quiet study hours are assigned to Addams Hall.
- Students who are under 21 years old and who do not request a residence hall with quiet study hours are assigned to Grant Hall.
- Students who are 21 years old and over who request a residence hall with quiet study hours are assigned to Lincoln Hall.
- Students who are 21 years old and over who do not request a residence hall with quiet study hours also are assigned to Lincoln Hall.

You can create a program that assigns each student to the appropriate residence hall and prints a list of students along with each student's hall assignment. The mainline logic for this program could look exactly like the mainline logic shown for the employee medical and dental benefits program in Figure 5-11, or you can choose new module names as shown in Figure 5-32. The programs are similar in that each performs start-up or housekeeping tasks, a main loop that acts repeatedly, once for each input record, and a finishing module that closes the open files. The general shape of the mainline logic modules in many computer programs look very similar; the individual module names can be any appropriate names you choose.

The **getReady()** module for the program that produces the residence hall report is shown in Figure 5-33.

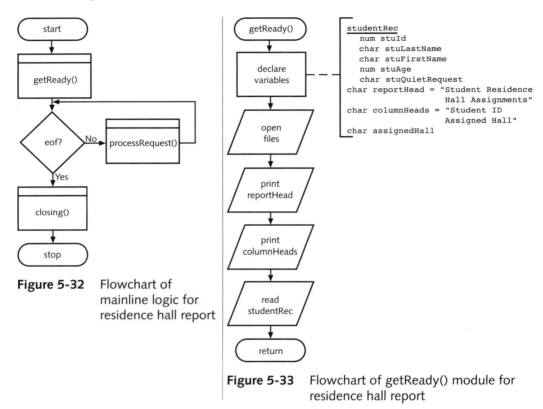

Figure 5-32   Flowchart of mainline logic for residence hall report

Figure 5-33   Flowchart of getReady() module for residence hall report

Before you draw a flowchart or write the pseudocode for the **processRequest()**, you can create a decision table to help you manage all the decisions. You can begin to create a decision table by listing all possible conditions. They are:

- stuAge < 21, or not
- stuQuietRequest = "Y", or not

Next determine how many possible Boolean value combinations exist for the conditions. In this case there are four possible combinations shown in Figure 5-34. A student can be under 21, request a residence hall with quiet hours, both, or neither. Since each condition has two outcomes and there are two conditions, there are 2 * 2 or four possibilities. Three conditions would produce eight possibilities (2 * 2 * 2); four conditions would produce 16 possible outcome combinations (2 * 2 * 2 * 2), and so on.

Condition	Outcome			
stuAge < 21	T	T	F	F
stuQuietRequest = "Y"	T	F	T	F

Figure 5-34   Possible outcomes of residence hall request conditions

Next, add rows to the decision table to list the possible outcome actions. A student might be assigned to Addams, Grant, or Lincoln Hall. Figure 5-35 shows these three possible outcomes.

Condition	Outcome			
stuAge < 21	T	T	F	F
stuQuietRequest = "Y"	T	F	T	F
assignedHall = "Addams"				
assignedHall = "Grant"				
assignedHall = "Lincoln"				

Figure 5-35   Possible outcome actions of residence hall requests

Choose one required outcome for each possible combination of conditions. As shown in Figure 5-36, place an X in the Addams Hall row when **stuAge** is less than 21 and the student requests a residence hall with quiet study hours.

Condition	Outcome			
stuAge < 21	T	T	F	F
stuQuietRequest = "Y"	T	F	T	F
assignedHall = "Addams"	X			
assignedHall = "Grant"				
assignedHall = "Lincoln"				

Figure 5-36   Decision table for residence hall selection, part 1 of 3

Next, place an X in the Grant Hall row under the condition when a student is under 21 but does not request a residence hall with quiet hours. See Figure 5-37.

Condition	Outcome			
stuAge < 21	T	T	F	F
stuQuietRequest = "Y"	T	F	T	F
assignedHall = "Addams"	X			
assignedHall = "Grant"		X		
assignedHall = "Lincoln"				

Figure 5-37 Decision table for residence hall selection, part 2 of 3

Finally, place Xs in the Lincoln Hall row for both situations when a student is not under 21 years old—only one residence hall is available for students 21 and over, whether they have requested a hall with quiet hours or not. See Figure 5-38.

Condition	Outcome			
stuAge < 21	T	T	F	F
stuQuietRequest = "Y"	T	F	T	F
assignedHall = "Addams"	X			
assignedHall = "Grant"		X		
assignedHall = "Lincoln"			X	X

Figure 5-38 Decision table for residence hall selection, part 3 of 3

The decision table is complete (count the Xs—there are four possible outcomes). Take a moment and confirm that each residence hall selection is the appropriate value based on the original specifications. Now you can start to plan the logic.

If you choose to use a flowchart to express the logic, you start by drawing a path to the outcome shown in the first column. This result (which occurs when stuAge < 21 and stuQuietRequest = "Y") sets the residence hall to "Addams". See Figure 5-39.

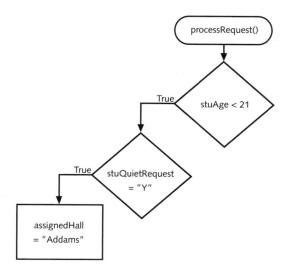

Figure 5-39 Flowchart for residence hall selection, part 1 of 5

Next, add the resulting action shown in the second column of the decision table, which occurs when `stuAge < 21` is true and `stuQuietRequest = "Y"` is false. See Figure 5-40.

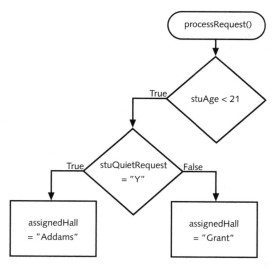

Figure 5-40 Flowchart for residence hall selection, part 2 of 5

Add the resulting action shown in the third column of the decision table, which occurs when `stuAge < 21` is false and `stuQuietRequest = "Y"` is true. See Figure 5-41.

Finally, add the resulting action shown in the fourth column of the decision table, which occurs when both conditions are false, as in Figure 5-42.

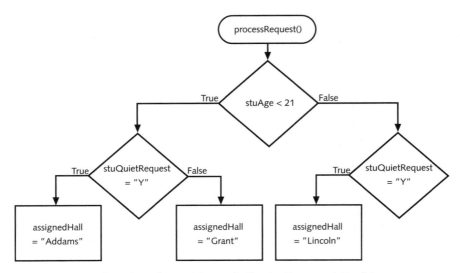

Figure 5-41 Flowchart for residence hall selection, part 3 of 5

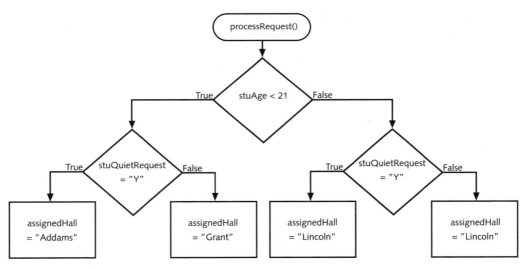

Figure 5-42 Flowchart for residence hall selection, part 4 of 5

The flowchart segment is now complete and accurately assigns each student to the correct residence hall. Just tie up the ends, print a student's ID number and residence hall assignment, and read the next record. However, if you examine the two rightmost result boxes, you see that the assigned residence hall is identical—Lincoln in both cases. When a student is not under 21, whether the **stuQuietRequest** equals "Y" or not, the residence hall assignment is the same; therefore, there is no point in asking the **stuQuietRequest** question. Additionally, many programmers prefer that the True or Yes side of a flowchart decision always appears on the right side. Figure 5-43 shows the complete program, including the `processRequest()` module with True results to the right of each selection.

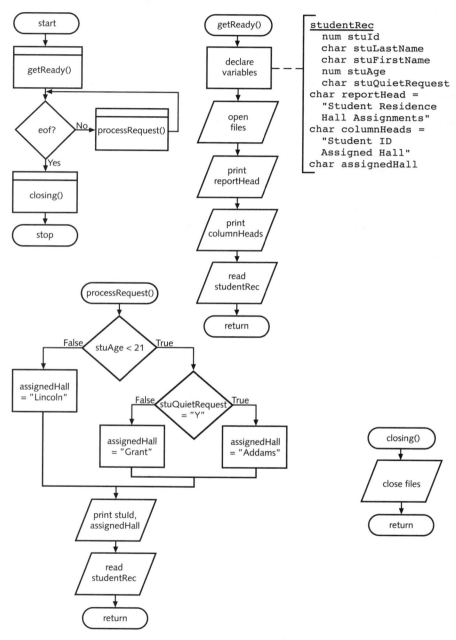

Figure 5-43 Flowchart for residence hall selection, part 5 of 5

Perhaps you could have created the final decision-making `processRequest()` module without creating the decision table first. If so, you need not use the table. Decision tables are more useful to the programmer when the decision-making process becomes more complicated. Additionally, they serve as a useful graphic tool when you want to explain the decision-making process of a program to a user who is not familiar with flowcharting symbols.

 In Appendix B, you can walk through the process used to create a larger decision table.

CHAPTER SUMMARY

- ❏ Every decision you make in a computer program involves evaluating a Boolean expression. You can use dual-alternative, binary selections, or if-then-else structures to choose between two possible outcomes. You also can use single-alternative, unary, or if-then selections when there is only one outcome for the question where action is required.

- ❏ For any two values that are the same type, you can use logical comparison operators to decide whether the two values are equal, the first value is greater than the second value, or the first value is less than the second value. The two values used in a Boolean expression can be either variables or constants.

- ❏ An AND situation occurs when two conditions must be true in order for a resulting action to take place. An AND situation requires a nested decision or a nested if.

- ❏ In an AND situation, first ask the question that is less likely to be true. This eliminates as many records as possible from having to go through the second decision and speeds up processing time.

- ❏ Most programming languages allow you to ask two or more questions in a single comparison by using a logical AND operator.

- ❏ When you must satisfy two or more criteria to initiate an event in a program, you must make sure that the second decision is made entirely within the first decision, and that you use a complete Boolean expression on both sides of the AND.

- ❏ An OR situation occurs when you want to take action when one *or* the other of two conditions is true.

- ❏ Errors occur in OR situations when programmers do not maintain structure. An additional source of errors that are particular to the OR situation stems from people using the word AND to express OR requirements.

- ❏ In an OR situation, first ask the question that is more likely to be true.

❑ Most programming languages allow you to ask two or more questions in a single comparison by using a logical OR operator.

❑ To perform a range check, make comparisons with either the lowest or highest value in each range of values you are using.

❑ Common errors that occur when programmers perform range checks include asking unnecessary and previously answered questions.

❑ A decision table is a problem-analysis tool that consists of conditions, possible combinations of Boolean values for the conditions, possible actions based on the conditions, and the actions that correspond to each Boolean value of each condition.

5

EXERCISES

1. Assume the following variables contain the values shown:

    numberRed = 100   numberBlue = 200   numberGreen = 300
    wordRed = "Wagon"   wordBlue = "Sky"   wordGreen = "Grass"

    For each of the following Boolean expressions, decide whether the statement is true, false, or illegal.

    a. numberRed = numberBlue?

    b. numberBlue > numberGreen?

    c. numberGreen < numberRed?

    d. numberBlue = wordBlue?

    e. numberGreen = "Green"?

    f. wordRed = "Red"?

    g. wordBlue = "Blue"?

    h. numberRed <= numberGreen?

    i. numberBlue >= 200?

    j. numberGreen >= numberRed + numberBlue?

2. a. A candy company wants a list of its best-selling items, including item number and name of candy. Best-selling items are those that sell over 2,000 pounds per month. Input records contain fields for the item number (three digits), the name of the candy (20 characters), the price per pound (four digits, two assumed decimal places), and the quantity in pounds sold last month (four digits, no decimals). Design the print chart, hierarchy chart, and flowchart.

    b. Write the pseudocode for the same problem.

    c. The candy company wants a list of its high-priced, best-selling items. Best-selling items are those that sell over 2,000 pounds per month. High-priced items are those that sell for $10 per pound or more. Design the print chart, hierarchy chart, and flowchart.

    d. Write the pseudocode for the same problem.

3. a. The Literary Honor Society needs a list of English majors who have a grade point average of 3.5 or higher. The student record file includes students' last names and first names (15 characters each), major (10 characters, for example "History" or "English"), and grade point average (two digits, one assumed decimal place). Design the print chart, hierarchy chart, and flowchart for this problem.

   b. Write the pseudocode for the same problem.

4. a. A telephone company charges 10 cents per minute for all calls outside the customer's area code that last over 20 minutes. All other calls are 13 cents per minute. The phone company has a file with one record for every call made in one day. (In other words, a single customer might have many such records on file.) Fields for each call include customer area code (three digits), customer phone number (seven digits), called area code (three digits), called number (seven digits), and call time in minutes (four digits). The company wants a report listing one detail line for each call, including the customer area code and number, the called area code and number, the minutes, and the total charge. Create a decision table to use with this problem.

   b. Design the print chart, hierarchy chart, and flowchart.

   c. Write the pseudocode for the same problem.

5. a. A nursery maintains a file of all plants in stock along with such data as price and characteristics. Only 20% of the nursery stock does well in shade and 50% does well in sandy soil. Create a decision table to use with this problem.

   b. Design a print chart, create an hierarchy chart, and draw the flowchart that would perform the most efficient search for a plant in a shady, sandy yard.

   c. Write the pseudocode for the same problem.

6. You have declared variables for an insurance company program as follows:

FIELD	POSITIONS	EXAMPLE
num custPolicyNumber	1–6	223356
char custLastName	7–20	Falkenburg
num custAge	21–23	25
num custDueMonth	24–25	06
num custDueDay	26–27	24
num custDueYear	28–31	2004
num custAccidents	32–34	2

   Draw the selection structures that print the `custPolicyNumber` and `custLastName` that satisfy the following requests for lists of policyholders:

   a. over 35 years old

   b. at least 21 years old

   c. no more than 30 years old

   d. due no later than March 15 any year

   e. due up to and including January 1, 2004

f. due by April 27, 2007

g. due as early as December 1, 2002

h. fewer than 11 accidents

i. no more than 5 accidents

j. no accidents

7. a. Student files contain an ID number (four digits), last and first names (15 characters each), and major field of study (10 characters). Draw the print chart, create the hierarchy chart, and draw the flowchart for a program that lists ID numbers and names for all French or Spanish majors.

   b. Write the pseudocode for the same problem.

8. a. A florist wants to send coupons to her best customers, so she needs a list of names and addresses for customers who placed orders more than three times last year or spent more than $200 last year. The input file description follows:

   File name: FLORISTCUSTS

FIELD DESCRIPTION	POSITIONS	TYPE	DECIMALS
Customer ID	1–3	Numeric	0
First Name	4–16	Character	
Last Name	17–30	Character	
Street Address	31–51	Character	
Orders Last Year	52–55	Numeric	0
Amount Spent Last Year	56–62	Numeric	2

   (Note: To save room, don't include city or state. Assume all the florist's best customers are in town.) Design the print chart, write the hierarchy chart, and draw the flowchart for this program.

   b. Write the pseudocode for the same problem.

9. a. A carpenter needs a program that computes the price of any desk a customer orders based on the following input fields: order number, desk length in inches and width in inches (three digits each, no decimals), type of wood (20 characters), and number of drawers (two digits). The price is computed as follows:

   ◘ The charge for all desks is a minimum $200.

   ◘ If the surface (length * width) is over 750 square inches, add $50.

   ◘ If the wood is "mahogany" add $150; for "oak" add $125. No charge is added for "pine."

   ◘ For every drawer in the desk, there is an additional $30 charge.

   Create a decision table to use with this problem.

   b. Design the print chart, write the hierarchy chart, and draw the flowchart for this program.

   c. Write the pseudocode for the same problem.

10. a. A company is attempting to organize carpools to save energy. Ten percent of the company's employees live in Wonder Lake. Thirty percent of the employees live in Woodstock. Since these towns are both north of the company, the company wants a list of employees who live in either town so it can recommend that these employees drive to work together. Create a flowchart that shows the most efficient process for selecting these employees, assuming there is a field called `empCity` in each employee's personnel record.

   b. Write pseudocode for the same process.

11. a. Create the logic to help plan your next vacation. Possible outcomes for destination are Hawaii, Grandma's house, and nowhere (stay home). If your bank balance is $1 million or more, you will go to Hawaii. If your bank balance is less than $1 million, and your boss says you must work, you will stay home. If your boss says you can go, you will go to Hawaii unless your bank account is below $2,000. In that case, you will go to Grandma's house. Assuming you have declared variables for `vacationDestination`, `vacationBossDecision`, and `vacationBankBalance`, create a flowchart that shows the decision-making process.

   b. Assuming you have declared variables for `vacationDestination`, `vacationBossDecision`, and `vacationBankBalance`, write pseudocode for the decision-making process from Exercise 11a.

12. a. A supervisor in a manufacturing company wants to produce a report showing which employees have increased their production this year over last year so that she can issue them a certificate of commendation. She wants to have a report with three columns: last name, first name, and either the word "UP" or blanks printed under the column heading PRODUCTION. "UP" is printed when this year's production is a greater number than last year's production. Input exists as follows:

```
PRODUCTION FILE DESCRIPTION
File name: PRODUCTION
FIELD DESCRIPTION          POSITIONS    DATA TYPE    DECIMALS
Last Name                  1-20         Character
First Name                 21-30        Character
Last Year's Production     31-34        Numeric      0
This Year's Production     35-38        Numeric      0
```

   Create the decision table that shows the logic for issuing the commendations, then create the print layout chart, hierarchy chart, and flowchart for this program.

   b. Write the pseudocode for the same problem.

   c. A supervisor in the same manufacturing company wants to produce a report from the PRODUCTION input file showing bonuses she is planning to give based on this year's production. She wants to have a report with three columns: last name, first name, and bonus. The bonuses will be distributed as follows.

If this year's production is:

❐ 1,000 units or fewer, the bonus is $25

❐ 1,001 to 3,000 units, the bonus is $50

❐ 3,001 to 6,000 units, the bonus is $100

❐ 6,001 units and up, the bonus is $200

Create the print layout chart, hierarchy chart, and either the flowchart or pseudocode for this program.

d. Modify Exercise 12c to reflect the following new facts, and have the program execute as efficiently as possible:

❐ Only employees whose production this year is higher than last year will receive bonuses. This is true for approximately 30% of the employees.

❐ Sixty percent of employees produce over 6,000 units per year, 20% produce 3,001 to 6,000, 15% produce 1,001 to 3,000 units, and only 5% produce fewer than 1,001.

5

6

LOOPING

After studying Chapter 6, you should be able to:

- ◆ Understand the advantages of looping
- ◆ Control a `while` loop using a loop control variable
- ◆ Increment a counter to control a loop
- ◆ Loop with a variable sentinel value
- ◆ Control a loop by decrementing a loop control variable
- ◆ Avoid common loop mistakes
- ◆ Use a `for` loop
- ◆ Use a `do until` loop
- ◆ Recognize the characteristics shared by all loops
- ◆ Nest loops
- ◆ Use a loop to accumulate totals

UNDERSTANDING THE ADVANTAGES OF LOOPING

If making decisions is what makes computers seem intelligent, it's looping that makes computer programming worthwhile. When you use a loop within a computer program, you can write one set of instructions that operates on multiple, separate sets of data. Consider the following set of tasks required for each employee in a typical payroll program:

- Determine regular pay
- Determine overtime pay, if any
- Determine federal withholding tax based on gross wages and number of dependents
- Determine state tax based on gross wages, number of dependents, and state of residence
- Determine insurance deduction based on insurance code
- Determine Social Security deduction based on gross
- Subtract federal tax, state tax, Social Security, and insurance from gross

In reality, this list is too short—companies deduct stock option plans, charitable contributions, union dues, and other items from checks in addition to the items mentioned in this list. Also, they might pay bonuses and commissions and provide sick days and vacation days that must be taken into account and handled appropriately. As you can see, payroll programs are complicated.

The advantage of having a computer perform payroll calculations is that all of the deduction instructions need to be written *only once* and can be repeated over and over again using a **loop**, (the structure that repeats actions while some condition continues).

USING A WHILE LOOP WITH A LOOP CONTROL VARIABLE

Recall the loop, or do-while structure that you learned about in Chapter 2. (See Figure 6-1.) In Chapter 3 you learned that almost every program has a **main loop**, or a basic set of instructions that are repeated for every record. The main loop is a typical loop—within it, you write one set of instructions that executes repeatedly while records continue to be read from an input file. Several housekeeping tasks execute at the start of most programs and a few clean-up tasks execute at the end. However, most of a program's tasks are located in a main loop; these tasks repeat over and over for many (sometimes hundreds, thousands, or millions) records.

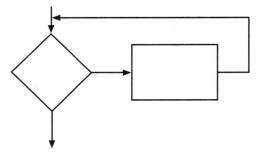

Figure 6-1 The while loop

In addition to this main loop, loops also appear within subroutines. They are used any time you need to perform a task several times and don't want to write identical or similar instructions over and over. Suppose for example, as part of a much larger program, you want to print a warning message on the computer screen when the user has made a potentially dangerous menu selection (say, "Delete all files"). To get the user's attention, you want to print the message four times. You can write this program segment as shown in Figure 6-2, but using a loop as shown in Figure 6-3 is much more efficient.

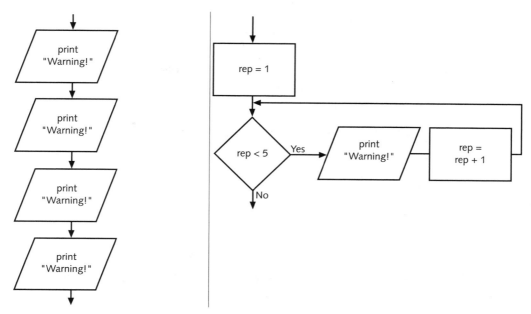

Figure 6-2: Printing four warning
messages in sequence

Figure 6-3: Printing four warning
messages in a loop

The flowchart segment in Figure 6-3 shows three steps that must occur in every loop:

1. You must initialize a variable that will control the loop. The variable in this case is named **rep**.

2. You must compare the variable to some value that stops the loop. In this case you compare **rep** to the value 5.

3. Within the loop, you must alter the variable. In this case, you alter **rep** by adding one to it.

On each pass through the loop, the value in the **rep** variable determines whether the loop will continue. Therefore variables like **rep** are known as **loop control variables**. Any variable that determines whether a loop will continue is a loop control variable. To stop a loop, you compare the loop control value to a **sentinel value** (also known as a limit, or ending value), in this case the value 5. The decision that controls every loop is always based on a Boolean comparison. You can use any of the six comparison operators that you learned about in Chapter 5 to control a loop.

 Just as with a selection, the Boolean comparison that controls a while loop must compare same-type values: numeric values are compared to other numeric values and character values to other character values.

The statements that execute within a loop are known as the **loop body**. The body of the loop might contain any number of statements, including subroutine calls, decisions, and other loops. Once your program enters the body of a structured loop, the entire loop body must execute. Your program can leave a structured loop only at the comparison that tests the loop control variable.

USING A COUNTER TO CONTROL LOOPING

Suppose you own a factory and have decided to place a label on every product you manufacture. The label contains the words "Made for you personally by" followed by the first name of one of your employees. For one week's production, you need 100 personalized labels for each employee.

Assume you already have a personnel file that can be used for input. This file has more information than you'll need for this program: an employee last name, first name, Social Security number, address, date hired, and salary. The important feature of the file is that it does contain each employee's name stored in a separate record. The input file description appears in Figure 6-4.

File Name: EMPLOYEES			
FIELD DESCRIPTION	POSITIONS	DATA TYPE	DECIMALS
Employee Last Name	1—20	Character	
Employee First Name	21—35	Character	
Social Security Number	36—44	Numeric	0
Address	45—60	Character	
Date Hired	61—68	Numeric	0
Hourly Salary	69—72	Numeric	2

Figure 6-4   Employee data file description

In the mainline of this program, you perform three subroutines: a housekeeping subroutine (`housekeep()`), a main loop (`mainLoop()`), and a finish routine (`finishUp()`). See Figure 6-5.

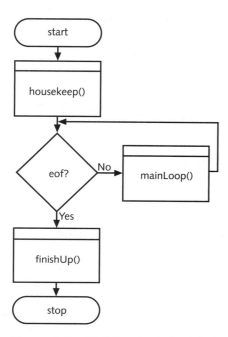

Figure 6-5 Mainline logic for label program

The first task for the label program involves naming the fields on the input record so you can refer to them within the program. As a programmer, you can choose any variable names you like, for example: `inLastName`, `inFirstName`, `inSSN`, `inAddress`, `inDate`, and `inSalary`.

 In Chapter 4 you learned that starting all field names in the input record with the same prefix, such as `in`, is a common programming technique to help identify these fields in a large program and differentiate them from work areas and output areas that will have other names. Another benefit to using a prefix like `in` is that some language compilers also produce a dictionary of variable names when you compile your program. These dictionaries show at which lines in the program each data name is referenced. If all your input field names start with the same prefix, they will be together alphabetically in the dictionary and perhaps be easier to find and work with.

You also can set up a variable to hold the characters "Made for you personally by" and name it `labelLine`. You eventually will print this `labelLine` variable followed by the employee's first name (`inFirstName`).

You will need one more variable: a location called a counter. A **counter** is any numeric variable you use to count the number of times an event has occurred; in this example you need a counter to keep track of how many labels have been printed at any point.

Each time you read an employee record, the counter variable is set to zero. Then every time a label is printed, you add one to the counter. Adding one to a variable is called **incrementing** the variable. Before the next employee label is printed, the program checks the variable to see if it has reached 100 yet. When it has, that means 100 labels have been printed and the job is done for that employee. While the counter remains below 100, you continue to print labels. As with all variables, the programmer can choose any name for a counter; this program uses `labelCounter`. In this example, `labelCounter` is the loop control variable.

The `housekeep()` routine for the label program, shown in Figure 6-6, includes a step to open the files: the employee file and the printer. Unlike a program that produces a report, this program has no headings, so the next and last task performed in **housekeep()** is to read the first input record.

 Remember, you can give any name you like to subroutines within your programs. This program uses `housekeep()` for its first routine, but `housekeeping()`, `startUp()`, `prep()`, or any other name with the same general meaning could be used.

 If you don't know why the first record is read in the `housekeep()` module, go back and review the concept of the priming read presented in Chapter 2.

Figure 6-6   housekeep() module for label program

When `housekeep()` is done, the logical flow returns to the `eof` question in the main-line. If for some reason you attempt to read the first record at the end of `housekeep()` and there is no record, the answer to `eof?` is Yes, so then the `mainLoop()` is never entered; instead, the logic of the program flows directly to the `finishUp()` module.

Usually, however, employee records will exist and the program will enter the `mainLoop()` module. When this happens, the first employee record is sitting in memory waiting to be processed. During one execution of the `mainLoop()` module, 100 labels will be printed for one employee. As the last event within `mainLoop()` module, the program reads the next employee record. Control of the program then returns to the `eof` question. If the new read process does not result in the `eof` condition, control returns to the `mainLoop()` module where 100 more labels print for a new employee.

The `mainLoop()` of this label program contains three parts:

- Set the `labelCounter` to 0.
- Compare the `labelCounter` to 100.
- While the `labelCounter` is less than 100, print the `labelLine` and the `inFirstName`, and add one to the `labelCounter`.

When the first employee record enters the `mainLoop()` module, the `labelCounter` is set to zero. Comparing the `labelCounter` to 100 results in a true condition, so the record enters the label-making loop. One label prints for the first employee, the `labelCounter` increases by one, and the logical flow returns to the question `labelCounter < 100?`. After the first label is printed, the `labelCounter` holds a value of only 1. It is nowhere near 100 yet, so the value of the Boolean expression is true and the loop is entered for a second time, thus printing a second label.

After the second printing `labelCounter` holds a value of 2. After the third printing, it holds a value of 3. Finally, after the 100th label prints, `labelCounter` has a value of 100. When the question `labelCounter < 100?` is asked, the answer will finally be no and the loop will exit.

Before leaving `mainLoop()`, and after the program prints 100 labels for an employee, there is one final step: the next input record is read from the EMPLOYEES file. When `mainLoop()` is over, control returns to the `eof` question in the mainline of the logic. If it is not `eof` (if another employee record is present), the program enters `mainLoop()` again, resets `labelCounter` to 0, and prints 100 new labels with the next employee's name. Figure 6-7 shows the complete `mainLoop()`.

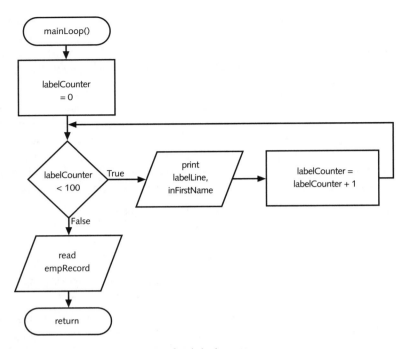

Figure 6-7 `mainLoop()` for label program

At some point while attempting to read a new record you encounter the end of the file, the `mainLoop()` is not entered again and control passes to the `finishUp()` module. In this program the `finishUp()` module simply closes the files. See Figure 6–8.

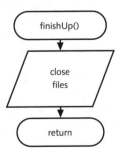

Figure 6-8 `finishUp()` module for label program

LOOPING WITH A VARIABLE SENTINEL VALUE

Sometimes you don't want to be forced to repeat every pass through a loop the same number of times. For example, instead of printing 100 labels for each employee, you might want to vary the number of labels based on how many items a worker actually produces. That way, high-achieving workers won't run out of labels and less productive workers won't have too many. Instead of printing the same number of labels for every employee, a more sophisticated program prints a different number of labels for each employee, depending on that employee's previous week's production. For example, you might decide to print enough labels to cover 110% of each employee's production rate from the previous week; this ensures that the employee will have enough labels for the week even if his or her production level improves.

For example, assume that employee production data exists on an input file called EMPPRODUCTION in the format shown in Figure 6-9.

```
File Name: EMPPRODUCTION
FIELD DESCRIPTION        POSITIONS     DATA TYPE      DECIMALS
Last Name                1—20          Character
First Name               21—35         Character
Production Last Week     36—38         Numeric        0
```

Figure 6-9 Employee production file description

A real-life production file would undoubtedly have more fields in each record, but these fields supply more than enough information to produce the labels. You need the first name to print on the label, and you need the field that holds production for the last week in order to calculate the number of labels to print for each employee. This field can contain any number from 0 through 999.

To write a program that produces an appropriate number of labels for each employee, you can make some minor modifications to the original label-making program. For example, the input file variables have changed; you must declare a variable for an inLastProduction field. Additionally, you might want to create a numeric field named labelsToPrint that can hold a value equal to 110% of a worker's inLastProduction.

The major modification to the original label-making program is in the question that controls the label-producing loop. Instead of asking if labelCounter < 100, you now can ask if labelCounter < labelsToPrint. The sentinel or limit value can be a variable just as easily as it can be a constant. See Figure 6-10 for the flowchart as well as the pseudocode.

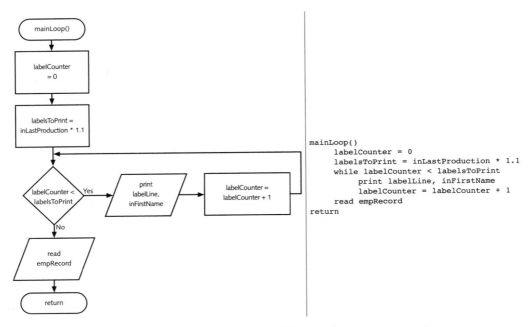

Figure 6-10   Flowchart and pseudocode for label-making mainLoop()

 The statement `labelsToPrint = inLastProduction * 1.1` calculates `labelsToPrint` as 110% of `inLastProduction`. Alternatively, you can perform the calculation as `labelsToPrint = inLastProduction + .10 * inLastProduction`. The mathematical result is the same.

LOOPING BY DECREMENTING

Rather than increasing a loop control variable until it passes some sentinel value, sometimes it is more convenient to reduce a loop control variable on every cycle through a loop. For example, again assume you want to print enough labels for every worker to cover 110% production. As an alternative to setting a `labelCounter` variable to 0 and increasing it after each label prints, you initially can set `labelCounter` equal to `inLastProduction * 1.1`, and subsequently reduce the `labelCounter` value every time a label prints. You continue printing labels and reducing the `labelCounter` until you have counted down to zero. Decreasing a variable by one is called **decrementing** the variable.

For example, when you write the following you produce enough labels to equal 110% of `inLastProduction`:

```
labelCounter = inLastProduction * 1.1
while labelCounter > 0
    print labelLine, inFirstName
    labelCounter = labelCounter - 1
```

When you decrement, you can avoid declaring a special variable for the `labelsToPrint`. The `labelCounter` variable starts with a value that represents the labels to print, and works its way down to zero.

Yet another alternative would allow you to eliminate the `labelCounter` variable. You could use the `inLastProduction` variable itself to keep track of the labels. For example, the following pseudocode segment also produces a number of labels equal to 110% of each worker's `inLastProduction` value:

```
inLastProduction = inLastProduction * 1.1
while inLastProduction > 0
    print labelLine, inFirstName
    inLastProduction = inLastProduction - 1
```

In this example, `inLastProduction` is first increased by 10%. Then, while it remains above zero, there are more labels to print. However, you can't use this method if you need the value of `inLastProduction` for this record later in the loop. By decrementing the variable, you are changing its value on every cycle through the loop; when you have finished, the original value in `inLastProduction` has been lost.

> Do not think the value of `inLastProduction` is gone forever when you alter it. The original value still exists within the data file. It is the main memory location called `inLastProduction` that is being reduced.

AVOIDING COMMON LOOP MISTAKES

The two mistakes programmers make most often with loops are:

- Neglecting to initialize the loop control variable
- Neglecting to alter the loop control variable

For example, assume you remove the statement `labelCounter = 0` from the program illustrated in Figure 6-10. When `labelCounter` is compared to `labelsToPrint` at the start of the `while` loop, it is impossible to predict whether any labels will print. Because uninitialized values contain unknown, unpredictable garbage, comparing such a variable to another value is meaningless. Even if you initialize `labelCounter` to zero in the `housekeep()` module of the program, you must reset `labelCounter` to zero for each new record that is processed within the `while` loop. If you fail to reset the `labelCounter`, it just keeps increasing through the life of the program and does not accurately reflect the number of labels printed for each employee.

A different sort of error will occur if you remove the statement that adds one to the `labelCounter` from the program in Figure 6-10. This error will result in the following code:

```
while labelCounter < labelsToPrint
    print labelLine, inFirstName
```

Following this logic, if `labelCounter` is zero and `labelsToPrint` is, for example 110, then `labelCounter` will be less than `labelsToPrint` forever. Nothing in the loop changes either variable, so labels will continue to print. A loop that never stops executing is called an **infinite loop**. It is always incorrect to create a loop that cannot terminate.

When you run a computer program that uses the loop in Figure 6-10, hundreds or thousands of employee records might pass through the `mainLoop()`. If there are 100 employee records, then `labelCounter` is set to zero exactly 100 times; it must be reset to zero once for each employee in order to count each employee's labels correctly. Similarly, `labelsToPrint` is set to 1.1 times `inLastProduction`, once for each employee.

If the average employee produces 100 items during a week, then the loop within the `mainLoop()`, the one controlled by the statement `while labelCounter < labelsToPrint`, executes 11,000 times—110 times each for 100 employees. Again, this number of repetitions is necessary in order to print the correct number of labels.

A repetition that is *not* necessary would be to execute 11,000 separate multiplication statements to recalculate the `labelCounter`. See Figure 6-11.

```
mainLoop()
    labelCounter = 0
    while labelCounter < inLastProduction * 1.1
        print labelLine, inFirstName
        labelCounter = labelCounter + 1
    read empRecord
return
```

Figure 6-11   Inefficient pseudocode for label-making mainLoop()

Although the pseudocode shown in Figure 6-11 will produce the correct number of labels for every employee, the statement `while labelCounter < inLastProduction * 1.1` executes an average of 110 times for each employee. That means that the multiplication of `inLastProduction` by 1.1 occurs 110 separate times for each employee. Performing the same calculation that results in the same mathematical answer 110 times in a row is inefficient. Instead, it is superior to perform the multiplication just once for each employee and use the result 110 times, as shown in the original version of the program in Figure 6-10. In the pseudocode in Figure 6-10, you still must recalculate `labelCounter` once for each record, but not once for each label, so you have improved the program's efficiency.

The modules illustrated in Figures 6-10 and 6-11 do the same thing: print enough labels for every employee to cover 110% of production. As you become more proficient at programming, you will recognize many opportunities to perform the same tasks in alternative, more elegant, and more efficient ways.

Another common error made by beginning programmers involves initializing a variable that does not require initialization. When declaring variables for the label-making program, you might be tempted to declare num `labelCounter = inLastProduction * 1.1`. It seems as though this declaration statement indicates that the value of the `labelCounter` will always be 110% of the `inLastProduction` figure. However, this approach is incorrect for two reasons. First, at the time `labelCounter` is declared, the first employee record has not yet been read into memory, so the value of `inLastProduction` is garbage; therefore the result in `labelCounter` after multiplication will also be garbage. Secondly, even if you read the first `empRecord` into memory before declaring the `labelCounter` variable, the mathematical calculation of the `labelCounter` within the `housekeep()` module would be valid for the first record only. The value of `labelCounter` must be recalculated for each employee record in the input file. Therefore, calculation of the `labelCounter` correctly belongs within the `mainLoop()` as shown in Figure 6-10.

6

USING THE FOR LOOP

The label-making programs discussed in this chapter each contain two loops. For example, Figures 6-12 and 6-13 show the loop within the mainline program as well as the loop within the `mainLoop()` module for the program that produces 100 labels for each employee.

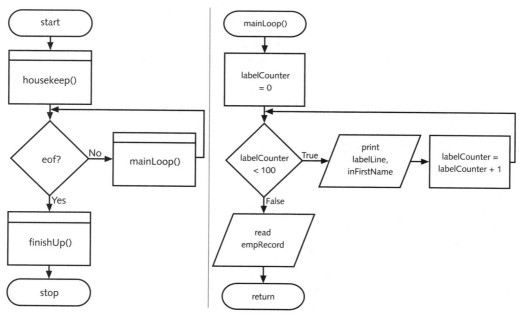

Figure 6-12: Mainline logic for label-making program

Figure 6-13: mainLoop() logic for label-making program

Entry to the `mainLoop()` in the mainline logic is controlled by the `eof` decision. Within the `mainLoop()`, label production is controlled by the `labelCounter`. When you execute the mainline logic, you cannot predict how many times the `mainLoop()` module will execute. Depending on the size of the input file, any number of records might be processed; while the program runs you don't know what the total number of records finally will be. Until you attempt to read a record and encounter the end of the file, you don't know if more records are going to become available. Because you can't determine ahead of time how many records there might be, the mainline loop in the label-making program is called an **indeterminate** or **indefinite loop**.

With some loops, you know exactly how many times they will execute. If every employee needs 100 printed labels, then the loop within the `mainLoop()` module executes exactly 100 times for each employee. This kind of loop, in which you definitely know the repetition factor, is a **definite loop**.

Every high-level computer programming language contains a **while statement** that you can use to code any loop, including indefinite loops (like the mainline loop) and definite loops (like the label-printing loop). You can write statements like the following:

```
while not eof perform mainLoop()
```

and

```
while labelCounter < 100
     print labelLine, inFirstName
     add 1 to labelCounter
```

In addition to the `while` statement, most computer languages also support a `for` statement. You can use the **for statement** or **for loop** with definite loops when you know how many times a loop will repeat. The `for` statement provides you with three actions in one compact statement. The `for` statement uses a loop control variable that it automatically:

- initializes
- evaluates
- increments

The `for` statement usually takes the form:

```
for initialValue to finalValue
     do something
```

For example, to print 100 labels you can write:

```
for labelCounter = 0 to 99
     print labelLine, inFirstName
```

This `for` statement accomplishes several tasks at once in a compact form:

- The `for` statement initializes the `labelCounter` to 0.

- The `for` statement checks the `labelCounter` against the limit value 99 and makes sure that the `labelCounter` is less than or equal to that value.

- If the evaluation is true, the `for` statement body that prints the label executes.

- After the `for` statement body executes, the `labelCounter` increases by one and the comparison to the limit value is made again.

As an alternative to using the loop for `labelCounter = 0 to 99`, you can use for `labelCounter = 1 to 100`. You can use any combination of values, as long as there are 100 whole number values between the two limits.

You never are required to use a `for` statement; the label loop executes correctly using a `while` statement with `labelCounter` as a loop control variable. However, when a loop is based on a loop control variable progressing from a known starting value to a known ending value in equal increments, the `for` loop presents you with a convenient shorthand.

6

The programmer needs to know neither the starting nor the ending value for the loop control variable; only the program must know those values. For example, you don't know the value of a worker's `inLastProduction` value, but when you tell the program to read a record, the program knows. To do so, you can write a for loop that begins for `labelCounter = 1 to inLastProduction`.

In several languages, you can provide a for loop with a step value. A step value is a number you use to increase a loop control variable on each pass through a loop. In most programming languages, the default loop step value is one. You specify a step value when you want each pass through the loop to change the loop control variable by a value other than one.

USING THE DO UNTIL LOOP

When you use either a `while` or a `for` loop, the body of the loop may never execute. For example, in the mainline logic in Figure 6-5, the last action in the `housekeep()` module is to read an input record. If the input file contains no records, the result of the `eof` decision is true, and the program executes the `finishUp()` module without ever entering the `mainLoop()` module.

Similarly, when you produce labels within the `mainLoop()` module shown in Figure 6-10, labels are produced `while labelCounter < labelsToPrint`. Suppose an employee record contains a zero in the `inLastProduction` field—for example, in the case of a new employee or an employee who was on vacation. In such a case, the value of `labelsToPrint` would be zero, and the label-producing body of the loop might never execute. With a `while` loop, you evaluate the loop control variable prior to executing the loop body, and the evaluation might indicate that you can't enter the loop.

When you want to ensure that a loop's body executes at least one time, you can use a do until loop. In a do until loop, the loop control variable is evaluated after the loop body executes. Therefore, the body always executes at least one time.

 You first learned about the do until loop in Chapter 2. Review Chapter 2 to reinforce your understanding of the differences between a while loop and a do until loop.

 Because the question that controls the loop is asked before you enter the loop body, programmers say a while loop has a pretest. Because the question that controls a do until loop occurs after the loop body executes, programmers say the do until loop contains a posttest.

For example, suppose you want to produce one label for each employee to wear as identification before you produce enough labels to cover 110% of last week's production. You can write the do until loop that appears in Figure 6-14.

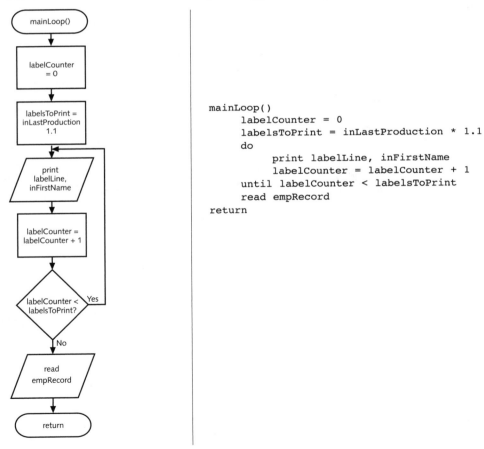

```
mainLoop()
     labelCounter = 0
     labelsToPrint = inLastProduction * 1.1
     do
          print labelLine, inFirstName
          labelCounter = labelCounter + 1
     until labelCounter < labelsToPrint
     read empRecord
return
```

Figure 6-14   do until loop for producing one extra label

Of course, you could achieve the same results by printing one label, then entering a `while` loop as in Figure 6-15.

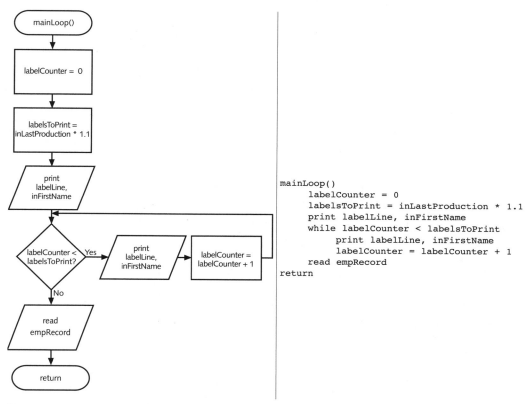

```
mainLoop()
    labelCounter = 0
    labelsToPrint = inLastProduction * 1.1
    print labelLine, inFirstName
    while labelCounter < labelsToPrint
        print labelLine, inFirstName
        labelCounter = labelCounter + 1
    read empRecord
return
```

Figure 6-15   Printing one label, then printing enough to cover production

RECOGNIZING THE CHARACTERISTICS SHARED BY ALL LOOPS

You can see from Figure 6-15 that you never are required to use a `do until` loop. The same results always can be achieved by performing the loop body steps once before entering a `while` loop. If you follow the logic of either of the loops shown in Figures 6-14 and 6-15, you will discover that when an employee has an `inLastProduction` value of 3, then exactly four labels print. Likewise, when an employee has an `inLastProduction` value of 0, then in both cases exactly one label prints. You can accomplish the same results with either type of loop; the `do until` loop is simply a convenience when you need a loop to execute at least one time.

In some languages, the do until loop is called a repeat until loop.

If you can express the logic you want to perform by saying "while a is true, keep doing b," you probably want to use a while loop. If what you want to accomplish seems to fit the statement, "do a until b is true," you can probably use a do until loop.

As you examine Figures 6-14 and 6-15, notice that with the do until loop the loop-controlling question is placed at the *end* of the sequence of the steps that repeat. With the while loop, the loop-controlling question is placed at the *beginning* of the steps that repeat. All structured loops share these characteristics:

- The loop-controlling question provides either entry to or exit from the repeating structure.

- The loop-controlling question provides *the only* entry to or exit from the repeating structure.

You should also notice the difference between *unstructured* loops and the structured do until and while loops. Figure 6-16 diagrams the outline of two unstructured loops. In each case, the decision labeled X breaks out of the loop prematurely. In each case, the loop control variable, (labeled **LC**), does not provide the only entry to or exit from the loop.

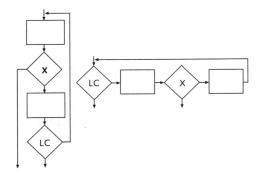

Figure 6-16   Examples of unstructured loops

NESTING LOOPS

Program logic gets more complicated when you must use loops within loops, or **nesting loops**. For example, suppose your worker records contain average *daily* production figures instead of weekly figures. But suppose you still want to print a week's worth of labels for each worker. If your company operates on a five-day work week, then within the mainLoop() of this program you must produce enough labels to cover 110% of each worker's daily label count five times. To accomplish this, you need two counters. You have declared a `labelCounter` to count labels, but now you want to produce 110% of the daily label count five times. You can declare a variable to count the days and name it `dayCounter`. Assuming you declare a variable that holds `inDailyProduction`, the `mainLoop()` logic looks like Figure 6-17.

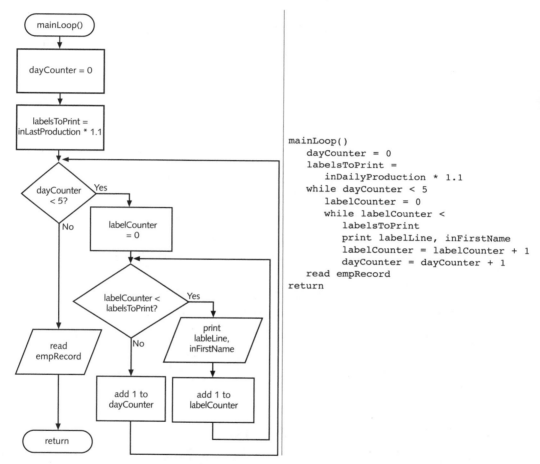

```
mainLoop()
   dayCounter = 0
   labelsToPrint =
      inDailyProduction * 1.1
   while dayCounter < 5
      labelCounter = 0
      while labelCounter <
         labelsToPrint
         print labelLine, inFirstName
         labelCounter = labelCounter + 1
         dayCounter = dayCounter + 1
   read empRecord
return
```

Figure 6-17: Flowchart and pseudocode for labels based on five daily production counts

When you examine Figure 6-17, you see that for each new employee record, the `dayCounter` is initialized to zero and the `labelsToPrint` is set to 110% of the daily production figure. For each new day, the `labelCounter` is reset to zero. While the `dayCounter` remains under 5, you produce the daily quota of labels. When the daily quota is complete, that is, when `labelCounter` is no longer less than `labelsToPrint`, you have printed one day's worth of labels, so you add one to the dayCounter and loop back to see if dayCounter has reached 5 yet. If not, you enter the loop body and print another day's worth of labels.

In this example, if a worker's daily production is 10, the worker needs 55 labels. Because all the labels are identical, you can achieve the same results without a nested loop. You can print the necessary labels for an employee by multiplying 110% of the worker's daily average figure by five, storing the result in labelsToPrint, and executing a single loop. However, if you want the labels to indicate the day of the week, then you must use nested loops, as in Figure 6-18. Each label prints a day number (0 through 4) along with the labelLine message and the employee's first name.

```
mainLoop()
    dayCounter = 0
    labelsToPrint = inDailyProduction * 1.1
    while dayCounter < 5
        labelCounter = 0
        while labelCounter < labelsToPrint
            print "DAY: ", dayCounter, labelLine, inFirstName
            labelCounter = labelCounter + 1
        dayCounter = dayCounter + 1
    read empRecord
return
```

Figure 6-18   Required nested loops for printing labels that include a day number

 To print day numbers 1 through 5 (instead of 0 through 4), you can print dayCounter + 1 on each label.

When nesting loops, you must maintain two individual loop control variables and alter each at the appropriate time.

USING A LOOP TO ACCUMULATE TOTALS

Business reports often include totals. The supervisor who wants a list of employees who participate in the company dental plan often is as interested in *how many* such employees there are as in *who* they are. When you receive your telephone bill at the end of the month, you are usually more interested in the total than in the charges for the individual calls. Some business reports list no individual detail records, just totals. Such reports are called **summary reports**.

For example, a real estate broker might maintain a file of company real estate listings. Each record in the file contains the street address and the asking price of a property for sale. The broker wants a listing of all the properties for sale; she also wants a total value for all the company's listings. The print chart appears in Figure 6-19.

Figure 6-19   Print chart for real estate report

When you read a real estate listing record, besides printing it you must add its value to an accumulator. An **accumulator** is a variable that you use to gather or accumulate values. An accumulator is very similar to a counter. The difference lies in the value that you add to the variable; usually you add just one to a counter, whereas you add some other value to an accumulator. If the real estate broker wants to know how many listings the company holds, you count them. When she wants to know total real estate value, you accumulate it.

In order to accumulate total real estate prices, you declare a numeric variable at the beginning of the program, as shown in Figure 6-20. You must initialize the accumulator, `accumValue`, to zero. In Chapter 4, you learned that when using most programming languages declared variables do not automatically assume any particular value; the unknown value is called garbage. When you read the first real estate record, you will add its value to the accumulator. If the accumulator contains garbage, the addition will not work. Some programming languages issue an error message if you don't initialize a variable you use for accumulating; others let you accumulate, but the results are worthless because you start with garbage.

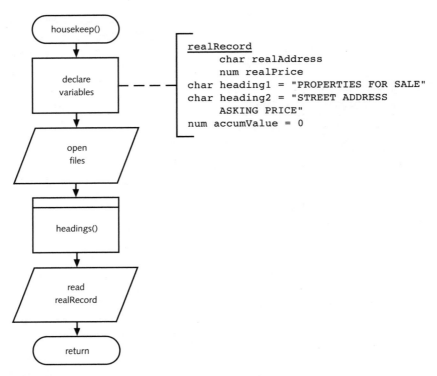

Figure 6-20   housekeep() module for real estate program

If you name the input record fields `realAddress` and `realPrice`, then the `mainLoop()` module of the real estate listing program can be written as shown in Figure 6-21. For each real estate record, you print it and add its value to the accumulator `accumValue`. Then you can read the next record.

Figure 6-21   Flowchart for mainLoop() of real estate listing program

After the program reaches the end of the file, the accumulator will hold the grand total of all the real estate values. When you reach the end of the file, the `finishUp()` module executes, and it is within the `finishUp()` module that you print the accumulated value, `accumValue`. After printing the total, you can close both the input and the output files and return to the mainline where the program ends. See Figure 6-22.

Figure 6-22   finishUp() module for real estate program

New programmers often want to reset the `accumValue` to zero after printing it. Although you *can* take this step without harming the execution of the program, it does not serve any useful purpose. You cannot set `accumValue` to zero in anticipation of having it ready for the next program. Program variables exist only for the life of the program, and even if a future program happens to contain a variable named `accumValue`, the variable will not necessarily occupy the same memory location. Even if you run the program a second time, the variables might occupy physical memory locations different from those they occupied during the first run. At the beginning of the program, it is the programmer's responsibility to initialize all variables that must start with a specific value. There is no benefit to changing a variable's value when it will never be used again during the current execution of the program.

CHAPTER SUMMARY

- ❑ When you use a loop within a computer program, you can write one set of instructions that operates on multiple, separate sets of data.

- ❑ Three steps must occur in every loop: You must initialize a loop control variable, compare the variable to some value that stops the loop, and alter the variable within the loop.

- ❑ A counter is a numeric variable you use to count the number of times an event has occurred. You can count occurrences by incrementing a variable.

- ❑ You can use a variable sentinel value to control a loop.

- ❑ Sometimes it is convenient to reduce or decrement a loop control variable on every cycle through a loop.

- ❑ The two mistakes programmers make most often with loops are neglecting to initialize the loop control variable, and neglecting to alter the loop control variable. Additionally, when a calculation can be performed once before entering a loop, it is inefficient to place the calculation within the loop. It is incorrect to attempt to initialize a variable by using data values that have not been read into memory yet.

- ❑ Most computer languages support a `for` statement or `for` loop that you can use with definite loops when you know how many times a loop will repeat. The `for` statement uses a loop control variable that it automatically initializes, evaluates, and increments.

- ❑ When you want to ensure that a loop's body executes at least one time, you can use a `do until` loop in which the loop control variable is evaluated after the loop body executes.

- ❑ All structured loops share these characteristics: The loop controlling question provides either entry to or exit from the repeating structure, and the loop controlling question provides *the only* entry to or exit from the repeating structure.

❐ When you must use loops within loops, you use nesting loops. When nesting loops, you must maintain two individual loop control variables and alter each at the appropriate time.

❐ Business reports often include totals. Summary reports list no detail records—only totals. An accumulator is a variable that you use to gather or accumulate values.

EXERCISES

1. Write pseudocode for the label-making program that is flowcharted in Figures 6-5 through 6-8.

2. a. Design the logic for a module that would print every number from 1 through 10 along with its square and cube. Design the print layout chart and create the flowchart for this module.

   b. Write pseudocode for the problem in Exercise 2a.

3. a. Design a program that reads credit card account records and prints payoff schedules for customers. Input records contain an account number, customer name, and balance due. For each customer, print the account number and name; then print the customer's projected balance each month for the next 10 months. Assume that there is no finance charge on this account, that the customer makes no new purchases, and that the customer pays off the balance with equal monthly payments, which are 10% of the original bill. Design the print chart, hierarchy chart, and flowchart for this program.

   b. Write pseudocode for the problem in Exercise 4a.

4. a. Design a program that reads credit card account records and prints payoff schedules for customers. Input records contain an account number, customer name, and balance due. For each customer, print the account number and name; then print the customer's payment amount and new balance each month until the card is paid off. Assume that when the balance reaches $10 or less, the customer can pay off the account. At the beginning of every month 1.5% interest is added to the balance, then the customer makes a payment equal to 5% of the current balance. Assume the customer makes no new purchases. Design the print chart, hierarchy chart, and flowchart for this program.

   b. Write pseudocode for the problem in Exercise 4a.

5. a. Assume you have a bank account that compounds interest on a yearly basis. In other words, if you deposit $100 for two years at 4% interest, at the end of one year you will have $104. At the end of two years, you will have the $104 plus 4% of that, or $108.16. Draw the logic for a program that would read in records containing a deposit amount, a term in years, and an interest rate, and for each record print the running total balance for each year of the term.

   b. Write pseudocode for the problem in Exercise 5a.

6. a. A school maintains class records in the following format:

```
CLASS FILE DESCRIPTION
File name: CLASS
FIELD DESCRIPTION  POSITIONS  DATA TYPE  DECIMALS EXAMPLE
Class Code         1—6        Character           CIS111
Section No.        7—9        Numeric    0        101
Teacher            10—29      Character           Gable
Enrollment         30—31      Numeric    0        24
Room               32—35      Character           A213
```

There is one record for each class section offered in the college. Design the program that would print as many stickers as a class needs to provide one for each enrolled student, plus one for the teacher. Each sticker would leave a blank for the student's (or teacher's) name like this:

This border is preprinted, but you must design the program to print all the text you see on the sticker.

Create the hierarchy chart and flowchart for this problem.

b. Write pseudocode for the problem in Exercise 6a.

7. a. A mail-order company often sends multiple packages per order. For each customer order, print enough mailing labels to use on each of the separate boxes that will be mailed. The mailing labels contain the customer's complete name and address along with a box number in the form "Box 9 of 9". For example, an order that requires three boxes produces three labels: "Box 1 of 3", Box 2 of 3", and "Box 3 of 3". The file description is as follows:

```
SHIPPING FILE DESCRIPTION
File name: ORDERS
FIELD DESCRIPTION  POSITIONS  DATA TYPE  DECIMALS EXAMPLE
Title              1—3        Character           Ms
First Name         4—14       Character           Kathy
Last Name          15—25      Character           Lewis
Street             26—40      Character           847 Pine
City               41—51      Character           Aurora
State              52—53      Character           IL
Boxes              54—55      Numeric    0        3
Balance Due        56—61      Numeric    2        129.95
```

Design the print chart for the mailing label, draw the hierarchy chart, and draw the flowchart for this problem.

b. Write pseudocode for the problem in Exercise 7a.

c. Design a program that creates a report listing each customer in the order file, the number of boxes in the customer's order, and the customer's balance. At the end of the report print a total count of all boxes shipped and the grand total of all balances. Draw the print chart, hierarchy chart, and flowchart for this problem.

d. Write pseudocode for the problem in Exercise 7c.

8. a. A second-hand store is having a seven-day sale during which the price of any unsold item drops 10% each day. The inventory file includes an item number, description, and original price on day one. For example, an item that costs $10.00 on the first day costs 10% less, or $9.00, on the second day. On the third day the same item is 10% less than $9.00, or $8.10. Produce a report that shows the price of the item on each day, one through seven. Draw the print chart, hierarchy chart, and flowchart for this problem.

b. Write pseudocode for the problem in Exercise 8a.

9. a. The state of Florida maintains a census file in which each record contains the name of a county, the current population, and a number representing the rate at which population is increasing per year. The governor wants a report listing each county and the number of years it will take for the population of the county to double, assuming the present rate of growth remains constant.

CENSUS FILE DESCRIPTION
File name: CENSUS

FIELD DESCRIPTION	POSITIONS	DATA TYPE	DECIMALS	EXAMPLE
County Name	1–20	Character		Dade
Current Population	21–28	Numeric	0	525000
Rate of Growth	29–30	Numeric	2	.07

Design the print chart for the report label, draw the hierarchy chart, and draw the flowchart for this problem.

b. Write pseudocode for the problem in Exercise 9a.

10. a. A Human Resources department wants a report that shows its employees the benefits of saving for retirement. Produce a report that shows twelve predicted retirement account values for each employee—the values if the employee saves 5, 10, or 15% of his or her annual salary for 10, 20, 30, or 40 years. The department maintains a file in which each record contains the name of an employee and the employee's current annual salary. Assume that savings grow at a rate of 8% per year. Design the print chart for the report label, draw the hierarchy chart, and draw the flowchart for this problem.

b. Write pseudocode for the problem in Exercise 10a.

11. a. Randy's Recreational Vehicles pays it salespeople once every three months. Salespeople receive one quarter of their annual base salary plus 7% of all sales made in the last three-month period. Randy creates an input file with four records for each salesperson. The first of the four records contains the salesperson's name and annual salary, while the three records that follow each contain the name of a month and the monthly sales figure. For example, the first eight records in the file might contain the following data:

Kimball	20000
April	30000
May	40000
June	60000
Johnson	15000
April	65000
May	78000
June	135500

Because the two types of records contain data in the same format, a character field followed by a numeric field, you can define one input record format containing two variables that you use with either type of record. Design the logic for the program that reads a salesperson's record, and if not at **eof**, reads the next three records in a loop, accumulating sales and computing commissions. For each salesperson, print the quarterly base salary, the three commission amounts, and the total salary, which is the quarterly base plus the three commission amounts. Design the print chart for the report, the hierarchy chart, and the flowchart for this problem.

b. Write pseudocode for the problem in Exercise 11a.

CONTROL BREAKS

After studying Chapter 7, you should be able to:

♦ Understand control break logic

♦ Perform single-level control breaks

♦ Use control data within the control break module

♦ Perform control breaks with totals

♦ Perform multiple-level control breaks

♦ Perform page breaks

UNDERSTANDING CONTROL BREAK LOGIC

A **control break** is a temporary detour in the logic of a program. In particular, programmers refer to a program as a **control break program** when a change in the value of a variable initiates special actions or causes special or unusual processing to occur. You usually write control break programs to organize output for programs that handle data records, which are organized logically in groups based on the value in a field. As you read in records, you examine the same field in each record, and when you encounter a record that contains a different value from the ones that preceded it, you perform a special action. If you have ever read a report that lists items in groups with each group followed by a subtotal, then you have read a type of **control break report**. Some other examples of control break reports produced by control break programs include:

- All employees listed in order by department number, in which a new page starts for each department

- All company clients listed in order by state of residence, with a count of clients after each state's client list

- All books for sale in a bookstore in order by category (such as reference or self-help), with a dollar total for the value of all books following each category of book

- All items sold in order by date of sale, switching ink color for each new month

Each of these reports shares two traits:

- The records used in each report are listed in order by a specific variable: department, state, category, or date.

- When that variable changes, the program takes special action: starts a new page, prints a count or total, or switches ink color.

To generate a control break report, your input records must be organized in sorted order based on the field that will cause the breaks. If you are going to write a program that prints employee records on separate pages based on their departments, then the records must be sorted in department-number order before you begin processing. As you grow more proficient in programming logic, you will learn techniques for writing programs that sort records; for now, assume that a sorting program has already been used to pre-sort your records.

 You will learn techniques for processing unsorted records in Chapter 8.

PERFORMING SINGLE-LEVEL CONTROL BREAKS

Suppose you want to print a list of employees, advancing to a new page for each department. Figure 7-1 shows the input file description, from which you can see that the employee department is a two-digit numeric field and that the file has been presorted in employee-department number order. Figure 7-2 shows the desired output—a simple list of employee names.

```
File name: EMPSBYDEPT
Sorted By: Department
FIELD DESCRIPTION      POSITIONS      DATA TYPE      DECIMALS
Department             1—2            Numeric        0
Last Name              3—14           Character
First Name             15—26          Character
```

Figure 7-1   Employee file description

```
        1111111111222222222233333333334444444444555555555
 1234567890123456789012345678901234567890123456789012345 67
1
2   EMPLOYEES BY DEPARTMENT
3
4   LAST NAME              FIRST NAME
5
6     XXXXXXXXXXXXX          XXXXXXXXXXXXX
7     XXXXXXXXXXXXX          XXXXXXXXXXXXX
8     XXXXXXXXXXXXX          XXXXXXXXXXXXX
```

Figure 7-2   Print chart for employees listed by department

The basic logic of the program works like this: When you read each employee record from the input file, you will determine whether the employee belongs to the same department as the previous employee. If so, you simply print the employee and read another record. If there are 20 employees in a department, these steps are repeated 20 times in a row—read an employee in and print the employee out. However, eventually you will read in an employee who does not belong to the same department. At that point, before you print the employee who is in the new department, you must print headings on the top of a new page. Then you can proceed to print employees who belong to the new department.

However, there is a slight problem you must solve before you can determine whether a newly input record contains the same department number as the previously input record. When you read a record from an input file, the data that represent department, last name, and first name occupy specific physical locations in computer memory. For each new record, new data must occupy the same positions and the previous set of data is lost. For example, if you read a record containing data for Alan Andrews in Department 1, when you read the next record for Barbara Bailey in Department 2, "Barbara" replaces "Alan", "Bailey" replaces "Andrews", and 2 replaces 1. After you read in a new record, there is no way to look back at the previous record to determine whether that record had a different department number. The previous record's data has been replaced by the new record's data.

The technique you must use to "remember" the old department number is to create a special variable, called a **control break field**, to hold the previous department number. With a control break field, every time you read in a record and print it, you also can save the crucial part of the record that will signal the change or control the program break. In this case, you want to store the department number in this specially created variable. Comparing the new and old department-number values will determine when it is time to print headings at the top of a new page.

The mainline logic for the Employees by Department report is the same as the mainline logic for all the other programs you've analyzed so far. It performs a `housekeeping()` module, after which an `eof` question controls execution of a `mainLoop()`. At `eof`, a `finish()` module executes. See Figure 7-3.

7

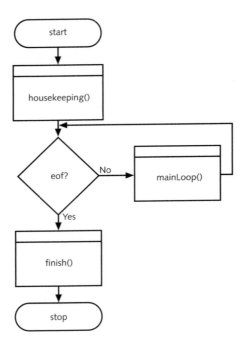

Figure 7-3   Mainline logic for Employees by Department report program

The housekeeping() module begins similarly to others you have seen. You declare variables as shown in Figure 7-4, including those you will use for the input data: empDept, empLast, and empFirst. You can also declare variables to hold the headings, and an additional variable that is named oldDept in this example. The purpose of oldDept is to serve as the control break field. Every time you read a record, you can save its department number in oldDept before you read the next record.

Note that it would be incorrect to initialize oldDept to the value of empDept when you declare oldDept. When you declare variables at the beginning of the housekeeping() module, you have not yet read in the first record, therefore empDept does not yet have any usable value. You use the value of the first empDept only after you read the first input record.

In the housekeeping() module you also open files, print headings, and read the first input record. However, before you leave housekeeping(), you can set the oldDept variable to equal the empDept value in the first input record. You will write the mainLoop() of the program to check for any change in department number; that's the signal to print headings at the top of a new page. Because you just printed headings and read in the first record, you do not want to print headings again for this record—you want to ensure that the empDept and oldDept are equal within the mainLoop().

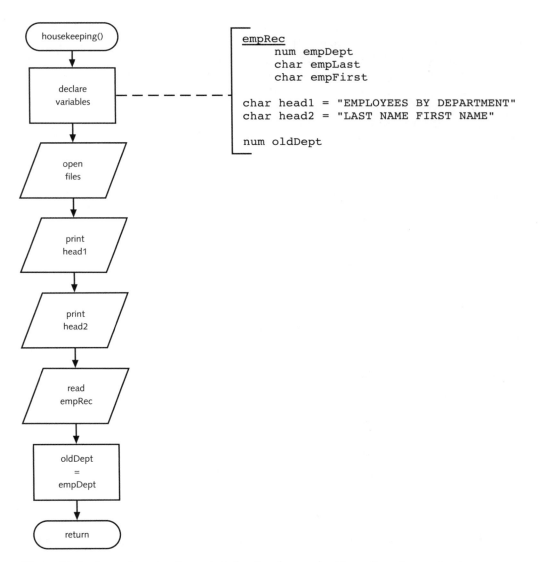

Figure 7-4 housekeeping() module for Employees by Department report program

As an alternative to the housekeeping() logic shown here, you can remove printing headings from the housekeeping() module and set the oldDept to any impossible value, for example, -1. Then in the mainLoop() the first record will force the control break and the headings will print in the newPage() control break routine.

The first task within the mainLoop() is to check whether the empDept holds the same value as oldDept. For the first record, on the first pass through the mainLoop(), the

values are equal; you set them to be equal in **housekeeping()**. Therefore you proceed, printing the employee's record and reading a second record. At the end of the
mainLoop() shown in Figure 7-5, the logical flow returns to the mainline logic shown
in Figure 7-3. If it is not **eof**, the flow travels back into the **mainLoop()** module. There
you compare the second record's **empDept** to **oldDept**. If the second record holds an
employee from the same department, then you simply print that employee's record, and
read a third record into memory. As long as each new record holds the same **empDept**
value, you continue reading and printing.

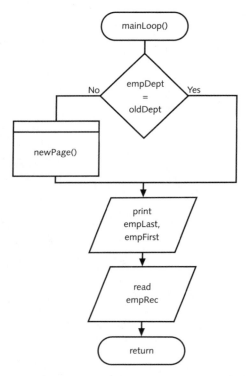

Figure 7-5   mainLoop() module for Employees by Department report program

Eventually, you will read in an employee whose **empDept** is not the same as **oldDept**.
That's when the control break routine, **newPage()**, executes. The **newPage()** module
must perform two tasks:

- It must print headings on top of a new page.

- It must update the control break field.

Figure 7-6 shows the **newPage()** module.

Figure 7-6   The newPage() module for Employees by Department report program

In Chapter 4 you learned that specific programming languages provide you with a means to physically advance printer paper to the top of a page. For this book, if a print chart shows a heading printing at the top of the page, then you can assume printing the heading causes the paper in the printer to advance to the top of a new page. The appropriate language-specific codes can be added when you code the program.

When you read an employee whose **empDept** is not the same as **oldDept**, you cause a break in the normal flow of the program. The new employee record must "wait" while headings print and the control break field **oldDept** acquires a new value. When the control break module ends, the waiting employee record prints on the new page. When you read the *next* employee record, the employee's **empDept** is compared to the updated **oldDept**, and if the new employee works in the same department as the one just preceding, then normal control continues with the print-and-read statements.

The **newPage()** module performs two tasks required in all control break routines:

- Performs any necessary processing for the new group—in this case, writes headings
- Updates the control break field

As an alternative to updating the control break field within the control break routine, you could set the oldDept equal to empDept just before you read each record. However, if there are 200 employees in Department 55, then you set the oldDept to the same value 200 times. It's more efficient to set oldDept to a different value only when there is a change.

The finish() module for the Employees by Department report program requires only that you close the files. See Figure 7-7.

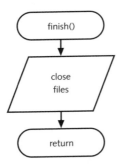

Figure 7-7   The finish() module for Employees by Department report program

USING CONTROL DATA WITHIN THE CONTROL BREAK MODULE

In the Employees by Department report program example, the control break routine printed constant headings at the top of each new page, but sometimes you need to use control data within a control break module. For example, consider the report layout shown in Figure 7-8.

```
                    1111111111222222222233333333334444444444555555555
      1234567890123456789012345678901234567890123456789012345678901234567
1
2        EMPLOYEES FOR DEPARTMENT 99
3
4        LAST NAME                    FIRST NAME
5
6        XXXXXXXXXXXXX                XXXXXXXXXXXXX
7        XXXXXXXXXXXXX                XXXXXXXXXXXXX
8        XXXXXXXXXXXXX                XXXXXXXXXXXXX
```

Figure 7-8   Print chart for employees listed by department identified in heading

The difference between Figure 7-2 and Figure 7-8 lies in the heading. Figure 7-8 shows variable data in the heading—the department number prints at the top of each page of employees. To create this kind of program, the one change you must make in the existing program is to modify the newPage() module, as shown in Figure 7-9. Instead of printing a fixed heading, you print a heading that contains two parts: a constant beginning ("EMPLOYEES FOR DEPARTMENT") with a variable ending (the department number for the employees who appear on the page). Notice that you use the `empDept` number that belongs to the employee record that is waiting to be printed while this control break module executes. Additionally, you must ensure that the first heading on the report prints correctly. You can modify the `housekeeping()` module in Figure 7-4 so that you read the first `empRec` prior to printing the headings.

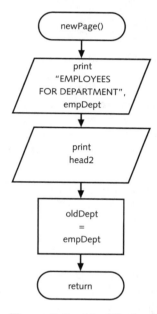

Figure 7-9   Modified newPage() module that prints department number in heading

Figure 7-10 shows a different print chart. For this report, the department number prints *following* the employee list for the department. A message that prints at the end of a page is called a **footer**. Headings usually require information about the *next* record; footers usually require information about the *previous* record.

			1 1 1 1 1 1 1 1 1 1 2 2 2 2 2 2 2 2 2 2 3 3 3 3 3 3 3 3 3 3 4 4 4 4 4 4 4 4 4 4 5 5 5 5 5 5 5 5
	1 2 3 4 5 6 7 8 9 0 1 2 3 4 5 6 7 8 9 0 1 2 3 4 5 6 7 8 9 0 1 2 3 4 5 6 7 8 9 0 1 2 3 4 5 6 7 8 9 0 1 2 3 4 5 6 7	

1	
2	EMPLOYEES BY DEPARTMENT
3	
4	LAST NAME FIRST NAME
5	
6	XXXXXXXXXXXX XXXXXXXXXXXX
7	XXXXXXXXXXXX XXXXXXXXXXXX
8	XXXXXXXXXXXX XXXXXXXXXXXX
9	
10	END OF DEPARTMENT 99

Figure 7-10   Print chart for employees listed by department identified in footer

Figure 7-11 shows the `newPage()` module required to print the department number in an Employees by Department report footer. When you write a program that produces the report shown in Figure 7-10, you continuously read records with `empLast`, `empFirst`, and `empDept` fields. Each time an `empDept` does not equal the `oldDept`, it means that you have reached a department break and that you should perform the `newPage()` module. The `newPage()` module has three tasks:

- It must print the footer for the previous department at the bottom of the employee list.
- It must print headings on top of a new page.
- It must update the control break field.

When the `newPage()` module prints the footer at the bottom of the old page, you must use the `oldDept` number. For example, assume you have printed several employees from Department 12. When you read a record with an employee from Department 13 (or any other department), the first thing you must do is print "END OF DEPARTMENT 12". You print the correct department number by accessing the value of the `oldDept`. Then you can print the other headings at the top of a new page and update `oldDept` to the current `empDept`, which is 13.

Now the `newPage()` module performs three tasks required in all control break routines:

- It performs any necessary processing for the previous group—in this case, writes the footer.
- It performs any necessary processing for the new group—in this case, writes headings.
- It updates the control break field.

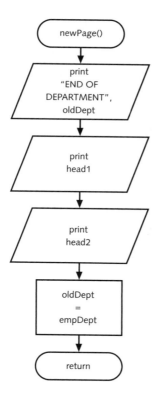

Figure 7-11   Modified newPage() module that prints department number in footer

The `finish()` module for the new program containing footers also requires an extra step. Imagine that the last five records on the input file include two employees from Department 78, Amy and Bill, and three employees from Department 85, Carol, Don, and Ellen. The logical flow proceeds as follows:

1. After the first Department 78 employee (Amy) prints, you read in the second Department 78 employee (Bill).

2. At the top of the `mainLoop()` module, Bill's department compares to `oldDept`. The departments are the same, so the second Department 78 employee (Bill) is printed. Then you read in the first Department 85 employee (Carol).

3. At the top of the `mainLoop()`, Carol's `empDept` and the `oldDept` are different, so you perform the `newPage()` module, while Carol's record waits in memory.

4. In the `newPage()` module, you print "END OF DEPARTMENT 78". Then you print headings for the top of the next page. Finally, you set `oldDept` to 85, and then return to the `mainLoop()`.

5. Back in the `mainLoop()`, you print a line of data for the first Department 85 employee (Carol), whose record waited while `newPage()` executed. Then you read in the record for the second Department 85 employee (Don).

6. At the top of `mainLoop()`, you compare Don's department number to `oldDept`. The numbers are the same, so you print Don's employee data and read in the last Department 85 employee (Ellen).

7. At the top of `mainLoop()` you determine that Ellen has the same department number, so you print Ellen's data and attempt to read from the input file where you encounter `eof`.

8. The `eof` decision in the mainline logic sends you to the `finish()` module.

You have printed the last Department 85 employee (Ellen), but the department footer for Department 85 has not printed. That's because every time you attempt to read an input record, you don't know whether there will be more records. The mainline logic checks for the `eof` condition, but if it determines that it is `eof`, the logic does not flow back into the `mainLoop()` where the `newPage()` module can execute.

To print the footer for the last department, you must print a footer one last time within the `finish()` routine. The `finish()` module in Figure 7-12 illustrates this. Taking this action is similar to printing the first heading in the `housekeeping()` module. The very first heading prints separately from all the others at the beginning; the very last footer must print separately from all the others at the end.

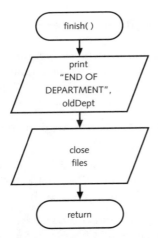

Figure 7-12   Modified finish() module for report program with footer

PERFORMING CONTROL BREAKS WITH TOTALS

Suppose you run a bookstore, and one of the files you maintain is called BOOKFILE, which has one record for every book title that you carry. Each record has fields such as `bookTitle`, `bookAuthor`, `bookCategory` (fiction, reference, self-help, and so on), `bookPublisher`, and `bookPrice`, as shown in this file description in Figure 7-13.

```
File name: BOOKFILE
Sorted by: Category
FIELD DESCRIPTION        POSITIONS        DATA TYPE        DECIMALS
Title                    1—30             Character
Author                   31—46            Character
Category                 47—56            Character
Publisher                57—72            Character
Price                    73—77            Numeric            2
```

Figure 7-13   BOOKFILE file description

Suppose you want to print out a list of all the books that your store carries with a total number of books at the bottom of the list, as shown in Figure 7-14. You can use the logic shown in Figure 7-15. In the main loop module, named `bookListLoop()`, you print a book title, add 1 to the `grandTotal`, and read the next record. At the end of the program, in the `closeDown()` module, you print the `grandTotal` before you close the files.

Figure 7-14   Print chart for book list

7

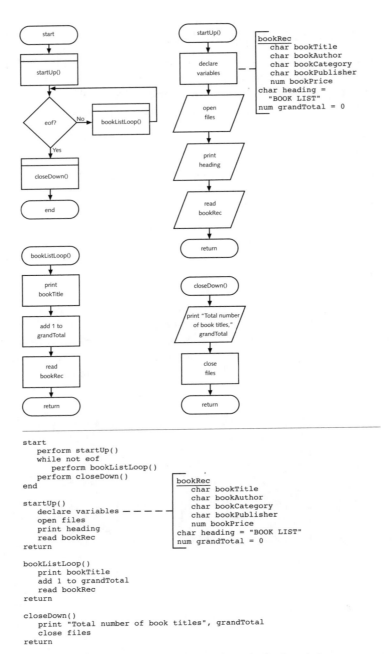

```
start
   perform startUp()
   while not eof
      perform bookListLoop()
   perform closeDown()
end

startUp()
   declare variables — — — —
   open files
   print heading
   read bookRec
return

bookListLoop()
   print bookTitle
   add 1 to grandTotal
   read bookRec
return

closeDown()
   print "Total number of book titles", grandTotal
   close files
return
```

```
bookRec
   char bookTitle
   char bookAuthor
   char bookCategory
   char bookPublisher
   num bookPrice
char heading = "BOOK LIST"
num grandTotal = 0
```

Figure 7-15   Flowchart and pseudocode for bookstore program

As you can see from the pseudocode in Figure 7-15, the `bookListLoop()` module performs three major tasks:

1. Prints a book title.

2. Adds 1 to the `grandTotal`.

3. Reads in the next book record.

The `closeDown()` module prints the `grandTotal`. You can't print `grandTotal` any earlier in the program because the `grandTotal` value isn't complete until the last record has been read.

The logic of the preceding program is pretty straightforward. Suppose, however, that you decide you want a count for each category of book rather than just one grand total. For example, in the categories of fiction, reference, and self-help the output would consist of a list of all fiction books first, followed by a count; then all reference books followed by a count; and finally all self-help books followed by a count. The report is a control break report and the control break field is the `bookCategory`.

To produce the report with subtotals by category, you must declare two new variables: `previousCategory` and `categoryTotal`. Every time you read in a book record, you compare `bookCategory` to `previousCategory`; when there is a category change, you print the count of books for the previous category. The `categoryTotal` variable holds that count. See Figure 7-16.

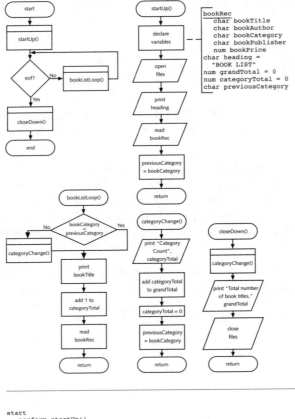

```
start
   perform startUp( )
   while not eof
      perform bookListLoop( )
   perform closeDown( )
end

startUp( )
   declare variables— — — — — —
   open files
   print heading
   read bookRec
   previousCategory = bookCategory
return

bookListLoop( )
   if bookCategory not equal to previousCategory then
      perform categoryChange( )
   endif
   print bookTitle
   add 1 to categoryTotal
   read bookRec
return

categoryChange( )
   print "Category count", categoryTotal
   add categoryTotal to grandTotal
   categoryTotal = 0
   previousCategory = bookCategory
return

closeDown( )
   perform categoryChange( )
   print "Total number of book titles", grandTotal
   close files
return
```

```
bookRec
   char bookTitle
   char bookAuthor
   char bookCategory
   char bookPublisher
   num bookPrice
char heading = "BOOK LIST"
num grandTotal = 0
num categoryTotal = 0
char previousCatergory
```

Figure 7-16   Flowchart and pseudocode for bookstore program with subtotals

When you draw a flowchart, it is usually clearer to ask questions positively, as in `bookCategory = previousCategory?` and draw appropriate actions on the Yes or No side of the decision. In pseudocode, when action occurs only on the No side of a decision, it is usually clearer to ask negatively, as in `bookCategory` *not* equal to `previousCategory`. Figure 7-16 uses these tactics.

When you read the first record from the input file, you save the value of `bookCategory` in the `previousCategory` variable. Every time a record enters the `bookListLoop()` module, the program checks to see if the current record represents a new category of work by comparing `bookCategory` to the variable called `previousCategory`. When you process the first record, the categories match, so the book title prints, the `categoryTotal` increases by one, and you read the next record. If this next record's `bookCategory` value matches the `previousCategory` value, processing continues as usual with printing a line and adding 1 to the `categoryTotal`.

At some point the `bookCategory` for an input record does not match the `previousCategory`. At that point, you perform the `categoryChange()` module. Within the `categoryChange()` module, you print the count of the previous category of books. Then you add the `categoryTotal` to the `grandTotal`. Adding a total to a higher-level total is called **rolling up the totals**.

You could write the `bookListLoop()` so that as you process each book, you add one to the `categoryTotal` and add one to the `grandTotal`. Then there would be no need to roll totals up in the `categoryChange()` module. If there are 120 fiction books, you add 1 to `categoryTotal` 120 times; you also would add 1 to `grandTotal` 120 times. This technique would yield correct results, but you can eliminate executing 119 addition instructions by waiting until you have accumulated all 120 category counts before adding the total figure to `grandTotal`.

This control break report containing totals performs four of the five tasks required in all control break routines that include totals:

- It performs any necessary processing for the previous group—in this case it prints the `categoryTotal`.

- It rolls up the current level totals to the next higher level—in this case it adds `categoryTotal` to `grandTotal`.

- It resets the current level's totals to zero—in this case the `categoryTotal` is set to zero.

- It performs any necessary processing for the new group—in this case there is none.

- It updates the control break field—in this case `previousCategory`.

The `closeDown()` routine for this type of program is more complicated than it might first appear. It seems as though you should print the `grandTotal`, close the files, and return to the mainline logic. However, when you read the last record, the mainline `eof` decision sends the logical flow to the `closeDown()` routine. You have not printed the last `categoryTotal`, nor have you added the count for the last category into the `grandTotal`. You must take care of both these tasks before printing the `grandTotal`. You can perform these two tasks as separate steps in `closeDown()`, but it is often simplest just to remember to perform the control break routine `categoryChange()` one last time. The `categoryChange()` module already executes after every previous category completes—that is, every time you encounter a new category during the execution of the program. You also can execute this module after the final category completes, at end of file. Encountering the end of the file is really just another form of break; it signals that the last category has finally completed. The `categoryChange()` module prints the category total and rolls the totals up to the `grandTotal` level.

When you call the `categoryChange()` module from within `closeDown()` it performs a few tasks you don't need, like setting the value of `previousCategory`. You have to weigh the convenience of calling the already-written `categoryChange()` module and executing a few unneeded statements, as opposed to taking the time to write a new module that would execute only the statements that are absolutely necessary.

It is very important to note that this control break program works whether there are three categories of books or 300. Note further that it does not matter what the categories of books are. For example, the program never asks `bookCategory = "fiction"`?. Instead, the control of the program breaks when the category field *changes* and it is in no way dependent on *what* that change is.

PERFORMING MULTIPLE-LEVEL CONTROL BREAKS

Let's say your bookstore from the last example is so successful that you have a chain of them across the country. Every time a sale is made you create a record with the fields `bookTitle`, `bookPrice`, `bookCity`, and `bookState`. You would like a report that prints a summary of books sold in each city and each state, similar to the one shown in Figure 7-17. A report such as this one that does not include any information about individual records, but instead includes group totals, is a **summary report**.

This program contains a **multiple-level control break**, that is, the normal flow of control (reading records and counting book sales) breaks away to print totals in response to more than just one change in condition. In this report a control break occurs in response to either of two conditions—when the contents of the `bookCity` variable changes as well as when the contents of the `bookState` variable changes.

Just as the file you use to create a single-level control break report must be presorted, so must the input file you use to create a multiple-level control break report. The input file that you use for the book sales report must be sorted by `bookCity` *within* `bookState`.

That is, all of one state's records, for example all records from IA, come first; then all the records from another state, such as IL, follow. Within any one state, all of one city's records come first, then all of the next city's records follow. For example, the input file that produces the report shown in Figure 7-17 contains 200 records for book sales in Ames, IA, followed by 814 records for book sales in Des Moines, IA. The basic processing entails reading a book sale record, adding one to a counter, and reading the next book sale record. At the end of any city's records, you print a total for that city; at the end of a state's records, you print a total for that state.

BOOK SALES BY CITY AND STATE

Ames	200
Des Moines	814
Iowa City	291
Total for IA	1305
Chicago	1093
Crystal Lake	564
McHenry	213
Springfield	365
Total for IL	2235
Springfield	289
Worcester	100
Total for MA	389
Grand Total	3929

Figure 7-17   Sample run of Book Sales by City and State report

The `housekeeping()` routine of the Book Sales by City and State report program looks similar to the `housekeeping()` routine in the last control break program. You declare variables, open files, and read the first record. This time, however, there are multiple fields to save and compare to the old fields. Here you declare two special variables, `prevCity` and `prevState`, as shown in Figure 7-18. In addition, the Book Sales report shows three kinds of totals, so you declare three special variables, `cityCounter`, `stateCounter`, and `grandTotal`, which are all set to zero.

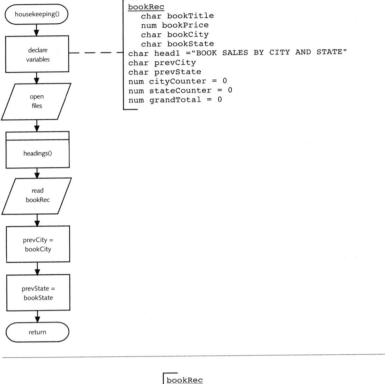

```
bookRec
    char bookTitle
    num bookPrice
    char bookCity
    char bookState
char head1 ="BOOK SALES BY CITY AND STATE"
char prevCity
char prevState
num cityCounter = 0
num stateCounter = 0
num grandTotal = 0
```

```
                              bookRec
                                  char bookTitle
                                  num bookPrice
                                  char bookCity
                                  char bookState
housekeeping()
    declare variables — — — char head1 = "BOOK SALES BY CITY AND STATE"
    open files                char prevCity
    perform headings()        char prevState
    read bookRec              num cityCounter = 0
    prevCity = bookCity       num stateCounter = 0
    prevState = bookState     num grandTotal = 0
return
```

Figure 7-18   Flowchart and pseudocode for housekeeping() module for Book Sales by City and State report program

This program prints both **bookState** and **bookCity** totals, so you need two control break modules, **cityBreak()** and **stateBreak()**. Every time there is a change in the **bookCity** field, the **cityBreak()** routine performs these standard control break tasks:

■ It performs any necessary processing for the previous group—prints totals for the previous city.

- It rolls up the current level totals to the next higher level—adds the city count to the state count.

- It resets the current level's totals to zero—sets the city count to zero.

- It performs any necessary processing for the new group—in this case there is none.

- It updates the control break field—sets `prevCity` to `bookCity`.

Within the `stateBreak()` module, you must perform one new type of task, as well as the control break tasks you are familiar with. The new task is the first task: within the `stateBreak()` module you must first perform a `cityBreak()` automatically (because if there is a change in the state, there must also be a change in the city). The `stateBreak()` module does the following:

- It processes the lower-level break, in this case `cityBreak()`.

- It performs any necessary processing for the previous group—prints totals for the previous state.

- It rolls up the current level totals to the next higher level—adds the state count to the grand total.

- It resets the current level's totals to zero—sets the state count to zero.

- It performs any necessary processing for the new group—in this case there is none.

- It updates the control break field—sets `prevState` to `bookState`.

The `mainLoop()` of this multiple-level control break program checks for any change in two different variables: `bookCity` and `bookState`. When the `bookCity` changes, a city total is printed, and when the `bookState` changes, a state total is printed. As you can see from the sample report in Figure 7-17, all city totals for each state print before the state total for the same state, so it might seem logical to check for a change in `bookCity` before checking for a change in `bookState`. However, the opposite is true. For the totals to be correct, you must check for any `bookState` change first. You do so because when a `bookCity` changes, the `bookState` also *might* be changing, but when the `bookState` changes, it means the `bookCity` *must* be changing.

Consider the sample input records shown in Figure 7-19, which are sorted by `bookCity` within `bookState`:

7

TITLE	PRICE	CITY	STATE
A Brief History of Time	20.00	Iowa City	IA
The Scarlet Letter	15.99	Chicago	IL
Math Magic	4.95	Chicago	IL
She's Come Undone	12.00	Springfield	IL
The Joy of Cooking	2.50	Springfield	IL
Walden	9.95	Springfield	MA
A Bridge Too Far	3.50	Springfield	MA

Figure 7-19   Sample data for Book Sales by City and State report

When you get to the point in the program where you read the first Illinois record (*The Scarlet Letter*), "Iowa City" is the value stored in the field `prevCity` and "IA" is the value stored in `prevState`. Since the values in the `bookCity` and `bookState` variables on the new record are both different from the `prevCity` and `prevState` fields, both a city and state total will print. However, consider the problem when you read the first record for Springfield, MA (*Walden*). At this point in the program `prevState` is "IL", but `prevCity` is the same as the current `bookCity`; both contain "Springfield." If you check for a change in `bookCity`, you won't find one at all, and no city total will print even though Springfield, MA is definitely a different city from Springfield, IL.

Because cities in different states can have the same name, writing your control break program to check for a change in city first, causes your program to not recognize that you are working with a new city. Instead, you should always check for the major-level break first. If the records are sorted by `bookCity` within `bookState`, then a change in `bookState` causes a **major-level break** and a change in `bookCity` causes a **minor-level break**. When the `bookState` value "MA", is not equal to the `prevState` value "IL", you force a `cityBreak()`, printing a city total for Springfield, IL before a state total for IL and before continuing with the Springfield, MA record. You check for a change in `bookState` first, and if there is one, you perform a `cityBreak()`. In other words, if there is a change in `bookState`, there is an implied change in `bookCity`, even if the cities happen to have the same name.

> If you need totals to print by `bookCity` within a field defined as `bookCounty` within `bookState`, you could say you have minor-, intermediate-, and major-level breaks.

Figure 7-20 shows the `mainLoop()` for the Book Sales by City and State Report program. You check for a change in the `bookState` value. If there is no change, you check for a change in the `bookCity` value. If there is no change there either, you add 1 to the counter for the city and read the next record. When there is a change in the `bookCity` value, you print the city total and add the city total to the state total. When there is a change in the **bookState** value, you perform the break routine for the last city in the state, then you print the state total and add it to the grand total.

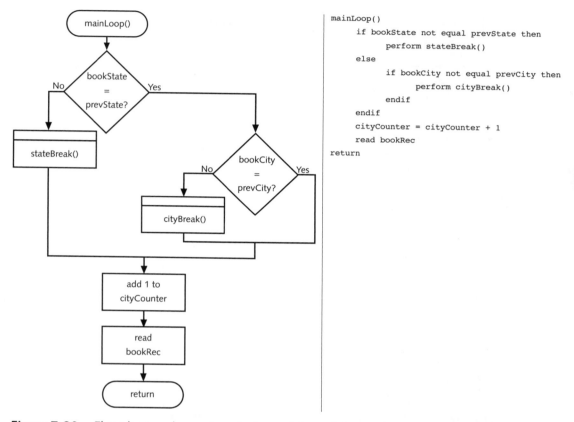

```
mainLoop()
        if bookState not equal prevState then
                perform stateBreak()
        else
                if bookCity not equal prevCity then
                        perform cityBreak()
                endif
        endif
        cityCounter = cityCounter + 1
        read bookRec
return
```

Figure 7-20   Flowchart and pseudocode for mainLoop() for Book Sales by City and State report

Figures 7-21 and 7-22 show the **stateBreak()** and **cityBreak()** modules. The two modules are very similar; the **stateBreak()** routine contains just one extra type of task. When there is a change in **bookState**, you perform the **cityBreak()** automatically before you perform any of the other necessary steps to change states.

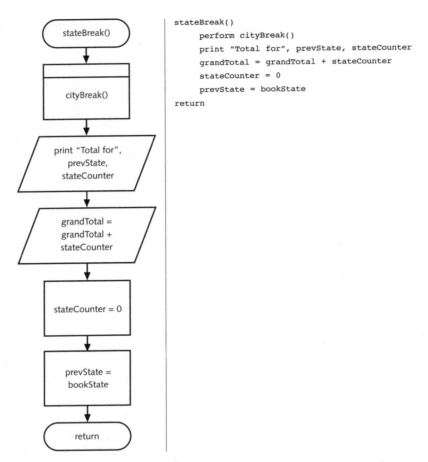

```
stateBreak()
    perform cityBreak()
    print "Total for", prevState, stateCounter
    grandTotal = grandTotal + stateCounter
    stateCounter = 0
    prevState = bookState
return
```

Figure 7-21   Flowchart and pseudocode for stateBreak() module

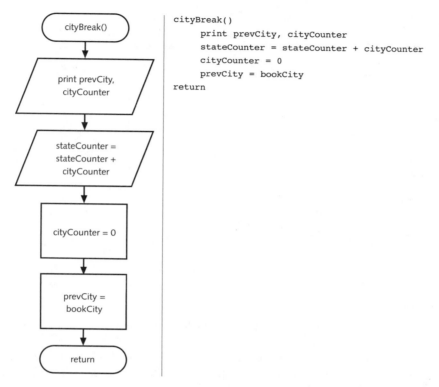

```
cityBreak()
    print prevCity, cityCounter
    stateCounter = stateCounter + cityCounter
    cityCounter = 0
    prevCity = bookCity
return
```

Figure 7-22   Flowchart and pseudocode for cityBreak() module

The sample report for the book sales by city and state shows that you print the grand total for all book sales, so within the `closeDown()` module, you must print the `grandTotal` variable. Before you can do so, however, you must perform both the `cityBreak()` and the `stateBreak()` modules one last time. You can accomplish this by performing `stateBreak()` because the first step within `stateBreak()` is to perform `cityBreak()`.

Consider the sample data shown in Figure 7-19. While you continue to read records for books sold in Springfield, MA, you continue to add to the `cityCounter` for that city. At the moment you attempt to read one more record past the end of the file, you do not know whether there will be more records; therefore, you have not yet printed either the `cityCounter` for Springfield or the `stateCounter` for MA. In the `closeDown()` module you perform `stateBreak()`, which immediately performs `cityBreak()`. Within `cityBreak()`, the count for Springfield prints and rolls up to the `stateCounter`. Then, after the logic transfers back to the `stateBreak()` module, the total for MA prints and rolls up to the `grandTotal`. Finally, you can print the `grandTotal`, as shown in Figure 7-23.

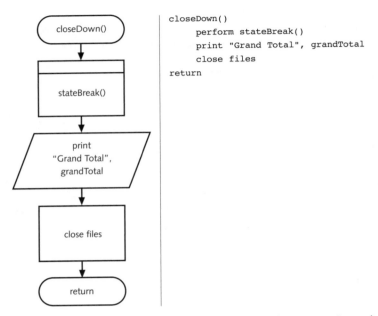

```
closeDown()
      perform stateBreak()
      print "Grand Total", grandTotal
      close files
return
```

Figure 7-23   Flowchart and pseudocode for closeDown() module

Every time you write a program, where you need control break routines, you should check whether you need to complete each of the following tasks within the modules:

- Performing the lower-level break, if any
- Performing any control break processing for the previous group
- Rolling up the current level totals to the next higher level
- Resetting the current level's totals to zero
- Performing any control break processing for the new group
- Updating the control break field

PERFORMING PAGE BREAKS

Many business programs use a control break to start a new page when a printed page fills up with output. In other words, you might want to start a new page based on the number of lines already printed rather than on the contents of an input field, such as department number. The logic in these programs involves counting the lines printed, pausing to print headings when the counter reaches some predetermined value, and then going on. This common business task is just another example of providing a break in the usual flow of control.

Some programmers may prefer to reserve the term *control break* for situations in which the break is based on the contents of one of the fields in an input record, rather than on the contents of a work field such as a line counter.

Let's say you have a file called CUSTOMERFILE that contains 1,000 customers with two character fields that you have decided to call `custLast` and `custFirst`. You want to print a list of these customers, 60 detail lines to a page. The mainline logic of the program is familiar. The only new feature is a variable called a line counter. You will use a **line-counter** variable to keep track of the number of printed lines so that you can break to a new page after printing 60 lines. See Figure 7-24.

```
start
     perform getReady()
     while not eof
           perform produceReport()
     perform cleanup()
end
```

Figure 7-24   Mainline logic of customer report program

 When creating a printed report, you need to clarify whether the user wants a specific number of *total* lines per page, including headings, or a specific number of *detail* lines per page following the headings.

Within the `getReady()` module (Figure 7-25), you declare the variables, open the files, print the headings, and read the first record. Within the `produceReport()` module (Figure 7-26), you compare the `lineCounter` to 60. When you process the first record, the `lineCounter` is zero, so you print the record, add one to the `lineCounter`, and read the next record.

```
getReady()
     open files
     print head1
     print head2
     read custRec
return
```

Figure 7-25   getReady() module for customer report

```
produceReport()
     if lineCounter = 60 then
         perform startNewPage()
     endif
     print custLast, custFirst
     add 1 to lineCounter
     read custRec
return
```

Figure 7-26   produceReport() module for customer report program

On every cycle through the **produceReport()** module, you check the line counter to see if it is 60 yet. When the first record is written, **lineCounter** is 1. You read the second record, and if there is a second record (that is, if it is not **eof**), you return to the top of the **produceReport()** module. In that module you compare **lineCounter** to 60, print another line, and add 1 to **lineCounter**, making it equal to 2.

After 60 records read and write, **lineCounter** holds a value of 60. When you read the sixty-first record (and if it is not **eof**), you enter the **produceReport()** module for the 61st time. The answer to the question **lineCounter = 60?** is yes, and you break to perform the **startNewPage()** module. The **startNewPage()** module is a control break routine.

The **startNewPage()** module must print the headings that appear at the top of a new page, and it must also set the **lineCounter** back to zero. If you neglect to reset the **lineCounter**, its value will increase with each successive record and never be equal to 60 again. When resetting the **lineCounter** for a new page, you force execution of the **startNewPage()** module after 60 more records (120 total) print.

```
startNewPage()
    print head1
    print head2
    lineCounter = 0
return
```

Figure 7-27   startNewPage() module for customer report

The **startNewPage()** module is simpler than many control break modules because no record counters or accumulators are being maintained. In fact, the **startNewPage()** module must perform only two of the tasks you have seen required by control break routines.

- It does not perform the lower-level break, because there is none.

- It does not perform any control break processing for the previous group, because there is none.

- It does not roll up the current level totals to the next higher level, because there are no totals.

- It does not reset the current level's totals to zero, because there are no totals (other than the **lineCounter**, which is the control break field).

- It does perform control break processing for the new group by writing headings at the top of the new page.

- It does update the control break field—the line counter.

You might want to employ one little trick that you can use to remove the statements that write the headings from the getReady() module. If you initialize lineCounter to 60 when defining the variables at the beginning of the program, on the first pass through mainLoop() you can "fool" the computer into printing the first set of headings automatically. When you initialize the lineCounter to 60, you can remove the statements print head1 and print head2 from the getReady() module. With this change, when you enter the produceReport() module for the first time, lineCounter already is set to 60 and the startNewPage() module prints the headings and resets the lineCounter to zero before processing the first record from the input file.

As within control break report programs that break based on the contents of one of a record's fields, in any program that starts new pages based on a line count, you always must update the line-counting variable which causes the unusual action. Using page breaks or control breaks (or both) within reports adds a new degree of organization to your printed output and makes it easier for the user to interpret and use.

7

CHAPTER SUMMARY

◻ A control break is a temporary detour in the logic of a program; programmers refer to a program as a control break program when a change in the value of a variable initiates special actions or causes special or unusual processing to occur. To generate a control break report, your input records must be organized in sorted order based on the field that will cause the breaks.

◻ You use a control break field to hold data from a previous record. You decide when to perform a control break routine by comparing the value in the control break field to the corresponding value in the current record. At minimum, the simplest control break routines perform necessary processing for the new group and update the control break field.

◻ Sometimes you need to use control data within a control break module, such as in a heading that requires information about the next record or in a footer that requires information about the previous record. The very first heading prints separately from all the others at the beginning; the very last footer must print separately from all the others at the end.

◻ A control break report that contains and prints totals for the previous group, rolls up the current level totals to the next higher level, resets the current level's totals to zero, performs any other needed control break processing, and updates the control break field.

◻ In a program containing a multiple-level control break, the normal flow of control breaks away for special processing in response to more than just one change in condition. You should always test for a major-level break before a minor-level break, and include a call to the minor break routine within the major break module.

❑ Every time you write a program in which you need control break routines, you should check whether you need to perform each of the following tasks within the routines: Any lower-level break, any control break processing for the previous group, rolling up the current level totals to the next higher level, resetting the current level's totals to zero, any control break processing for the new group, and updating the control break field.

❑ To perform page breaks, you count the lines printed and pause to print headings when the counter reaches some predetermined value.

EXERCISES

1. What fields would you want to use as the control break fields to produce a report that lists all inventory items in a grocery store? (For example, you might choose to group items by grocery store department.) Design the print chart for the report.

2. What fields would you want to use as the control break fields to produce a report that lists all the people you know? (For example, you might choose to group friends by city of residence.) Design the print chart for the report.

3. Write the pseudocode for the employees listed by department program that is flowcharted in Figures 7-3 through 7-7 earlier in this chapter.

4. A used-car dealer keeps track of sales in the following format:

```
AUTO SALES FILE DESCRIPTION
File name: AUTO
Sorted by: Salesperson
```

FIELD DESCRIPTION	POSITIONS	DATA TYPE	DECIMALS	EXAMPLE
Salesperson	1—20	Character		Miller
Make of Car	21—30	Character		Ford
Vehicle Type	31—40	Character		Sedan
Sale Price	41—45	Numeric	0	12500

By the end of the week, a salesperson may have sold no cars, one car, or many cars. Create the logic of a program that would print one line for each salesperson with that salesperson's total sales for the week and commission earned, which is 4% of the total sales. Create the print chart, hierarchy chart, and either the flowchart or the pseudocode.

5. A community college maintains student records in the following format:

```
STUDENT FILE DESCRIPTION
File name: STUDENTS
Sorted by: Hour of first class
```

FIELD DESCRIPTION	POSITIONS	DATA TYPE	DECIMALS	EXAMPLE
Student Name	1—20	Character		Danielle Erickson
City	21—30	Character		Woodstock
Hour of First Class	31—32	Numeric	0	08
Phone Number	33—42	Numeric	0	8154379823

The records have been sorted by hour of the day. The hour of first class is a two-digit number based on a 24-hour clock (that is, a 1 p.m. first class is recorded as 13).

Create a report that students can use to organize carpools. The report lists the names and phone numbers of students from the city of Huntley. Note that some students come from cities other than Huntley; these students should not be listed on the report.

Start a new page for each hour of the day so that all students starting classes at the same hour are listed on the same page. Include the hour that each page represents in the heading for that page.

Design the print chart and hierarchy chart, and then create the flowchart or pseudocode for this program.

6. The Stanton Insurance Agency needs a report summarizing the counts of life, health, and other types of insurance policies it sells. Input records contain policy number, name of insured, policy value, and type of policy and have been sorted in alphabetical order by type of policy. At the end of the report, display a count of all the policies. Design the print chart and hierarchy chart, and then create the flow-chart or pseudocode for this program.

7. If a university is organized into colleges (such as Liberal Arts), divisions (such as Languages), and departments (such as French), what would constitute the major, intermediate, and minor control breaks in a report that prints all classes offered by the university?

8. A zoo keeps track of the expense of feeding the animals it houses. Each record holds one animal's ID number, name, species (elephant, rhinoceros, tiger, lion, and so on), zoo residence (pachyderm house, large cat house, and so on), and weekly food budget. The records take the following form:

```
ANIMAL FEED RECORDS
File name: ANIMFOOD
Sorted by: Species within house
```

FIELD DESCRIPTION	POSITIONS	DATA TYPE	DECIMALS	EXAMPLE
Animal ID	1—4	Numeric	0	4116
Animal Name	5—29	Character		Elmo
Species	30—45	Character		Elephant
House	46—55	Character		Pachyderm
Weekly Food	56—59	Numeric	0	75
Budget in Dollars				

Design a report that lists each animal's ID, name, and budgeted food amount. At the end of each species group, print a total budget for the species. At the end of each house (for example, the species lion, tiger, and leopard are all in the large cat house), print the house total. At the end of the report, print the grand total. Draw the hierarchy chart and create the flowchart or pseudocode for this problem.

9. A soft-drink manufacturer produces several flavors of drink—for example, cola, orange, and lemon. Additionally, each flavor has several versions such as regular, diet, and caffeine-free. The manufacturer operates factories in several states. Assume you have input records that list version, flavor, yearly production in gallons and state. (For example: Regular Cola 5000 Kansas.) The records have been sorted in alphabetical order by version within flavor within state. Design the report that lists each version and flavor, with minor total production figures for each flavor and major total production figures for each state. Create the hierarchy chart and flowchart or pseudocode for this program.

10. An art shop owner maintains records for each item in the shop, including the title of the work, the artist who made the item, the medium (for example, watercolor, oil, or clay), and the monetary value. The records are sorted by artist within medium. Design a report that lists all items in the store with a minor total value following each artist's work, and a major total value following each medium. Allow only 40 detail lines per page. Create the hierarchy chart and flowchart or pseudocode for this program.

ARRAYS

UNDERSTANDING ARRAYS

An **array** is a series or list of variables in computer memory, all of which have the same name but are differentiated with special numbers called **subscripts**. Whenever you require multiple storage locations for objects, you are using a real-life counterpart of a programming array. For example, if you store important papers in a series of file folders and label each folder with a consecutive letter of the alphabet, then you are using the equivalent of an array. If you store mementos in a series of stacked shoeboxes, each labeled with a year, or if you sort mail into slots, each labeled with a name, then you are also using a real-life equivalent of a programming array.

When you look down the left side of a tax table to find your income level before looking to the right to find your income tax obligation, you are using an array. Similarly, if you look down the left side of a train schedule to find your station before looking to the right to find the train's arrival time, you also are using an array.

Each of these real-life arrays helps you organize real-life objects. You *could* store all your papers or mementos in one huge cardboard box, or find your tax rate or train's arrival time if both were printed randomly in one large book. However, using an organized storage and display system makes your life easier in each case. Using a programming array will accomplish the same results for your data.

Some programmers refer to an array as a *table* or a *matrix*.

HOW ARRAYS OCCUPY COMPUTER MEMORY

When you declare an array, you declare a programming structure that contains multiple variables. Each variable within an array has the same name and the same data type and each separate array variable is one **element** of the array. Each array element occupies an area in memory next to, or contiguous to, the others as shown in Figure 8-1. You indicate the number of elements an array will hold—the **size of the array**—when you declare the array along with your other variables.

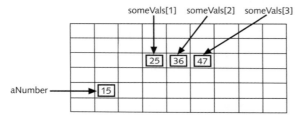

Figure 8-1   Appearance of a three-element array in computer memory

Every array element has the same group name, but also has a unique subscript indicating how far away the individual element is from the first element. Therefore any array's subscripts are always a sequence of integers such as 1 through 5 or 1 through 10. Depending on the syntax rules of the programming language you use, you place the subscript within either parentheses or square brackets following the group name; when writing pseudocode or drawing a flowchart, you can use either form of notation. This text will use square brackets to hold array element subscripts so that you don't mistake array names for method names. For example, Figure 8-1 shows how a single variable and an array are stored in computer memory. The single variable named **aNumber** holds the value 15. The array named **someVals** contains three elements, so the elements are **someVals[1]**, **someVals[2]**, and **someVals[3]**. The value stored in **someVals[1]** is 25; **someVals[2]** holds 36 and **someVals[3]** holds 47.

In general, older programming languages such as COBOL and RPG use parentheses to hold their array subscripts. Newer languages such as C#, C++, and Java use square brackets.

In some languages (for example, Java, C#, and C++) the first array element's subscript is 0; in others (for example, Visual Basic, COBOL, and RPG) it is 1. In Pascal you can identify the starting number as any value you like. In all languages, however, the subscripts must be integers (whole numbers) and sequential.

You are never required to use arrays within your programs, but learning to use arrays correctly can make many programming tasks far more efficient and professional. When you understand how to use arrays, you will be able to provide elegant solutions to problems that otherwise would require tedious programming steps.

When you describe people or events as "elegant," you mean they possess a refined gracefulness. Similarly, programmers use the term "elegant" to describe programs that are well designed and easy to understand and maintain.

MANIPULATING AN ARRAY TO REPLACE USING NESTED DECISIONS

Consider a program that keeps statistics for a recycling drive competition at a high school. The school is holding a competition between the freshman, sophomore, junior, and senior classes to see which class can collect the greatest number of aluminum cans. Each time a student brings in some cans, a clerk adds a record to a file in the following format, shown in Figure 8-2.

```
File name: STURECORDS
FIELD DESCRIPTION        POSITIONS        DATA TYPE         DECIMALS
Student class            1                Numeric           0
Cans collected           2—4              Numeric           0
```

Figure 8-2   File description for recycling records

For example, if a junior brings in 25 cans, one record is created with a 3 (for junior) in the class field and a 25 in the cans collected field. If a freshman brings in 10 cans, a record with 1 and 10 is created. If a second junior then brings in 20 more cans, the third record will contain a 3 and a 20.

At the end of the recycling competition after all the records have been collected, the file might contain hundreds of records, each holding a one-digit number representing a class and up to a three-digit number representing cans. You want to write a program that summarizes the total of the cans brought in by each class. The print chart for this report appears in Figure 8-3.

									1	1	1	1	1	1	1	1	1	1	2	2	2	2	2	2	2	2	2	2	3	3	3	3	3	3	3	3	3	3	4	4	4	4	4	4	4	4	4	4	5	5	5	5	5	5	5	5
		1	2	3	4	5	6	7	8	9	0	1	2	3	4	5	6	7	8	9	0	1	2	3	4	5	6	7	8	9	0	1	2	3	4	5	6	7	8	9	0	1	2	3	4	5	6	7	8	9	0	1	2	3	4	5	6	7
1																																																									
2			C	a	n		C	o	m	p	e	t	i	t	i	o	n		R	e	p	o	r	t																																	
3																																																									
4			C	l	a	s	s						C	a	n	s																																										
5					1								9	9	9	9	9																																									
6					2								9	9	9	9	9																																									
7					3								9	9	9	9	9																																									
8					4								9	9	9	9	9																																									

Figure 8-3   Print chart for can-recycling report

If all the records were sorted in order by the student's class, this report could be a control break report. You would simply read each record for the first (freshman) class, accumulating the number of collected cans in a variable. When you read the first record from a different class, you would print out the total for the previous class, reset the total to zero, and update the control break field before continuing.

 You learned about control break logic in Chapter 7.

Assume, however, that the records have not been sorted. Without using an array, could you write the program that would accumulate the four class can-recycling totals? Of course you could. The program would have the same mainline logic as the other programs you have seen, as flowcharted in Figure 8-4.

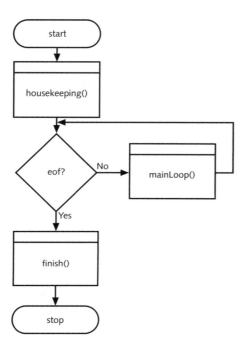

Figure 8-4   Flowchart for mainline logic of recycling program

 Later in this chapter you will see how to write the can-recycling program much more efficiently using arrays.

In the `housekeeping()` module (Figure 8-5), you declare variables including `stuClass` and `stuCans`. Then you open the files and read the first record into memory. The headings *could* print in `housekeeping()`, or, because no other printing takes place in this program until the `finish()` module, you can choose to wait and print the headings there.

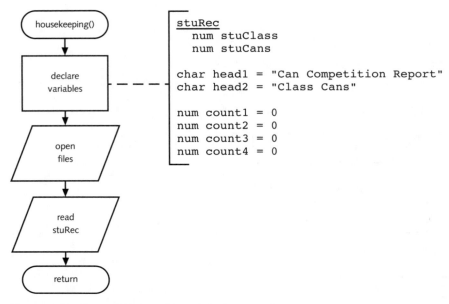

Figure 8-5   housekeeping() module for recycling program

You can use four variables, count1, count2, count3, and count4, to keep running counts of collected-can totals for the four different classes. All four of these counter variables need to be initialized to zero. You can tell by looking at the planned output that you need two heading lines, so head1 is defined as "Can Competition Report" and head2 as "Class Cans".

Eventually, four lines will be printed, each with a class number and a count of cans for that class. These lines cannot be printed until the finish() module, however, because you won't have a complete count of each class's cans until all input records have been read.

The logic within the mainLoop() module of the program requires adding a record's stuCans value to count1, count2, count3, or count4, depending on the stuClass. After one student's stuCans value has been added to one of the four accumulators you read the next record, and if it is not eof, you repeat the decision-making and accumulating process. When all records have been read you proceed to the finish() module, where you print the four summary lines with the four class counts. See Figures 8-6 and 8-7.

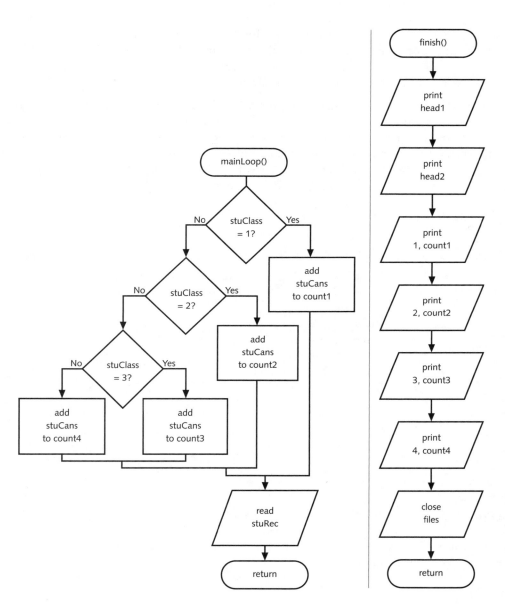

Figure 8-6   mainLoop() module for recycling program

Figure 8-7   finish() module for recycling program

The recycling program works just fine and there is absolutely nothing wrong with it logically. But what if the recycling drive is held at an elementary school with eight classes, in a school district with 12 grade levels, or in a company with 30 departments?

With any of these scenarios, the basic logic of the program would remain the same; however, you would need to declare many additional accumulator variables. You also would need many additional decisions within the **mainLoop()** module and many additional print statements within the **finish()** module in order to complete the processing.

Using an array provides an alternative approach to this programming problem, which greatly reduces the number of statements you need. When you declare an array, you provide a group name for a number of associated variables in memory. For example, the four can-collection count accumulators can be redefined as a single array named **count**. The individual elements become **count[1]**, **count[2]**, **count[3]**, and **count[4]** as shown in the new **housekeeping()** module in Figure 8-8.

Figure 8-8   Modified housekeeping() declaring count array

With the change to **housekeeping()** shown in Figure 8-8, the **mainLoop()** changes to the version shown in Figure 8-9.

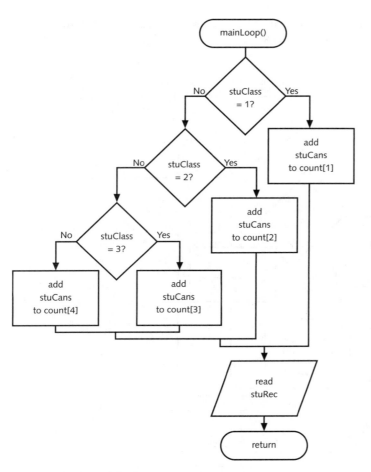

Figure 8-9   Modified mainLoop() using count array

Figure 8-9 shows that when the **stuClass** is 1, the **stuCans** are added to **count[1]**; when the **stuClass** is 4, the **stuCans** are added to **count[4]**. In other words, the value in **stuCans** is added to one of the elements of a **count** array instead of to a single variable named **count1**, **count2**, **count3**, or **count4**. Is this a big improvement over the original? Of course, it isn't. You still have not taken advantage of the benefits of using the array in this program.

The true benefit of using an array lies in your ability to use a variable as a subscript to the array rather than using a constant such as 1 or 4. Notice in the **mainLoop()** in Figure 8-9 that within each decision, the value you are comparing to **stuClass** and the constant you are using as a subscript in the resulting "Yes" process are always identical. That is, when the **stuClass** is 1, the subscript used to add **stuCans** to the **count** array is 1; when the **stuClass** is 2, the subscript used for the **count** array is 2; and so on. Therefore, why not just use `stuClass` as a subscript? You can rewrite the `mainLoop()` as shown in Figure 8-10.

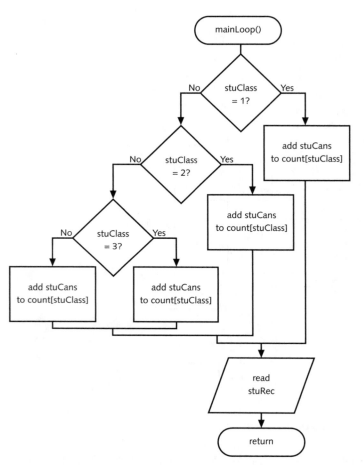

Figure 8-10   Modified mainLoop() using variable stuCans as a subscript

Of course, this flowchart segment looks no more efficient than the one in Figure 8-9. However, notice that in Figure 8-10 the process boxes after each decision are exactly the same. Each box contains `add stuCans to count[stuClass]`. If you are always going to take the same action no matter what the answer to a question is, why ask the question? Instead, you can write the `mainLoop()` module as shown in Figure 8-11.

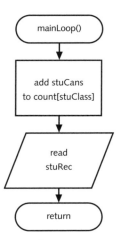

Figure 8-11   Modified mainLoop() eliminating decisions

The two steps in Figure 8-11 represent the *entire* **mainLoop()** module! When **stuClass** is 2, **stuCans** is added to **count[2]**; when **stuClass** is 4, **stuCans** is added to **count[4]**, and so on. *Now* you have a big improvement to the original **mainLoop()** from Figure 8-9. What's more, this **mainLoop()** does not change whether there are 8, 30, or any other number of classes and **count** array elements, as long as the classes are numbered sequentially. To use more than four accumulators, you would declare additional **count** elements in the **housekeeping()** module, but the **mainLoop()** logic would remain the same as it is in Figure 8-11.

The **finish()** module also can be improved. Instead of four separate print statements, you can use a variable to control a printing loop, as shown in Figure 8-12. Because the **finish()** module follows the **eof** condition, all input records have been used and **stuClass** is not currently holding any needed information. In **finish()** you can set **stuClass** to 1, then write **stuClass** and **count[stuClass]**). Then add 1 to **stuClass** and use the same set of instructions again. You can use **stuClass** as a loop control variable to print the four individual **count** values. The improvement in this **finish()** module over the one shown in Figure 8-7 is not as dramatic as the improvement in the **mainLoop()**; but in a program with more **count** elements, the only change to the **finish()** module would be in the constant value you use to control the loop. Twelve or 30 **count** values can print as easily as four if they are stored in an array.

8

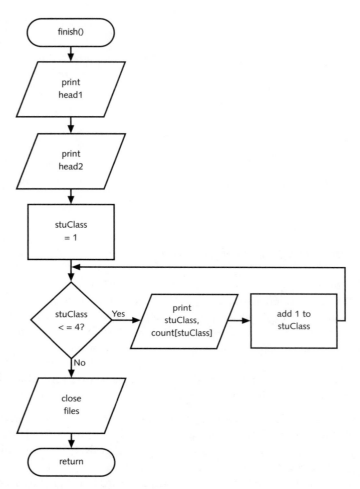

Figure 8-12   Modified `finish()` module that uses an array

Within the `finish()` module in Figure 8-12, the `stuClass` variable is handy to use as a subscript, but any variable could have been used as long as it was:

- Numeric with no decimal places

- Initialized to 1

- Incremented by 1 each time the logic passes through the loop

In other words, nothing is linking `stuClass` to the `count` array per se; within the `finish()` module you simply can use the `stuClass` variable as a subscript to indicate each successive element within the `count` array.

The can-recycling program *worked* when the `mainLoop()` contained a long series of decisions, but it is easier to write when you employ arrays. Additionally, the program is more efficient, easier for other programmers to understand, and easier to maintain. Arrays are never mandatory, but often they can drastically cut down on your programming time and make a program easier to understand.

ARRAY DECLARATION AND INITIALIZATION

In the can-recycling program, the four `count` array elements were declared and initialized to 0s in the `housekeeping()` module. The `count` values need to start at 0 so they can be added to during the course of the program. Originally (see Figure 8-8) you provided initialization in the `housekeeping()` module as:

```
num count[1] = 0
num count[2] = 0
num count[3] = 0
num count[4] = 0
```

Separately declaring and initializing each `count` element is acceptable only if there are a small number of `count`s. If the can-recycling program were updated to keep track of recycling in a company with 30 departments, you would have to initialize 30 separate fields. It would be too tedious to write 30 separate declaration statements.

Programming languages do not require the programmer to name each of the 30 `count`s: `count[1]`, `count[2]`, and so on. Instead, you can make a declaration such as one of those in Figure 8-13.

```
Declaration                           Programming Language
DIM COUNT(30)                         BASIC, Visual Basic
int count[30];                        C#, C++
int count = new int[30];              Java
COUNT OCCURS 30 TIMES PICTURE 9999.   COBOL
array count [1..30] of integer;       Pascal
```

Figure 8-13   Declaring a 30-element array named count in several common languages

 C, C++, Pascal, and Java programmers typically use lowercase variable names. COBOL, and BASIC programmers often use all uppercase. Visual Basic programmers are likely to begin with an uppercase letter.

 The terms `int` and `integer` in the code samples within Figure 8-13 both indicate that the `count` array will hold whole-number values. The value 9999 in the COBOL example indicates that each `count` will be a four-digit integer. These terms are more specific than the `num` identifier this book uses to declare all numeric variables.

All the declarations in Figure 8-13 have two things in common: They name the `count` array and indicate that there will be 30 separate numeric elements. For flowcharting or pseudocode purposes, a statement such as `num count[30]` will indicate the same thing.

Declaring a numeric array does not necessarily set its individual elements to zero (although it does in some programming languages like BASIC and Java). Most programming languages allow the equivalent of `num count[30] all set to 0`; you should use a statement like this to initialize an array in your flowcharts or pseudocode.

Alternatively, to start all array elements with the same initial value, you can use an initialization loop within the `housekeeping()` module. An **initialization loop** is a loop structure that provides initial values for every element in any array. To create an initialization loop, you must use a numeric field as a subscript. For example, if you declare a field named `sub`, and initialize `sub` to 1, then you can use a loop like the one shown in the `housekeeping()` module in Figure 8-14 to set all the array elements to zero.

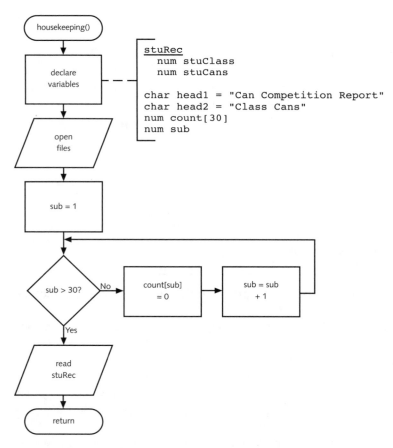

Figure 8-14   A housekeeping() module demonstrating one method of initializing array elements

RUN-TIME AND COMPILE-TIME ARRAYS

The array that you used to accumulate class counts in the can-recycling program is a **run-time array** or **execution-time array**, because the values that you want to use, the final can counts, are created during an actual run, or execution, of the program. In other words, if the freshman class is going to collect 1,000 cans, you don't know that fact at the beginning of the program. Instead, that value is accumulated during the execution of the program and not known until the end.

Some arrays are not run-time, but rather **compile-time arrays**. Recall from Chapter 1 that compiling is the act of translating a high-level language into machine code (1s and 0s). A compile-time array is one whose final desired values are fixed at the beginning of the program.

For example, let's say you own an apartment building with five floors and you have records for all your tenants with the information shown in Figure 8-15. The combination of each tenant's floor number and apartment letter provides you with a specific apartment—for example, apartment 3B.

```
File name: TENANTS
FIELD DESCRIPTION        POSITIONS       DATA TYPE       DECIMALS
Tenant name              1-40            Character
Floor number             41              Numeric         0
Apartment letter         42              Character
```

Figure 8-15   Tenant file description

Every month you print a rent bill for each tenant. Your rent charges are based on the floor of the building as shown in Figure 8-16.

```
Floor        Rent in $
1            350
2            400
3            475
4            600
5            1000 (the penthouse!)
```

Figure 8-16   Rents by floor

To create a computer program that prints each tenant's name and rent due, you could use five decisions concerning the floor number. However, it is more efficient to use a compile-time array to hold the five rent figures. The array is a compile-time array because you set its values once at the beginning of the program and they never change.

Remember that another name for an array is a *table*. If you can use paper and pencil to list the rents in a table format, using an array might be an appropriate programming option.

The mainline logic for this program is shown in Figure 8-17. The housekeeping module is named **prep()**. When you declare variables within the **prep()** module, you create an array for the five rent figures and set num **rent[1] = 350**, num **rent[2] = 400**, and so on. The rent amounts are **hard-coded** into the array; that is, they are explicitly assigned to the array elements. The **prep()** module is shown in Figure 8-18.

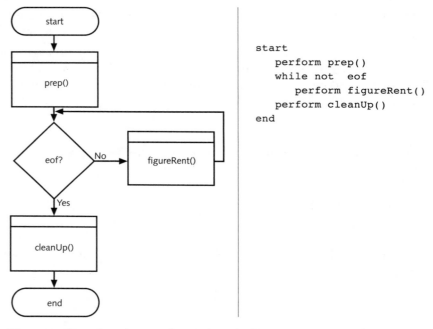

```
start
    perform prep()
    while not   eof
        perform figureRent()
    perform cleanUp()
end
```

Figure 8-17   Flowchart and pseudocode for mainline logic of rent program

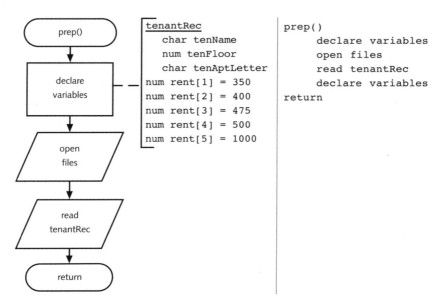

Figure 8-18 Flowchart and pseudocode for prep() module of rent program

As an alternative to defining `rent[1]`, `rent[2]`, and so on as in Figure 8-18, most programming languages allow a more concise version that takes the general form `num rent[5] = 350, 400, 475, 600, 1000`. When you use this form of array initialization, the first value you list is assigned to the first array element and the subsequent values are assigned in order. Most programming languages allow you to assign fewer values than there are array elements declared, but none allow you to assign more values.

At the end of the **prep()** module, you read a first record into memory. When it enters **figureRent()** (the main loop), you can print three items: "Dear", **tenName**, and ", Here is your monthly rent bill" (the quote begins with a comma that follows the recipient's name). Then you must print the rent amount. Instead of making a series of selections such as **if tenFloor = 1 then print rent[1]** and **if tenFloor = 2 then print rent[2]**, you want to take advantage of the **rent** array. The solution is to create a **figureRent()** module that looks like Figure 8-19. You use the **tenFloor** variable as a subscript to access the correct **rent** array element. When deciding what variable to use as a subscript with an array, ask yourself, "Of all the values available in the array, what does the correct selection depend on?" When printing a **rent** value, the rent you use depends on the floor on which the tenant lives, so the correct action is **print rent[tenFloor]**.

Every programming language provides ways to space your output for easy reading. For example, a common technique to separate "Dear" from the tenant's name is to include a space after the *r* in *Dear*, as in
`print "Dear ", tenName`.

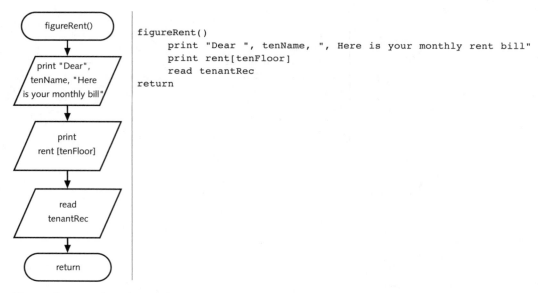

```
figureRent()
        print "Dear ", tenName, ", Here is your monthly rent bill"
        print rent[tenFloor]
        read tenantRec
return
```

Figure 8-19   Flowchart and pseudocode for the figureRent() module of the rent program

The **cleanup()** module for this program is very simple—just close the files. See Figure 8-20.

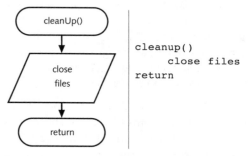

```
cleanup()
        close files
return
```

Figure 8-20   The cleanup() module for the rent program

Without a **rent** array, the **figureRent()** module would have to contain four decisions and five different resulting actions. With the **rent** array there are no decisions. Each tenant's rent is simply based on the **rent** element that corresponds to the **tenFloor** because the floor number indicates the positional value of the corresponding rent. Arrays can really lighten the load.

LOADING AN ARRAY FROM A FILE

Writing the rent program from the last section requires that you set values for five **rent** array elements within the **prep()** module. If you write the rent program for a skyscraper, you might have to initialize 100 array elements. Additionally, when the building management changes the rent amounts, you must alter the array element values within the program to reflect the new rent charges. If the rent values change frequently, it is inconvenient to have hard-coded values in your program. Instead, you can write your program so that it loads the array rent amounts from a file.

A file that contains all the rent amounts can be updated by apartment building management as frequently as needed. Suppose you receive a file named RENTFILE that always contains the current rent values. You can write the rent program so that it accepts all records from this input file within the **prep( )** module. Figure 8-21 shows how this is accomplished.

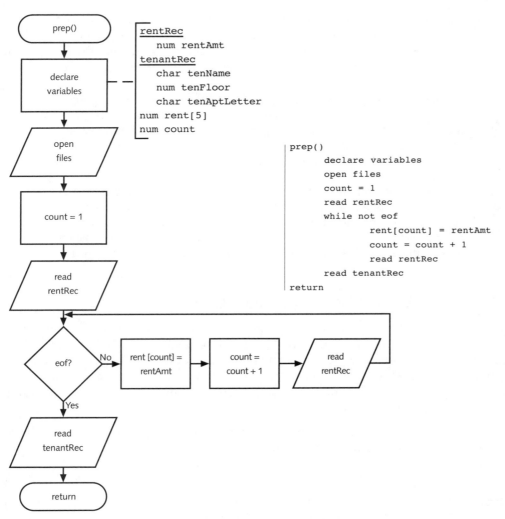

Figure 8-21   Flowchart and pseudocode for prep() module that reads rents from an
input file

In the prep( ) module in Figure 8-21, you set the variable count, to one and read a rentRec record from the RENTFILE. Each record in the RENTFILE contains just one field—a numeric rentAmt value. For this program, assume that the rent records in the RENTFILE are stored in order by floor. When you read in the first rentAmt you store it in the first element of the rent array. You increase the count to 2, read the second record, and assuming it's not eof, you store the second rent in the second element of the rent array. After the RENTFILE is exhausted you begin to read the file containing the tenantRec records, and then the program proceeds as usual.

When you use this method, reading the rents from an input file instead of hard-coding them into the program, clerical employees can update the rentRec values in the RENTFILE. Your program takes care of loading the rents into the program array from the most recent copy of the RENTFILE, assuring that each rent is always accurate and up-to-date.

Another way to organize the RENTFILE would be to include two fields within each record-for example, rentFloor and rentAmt. Then the records would not have to be read into your program in floor number order. Instead, you could use the rentFloor variable as a subscript to indicate which position in the array to use to store the rentAmt.

You might question how the program knows which file's eof condition is tested when a program uses two or more input files. In some programming languages, the eof condition is tested on the file most recently read. In many programming languages you would have to provide more specific information along with the eof question, perhaps rentRec eof? or tenantRec eof?.

SEARCHING FOR AN EXACT MATCH IN AN ARRAY

In both the can-recycling program and the rent program that you've seen in this chapter, the fields that the arrays depend on conveniently hold small whole numbers. The classes in the high school are 1 through 4 and the floors of the building are 1 through 5. Unfortunately, real life doesn't always happen in small integers. Sometimes you don't have a variable that conveniently holds an array position; sometimes you have to search through an array to find a value you need.

Consider a mail-order business in which orders come in with a customer name, address, item number ordered, and quantity ordered, as shown in Figure 8-22.

File name: CUSTREC			
FIELD DESCRIPTION	POSITIONS	DATA TYPE	DECIMALS
Customer name	1–20	Character	
Address	21–40	Character	
Item number	41–43	Numeric	0
Quantity	44–45	Numeric	0

Figure 8-22   Mail-order customer file description

The item numbers are three-digit numbers, but perhaps they are not consecutive 001 through 999. Instead, over the years items have been deleted and new items have been added. For example, there might no longer be an item with number 005 or 129. Sometimes there might be a hundred-number gap or more between items.

For example, let's say that this season you are down to the items shown in Figure 8-23.

```
ITEM NUMBER
006
008
107
405
457
688
```

Figure 8-23   Available items in mail-order company

8

When a customer orders an item you want to determine whether the customer has ordered a valid item number. You could use a series of six decisions to determine whether the ordered item is valid, but a superior approach is to create an array that holds the list of valid item numbers. Then you can search through the array for an exact match to the ordered item. If you search through the entire array without finding a match for the item the customer ordered, you can print an error message, for example "No such item."

Suppose you create an array with the six elements shown in Figure 8-24. If a customer orders item 107, a clerical worker can tell whether it is valid by looking down the list and verifying that 107 is a member of the list. In a similar fashion, you can use a loop to test each **validItem** against the ordered item number.

```
num validItem[1]  =  006
num validItem[2]  =  008
num validItem[3]  =  107
num validItem[4]  =  405
num validItem[5]  =  457
num validItem[6]  =  688
```

Figure 8-24   Array of valid item numbers

The technique for verifying that an item number exists involves setting a subscript to 1 and setting a flag variable to indicate that you have not yet determined whether the customer's order is valid. A **flag** is a variable that you set to indicate a true or false state. Typically, a variable is called a flag when its only purpose is to tell you whether some event has occurred. For example, you can set a character variable named **foundIt** to "N", indicating "No". Then you compare the customer's ordered item number to the first item in the array. If the customer-ordered item matches the first item in the array, you can set the flag variable to "Y", or any other value that is not "N". If the items do not match, you increase the subscript and continue to look down the list of numbers stored in the array. If you check all six valid item numbers and the customer item matches none of them, then the flag variable **foundIt** still holds the value "N". If the flag variable is "N" after you have looked through the entire list, you can issue an error message indicating that no match was ever found. Assuming you declare the customer item as **custItemNo** and the subscript as **x**, then Figure 8-25 shows a flowchart segment and the pseudocode that accomplishes the item verification.

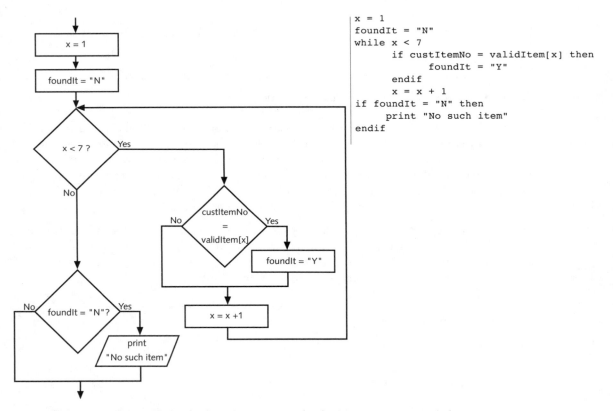

```
x = 1
foundIt = "N"
while x < 7
        if custItemNo = validItem[x] then
                foundIt = "Y"
        endif
        x = x + 1
if foundIt = "N" then
     print "No such item"
endif
```

Figure 8-25   Flowchart and pseudocode segments for finding an exact match for a customer item number

USING PARALLEL ARRAYS

In a mail-order company when you read in a customer's order, you usually want to accomplish more than to simply verify that the item exists. You want to determine the price of the ordered item, multiply that price by quantity ordered, and print a bill. Suppose you have prices for six available items as shown in Figure 8-26.

```
ITEM NUMBER          ITEM PRICE
006                      0.59
008                      0.99
107                      4.50
405                     15.99
457                     17.50
688                     39.00
```

Figure 8-26   Available items with prices for mail-order company

You *could* write a program in which you read in a customer order record and then use the customer's item number as a subscript to pull a price from an array. To use this method, you would need an array with at least 688 elements. If a customer orders item 405, the price is found at `validItem[custItemNo]`, which is `validItem[405]`, or the 405th element of the array. Such an array would need 688 elements, but because you sell only six items, you would waste 682 of the memory positions. Instead of reserving a large quantity of memory that remains unused, you can set up this program to use two arrays.

Consider the mainline logic in Figure 8-27 and the `ready()` routine in Figure 8-28. Two arrays are set up within the `ready()` module. One contains six elements named `validItem`; all six elements are valid item numbers. The other array also has six elements named `validItemPrice`; all six elements are prices. Each price in this `validItemPrice` array is conveniently in the same position as the corresponding item number in the other `validItem` array. Two corresponding arrays such as these are **parallel arrays** because each element in one array is associated with the element in the same relative position in the other array.

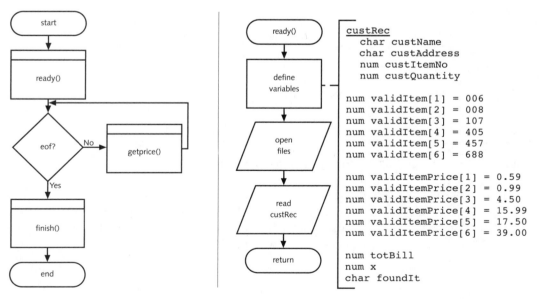

Figure 8-27   Mainline logic for price program

Figure 8-28   ready() module for price program

You can write the **getPrice()** module as shown in Figure 8-29. The general procedure is to read each item number, look through each of the **validItem** values separately, and when a match for the **custItemNo** on the input record is found, pull the corresponding parallel price out of the list of **validItemPrice**s.

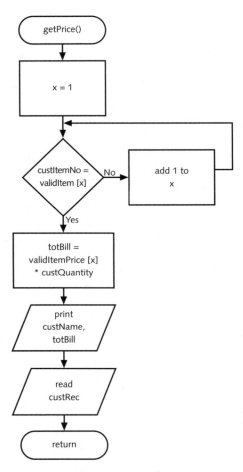

Figure 8-29   The getPrice() module for price program

You must create a variable to use as a subscript for the arrays. If you name the subscript **x**, then you can start by setting **x** equal to 1. Then if **custItemNo** is the same as **validItem[x]**, you can use the corresponding price from the other table, **validItemPrice[x]**, to calculate the customer's bill.

Some programmers object to using a cryptic variable name such as **x** because it is not descriptive. These programmers would prefer a name like **priceIndex**. Others approve of short names like **x** when the variable is used only in a limited area of a program, as it is used here, to step through an array. There are many style issues like this on which programmers disagree. As a programmer it is your responsibility to find out what conventions are used among your peers in your organization.

Within the **getPrice()** module, if **custItemNo** is *not* the same as **validItem[x]**, then add 1 to **x**. Because **x** now holds the value 2, next you compare the customer's requested item number to **validItem[2]**. The value of **x** keeps increasing, and eventually a match between **custItemNo** and some **validItem[x]** should be found.

Once you find a match for the **custItemNo** in the **validItem** array, you know that the price of that item is in the same position in the other array, **validItemPrice**. When **validItem[x]** is the correct item, **validItemPrice[x]** must be the correct price.

Suppose that a customer orders item 457 and walk through the flowchart yourself to see if you come up with the correct price.

8

REMAINING WITHIN ARRAY BOUNDS

The **getPrice()** module in Figure 8-29 is not perfect. The logic makes one dangerous assumption: that every customer will order a valid item number. If a customer is looking at an old catalog and orders item 007, the program will never find a match. The value of **x** will just continue to increase until it reaches a value higher than the number of elements in the array. At that point one of two things will happen. When you use a subscript value that is higher than the number of elements in an array, some programming languages will stop execution of the program and issue an error message. Other programming languages will not issue an error message but will continue to search through computer memory beyond the end of the array. Either way, the program doesn't end elegantly. When you use a subscript that is not within the range of acceptable subscripts, your subscript is said to be **out of bounds**. Ordering a wrong item number is a frequent error; a good program should be able to handle the mistake and not allow the subscript to go out of bounds.

You can improve the price-finding program by adding a flag variable and a test to the **getPrice()** module. You can set the flag when you find a valid item in the **validItem** array, and after searching the array, check whether the flag has been altered. See Figure 8-30.

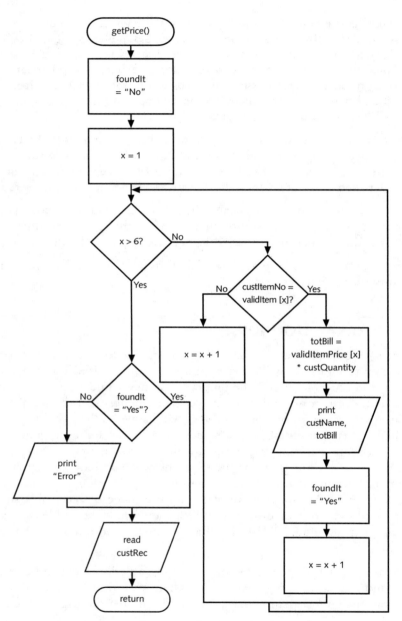

Figure 8-30   The getPrice() module using foundIt flag

In the `ready()` module, you can declare a variable named `foundIt` that acts as a flag. When you enter the `getPrice()` module you can set `foundIt` equal to "No". Then after setting `x` to 1, check to see if `x` is greater than 6 yet. If it is not, compare the `custItemNo` to `validItem[x]`. If they are equal, you know the position of the item's price and you can use the price to print the customer's bill and set the `foundIt` flag to "Yes". If the `custItemNo` is not equal to `validItem[x]`, you increase `x` by 1 and continue to search through the array. When `x` is 7, you shouldn't look through the array any more; you've gone through all six legitimate items and you've reached the end. If `foundIt` doesn't have a "Yes" in it at this point, it means you never found a match for the ordered item number; you never took the Yes path leading from the `custItemNo = validItem[x]?` question. If `foundIt` does not have "Yes" stored in it, you should print an error message; the customer has ordered a nonexistent item.

IMPROVING SEARCH EFFICIENCY USING AN EARLY EXIT

8

The mail-order program is still a little inefficient. The problem is that if lots of customers order item 006 or 008, their price is found on the first or second pass through the loop. The program continues searching through the item array, however, until `x` exceeds the value 6. To stop the search once the item has been found and `foundIt` is set to "Yes", force `x` to 7 immediately. Then, when the program loops back to check whether `x` is greater than 6 yet, the loop will be exited and the program won't bother checking any of the higher item numbers. Leaving a loop as soon as a match is found is called an **early exit**; it improves the program's efficiency. The larger the array, the more beneficial it becomes to exit the searching loop as soon as you find what you're looking for.

Figure 8-31 shows the final version of the `getPrice()` module. You search the `validItem` array, element by element. If an item number is not matched in a given location, the subscript is increased and the next location is checked. As soon as an item number is located in the array, you print a line, turn on the flag, and force the subscript to a high number (seven) so the program will not check the item number array any further.

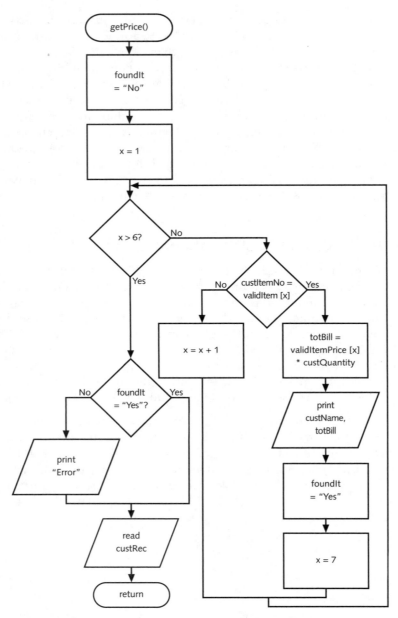

Figure 8-31 The getPrice() module with early exit

SEARCHING AN ARRAY FOR A RANGE MATCH

Customer item numbers need to match numbers in a table exactly in order to determine the correct price of an item. Sometimes, however, programmers want to work with ranges of values in arrays. A **range of values** is any set of contiguous values, for example 1 though 5.

Recall the customer file description from earlier in this chapter, shown again in Figure 8-32.

```
File name: CUSTREC
FIELD DESCRIPTION        POSITIONS        DATA TYPE        DECIMALS
Customer name            1–20             Character
Address                  21–40            Character
Item number              41–43            Numeric          0
Quantity                 44–45            Numeric          0
```

Figure 8-32   Customer file description

Suppose the company decides to offer quantity discounts as shown in Figure 8-33.

Number of items ordered	Discount %
1–9	0
10–24	10
25–48	15
49 or more	25

Figure 8-33   Discounts on orders by quantity

You want to be able to read in a record and determine a discount percentage based on the value in the quantity field. One ill-advised approach might be to set up an array with as many elements as any customer might ever order and store the appropriate discount for each possible number, as shown in Figure 8-34.

```
num discount[1] = 0
num discount[2] = 0
  .
  .
num discount[9] = 0
num discount[10] = 10
  .
  .
num discount[48] = 15
num discount[49] = 25
num discount[50] = 25
  .
  .
```

Figure 8-34   Usable—but inefficient—discount array

This approach has three drawbacks:

- It requires a very large array that uses a lot of memory.

- You must store the same value repeatedly. For example, each of the first nine elements receives the same value, zero.

- Where do you stop adding array elements? Is a customer order quantity of 75 items enough? What if a customer orders 100 or 1000 items? No matter how many elements you place in the array, there's always a chance that a customer will order more.

A better approach is to create just four discount array elements, one for each of the possible discount rates, as shown in Figure 8-35.

```
num discount[1] = 0
num discount[2] = 10
num discount[3] = 15
num discount[4] = 25
```

Figure 8-35   Superior discount array

With the new four-element `discount` array, you need a parallel array to search through to find the appropriate level for the discount. At first, beginning programmers might consider creating an array named `discountRange` and testing whether the quantity ordered equals one of the four stored values. For example:

```
num discountRange[1] = 1 through 9
num discountRange[2] = 10 through 24
num discountRange[3] = 25 through 48
num discountRange[4] = 49 and higher
```

However, you cannot create an array like the one above. Each element in any array is simply a single variable. A variable like `payRate` can hold 6 or 12, but it can't hold every value 6 *through* 12. Similarly, the `discountRange[1]` variable can hold a 1, 2, 9, or any other single value, but it can't hold 1 *through* 9; there is no such numeric value.

One solution is to create an array that holds only the low-end value of each range, as Figure 8-36 shows.

```
num discountRange[1] = 1
num discountRange[2] = 10
num discountRange[3] = 25
num discountRange[4] = 49
```

Figure 8-36   discountRange array using low end of each discount range

Now the process is to compare each `custQuantity` value with the *last* range limit (`discountRange[4]`). If the `custQuantity` is at least that value, 49, the customer gets the highest discount rate (`discount[4]`). If the `custQuantity` is not at least discountRange[4], then you check to see if it is at least discountRange[3], or 25. If so, the customer receives discount[3], and so on. If you declare a variable named rate to hold the correct discount rate, and another variable named sub to use as a subscript, then you can use the determineDiscount() module shown in Figure 8-37. This determineDiscount() module uses a loop to find the appropriate discount rate for an order, then calculates and prints a customer bill.

 An alternative approach is to store the high end of every range in an array. Then you start with the *lowest* element and check for values *less than or equal to* each array element value.

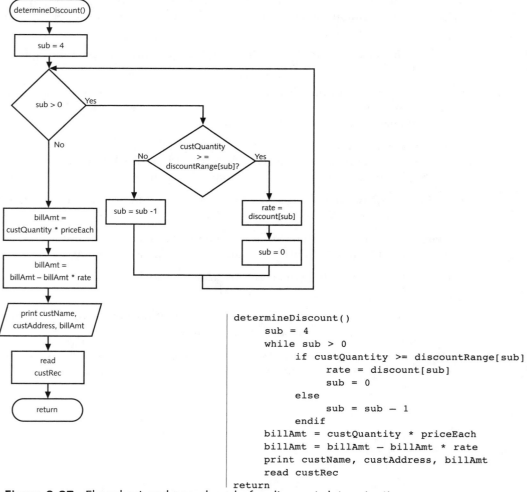

```
determineDiscount()
    sub = 4
    while sub > 0
        if custQuantity >= discountRange[sub]
            rate = discount[sub]
            sub = 0
        else
            sub = sub - 1
        endif
    billAmt = custQuantity * priceEach
    billAmt = billAmt - billAmt * rate
    print custName, custAddress, billAmt
    read custRec
return
```

Figure 8-37 Flowchart and pseudocode for discount determination

When using an array to store range limits, you use a loop to make a series of comparisons that would otherwise require many separate decisions. Your program is written using fewer instructions than would be required if you did not use an array, and modifications to your program will be easier to make in the future.

CHAPTER SUMMARY

- An array is a series or list of variables in computer memory, all of which have the same name but are differentiated with special numbers called subscripts.

- When you declare an array, you declare a programming structure that contains multiple elements, each of which has the same name and the same data type. Each array element has a unique integer subscript indicating how far away the individual element is from the first element.

- You often can use a variable as a subscript to an array, replacing multiple nested decisions.

- You can declare and initialize all of the elements in an array using a single statement that provides a type, a name, and a quantity of elements for the array. You also can initialize array values within an initialization loop.

- An array whose values are determined during the execution of a program is a runtime array, or execution-time array. An array whose final desired values are fixed at the beginning of the program is a compile-time array.

- You can load an array from a file. This step is often performed in a program's housekeeping module.

- Searching through an array to find a value you need involves initializing a subscript, using a loop to test each array element, and setting a flag when a match is found.

- In parallel arrays, each element in one array is associated with the element in the same relative position in the other array.

- Your programs should assure that subscript values do not go out of bounds, that is, take on a value out of the range of legal subscripts.

- When you need to compare a value to a range of values in an array, you can store either the low- or high-end value of each range for comparison.

EXERCISES

1. The city of Cary is holding a special census. The census takers collect one record for each citizen as follows:

```
CENSUS FILE DESCRIPTION
File name: CENSUS
Not sorted
FIELD DESCRIPTION        POSITIONS      DATA TYPE       DECIMALS
Age                      1—3            Numeric         0
Gender                   4              Character
Marital status           5              Character
Voting district          6—7            Numeric         0
```

The voting district field contains a number from 1 through 22.

Design the report, draw the hierarchy chart, and draw the logic of the program that would produce a count of the number of citizens residing in each of the 22 voting districts.

2. a. The Midville Park District maintains records containing information about players on its soccer teams. Each record contains a player's first name, last name, and team number. The teams are:

```
Soccer Teams
Team number        Team name
1                  Goal Getters
2                  The Force
3                  Top Guns
4                  Shooting Stars
5                  Midfield Monsters
```

Design the print chart, hierarchy chart, and flowchart or pseudocode for a report that lists all players along with their team numbers and team names.

   b. Create the logic for a program that produces a count of the number of players registered for each team listed in Exercise 2a.

3. a. An elementary school contains 30 classrooms numbered 1 through 30. Each classroom can contain any number of students up to 35. Each student takes an achievement test at the end of the school year and receives a score from 0 through 100. One record is created for each student in the school; each record contains a student ID, classroom number, and grade. Design the print chart, hierarchy chart, and logic for a program that lists the total points scored for each of the 30 classrooms.

   b. Modify Exercise 3a so that each classroom's average of the test scores prints rather than each classroom total.

   c. The school in Exercises 3a and 3b maintains a file containing the teacher's name for each classroom. Each record in this file contains a room number 1 through 30, and the last name of the teacher. Modify Exercise 3b so that the correct teacher's name appears on the list with his or her class's average.

8

4. A fast-food restaurant sells the following products:

```
Fast-Food Items
Product            Price
Cheeseburger       2.49
Pepsi              1.00
Chips               .59
```

Create a flowchart or pseudocode for a program that reads in a record containing a customer number and item name, then prints either the correct price or the message "Sorry, we do not carry that" as output.

5. Each week, the home office for a fast-food restaurant franchise distributes a file containing new prices for the items it carries. The file contains the item name and current price. Create a flowchart or pseudocode for a program that loads the current values into arrays. Then the program reads in a customer record containing a customer number and item name, and prints either the correct price or the message "Sorry, we do not carry that" as output.

6. The city of Redgranite is holding a special census. The census takers collect one record for each citizen as follows:

```
CENSUS FILE DESCRIPTION
File name: CENSUS
Not sorted
FIELD DESCRIPTION      POSITIONS      DATA TYPE      DECIMALS
Age                    1—3            Numeric        0
Gender                 4              Character
Marital status         5              Character
Voting district        6—7            Numeric        0
```

Design the report, draw the hierarchy chart, and draw the logic of the program that produces a count of the number of citizens residing in each of the following age groups: under 18, 18 through 30, 31 through 45, 46 through 64, and 65 and older.

7. a. A company desires a breakdown of payroll by department. Input records are as follows:

```
PAYROLL FILE DESCRIPTION
File name: PAY
FIELD DESCRIPTION      POSITIONS   DATA TYPE   DECIMALS   EXAMPLE
Employee last name     1—20        Character              Dykeman
First name             21—30       Character              Ellen
Department             31          Numeric     0          3
Hourly salary          32—36       Numeric     2          12.50
Hours worked           37—38       Numeric     0          40
```

Input records are organized in alphabetical order by employee, *not* in department number order.

The output is a list of the seven departments in the company (numbered 1 through 7) and the total gross payroll (rate times hours) for each department. Create the print layout chart, hierarchy chart, and flowchart or pseudocode for this program.

b. Modify Exercise 7a so that the report lists department names as well as numbers. The names are:

Department names and numbers

Department number	Department name
1	Personnel
2	Marketing
3	Manufacturing
4	Computer Services
5	Sales
6	Accounting
7	Shipping

c. Modify the report created in Exercise 7b so that it prints a line of information for each employee before printing the department summary at the end of the report. Each detail line must contain the employee's name, department number, department name, hourly wage, hours worked, gross pay, and withholding tax.

Withholding taxes are based on the following percentages of gross pay:

Withholding Taxes

Weekly salary	Withholding %
0.00—200.00	10
200.01—350.00	14
350.01—500.00	18
500.01—up	22

8. The Perfect Party Catering Company keeps records concerning the events it caters as follows:

EVENT RECORDS
File name: CATER

FIELD DESCRIPTION	POSITIONS	DATA TYPE	DECIMALS	EXAMPLES
Event number	1—5	Numeric	0	15621
Host name	6—25	Character		Profeta
Month	26—27	Numeric	0	10
Day	28—29	Numeric	0	15
Year	30—33	Numeric	0	2003
Meal selection	34	Numeric	0	4
Number of guests	35—40	Numeric	0	150

Additionally, a meal file contains the meal selection codes (such as 4), name of entree (such as "Roast beef"), and current price per guest (such as 19.50).

Design the print chart for a report that lists each event number, host name, date, meal, guests, gross total price for the party, and price for the party after discount. Print the month *name*—for example, "October"—rather than "10". Print the meal selection—for example, "Roast beef"—rather than "4". The gross total price for

8

the party is the price per guest for the meal, times the number of guests. The final price includes a discount based on the following table:

```
Discounts for Large Parties
Number of guests        Discount
1–25                    $0
26–50                   $75
51–100                  $125
101–250                 $200
251 and over            $300
```

Create the hierarchy chart and either the flowchart or pseudocode for this problem.

9. *Daily Life Magazine* wants an analysis of the demographic characteristics of its readers. The Marketing department has collected reader survey records in the following format:

```
MAGAZINE READER FILE DESCRIPTION
File name: MAGREADERS
Not sorted
```

FIELD DESCRIPTION	POSITIONS	DATA TYPE	DECIMALS	EXAMPLE
Age	1–3	Numeric	0	38
Gender	4	Character		F
Marital status	5	Character		M
Annual income	6–11	Numeric	0	45000

a. Create the logic for the program that would produce a count of readers by age groups as follows: under 20, 20–29, 30–39, 40–49, and 50 and older.

b. Create the logic for the program that would produce a count of readers by gender within age group—that is, under 20 females, under 20 males, and so on.

c. Create the logic for the program that would produce a count of readers by income groups as follows: under $20,000, $20,000–$24,999, $25,000–$34,999, $35,000–$49,000, and $50,000 and up.

10. Glen Ross Vacation Property Sales employs seven salespeople as follows:

Salespeople

ID Number	Name
103	Darwin
104	Kravitz
201	Shulstad
319	Fortune
367	Wickert
388	Miller
435	Vick

When a salesperson makes a sale, a record is created including the date, time, and dollar amount of the sale as follows: The time is expressed in hours and minutes, based on a 24-hour clock. The sale amount is expressed in whole dollars.

SALE Records
File name: SALES

FIELD DESCRIPTION	POSITIONS	DATA TYPE	DECIMALS	EXAMPLES
Salesperson	1–3	Numeric	0	319
Month	4–5	Numeric	0	02
Day	6–7	Numeric	0	21
Year	8–11	Numeric	0	2003
Time	12–15	Numeric	0	1315
Sale amount	16–22	Numeric	0	95900

Salespeople earn a commission that differs for each sale based on the following rate schedule:

Commission rates

Sale amount	Rate
$0–50,000	.04
$51,000–$125,000	.05
$126,000–$200,000	.06
$201,000 and up	.07

Design the print chart, hierarchy chart, and either the flowchart or pseudocode that produces each of the following reports:

a. A report listing each salesperson number, name, total sales, and total commissions.

b. A report listing each month of the year as both a number and a word (for example, "01 January"), and the total sales for the month for all salespeople.

c. A report listing total sales as well as total commissions earned by all salespeople for each of the following time frames based on hour of the day: 00–05, 06–12, 13–18, and 19–23.

8

A

A DIFFICULT STRUCTURING PROBLEM

In Chapter 2 you learned that you can solve any logical problem using only the three standard structures—sequence, selection, and looping. Often it is a simple matter to modify an unstructured program to make it adhere to structured rules. Sometimes, however, it is a challenge to structure a more complicated program. Still, no matter how complicated, large, or poorly structured a problem is, the same tasks can *always* be accomplished in a structured manner.

Consider the flowchart segment in Figure A-1. Is it structured?

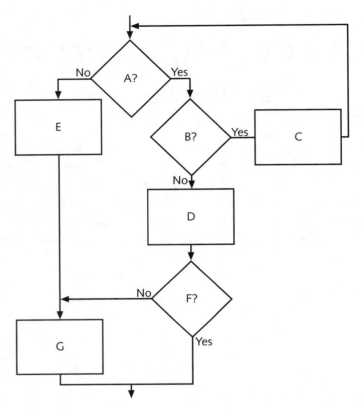

Figure A-1   Unstructured flowchart

No, it's not. Let's straighten it out. You can use the "spaghetti" method to enforce structure. Start at the beginning with the decision labeled A, shown in Figure A-2. This must represent the beginning of either a selection or a loop, because a sequence would not contain a decision.

Figure A-2   Structuring Step 1

If you follow the logic on the "No" or left side of the question, you can pull up on the left branch of the decision. You get process E, followed by G, followed by the end, as shown in Figure A-3.

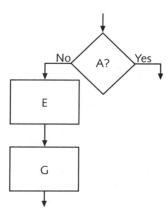

Figure A-3   Structuring Step 2

Now continue on the right or "Yes" side of decision A. When you follow the flowline, you encounter a decision symbol, labeled B. Pull on B's left side, and a process, D, comes up next. See Figure A-4.

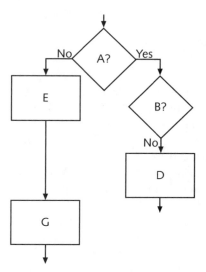

Figure A-4   Structuring Step 3

After D, a decision labeled F comes up. Pull on its left side and get a process, G, and then the end. When you pull on F's right side, you simply reach the end, as shown in Figure A-5.

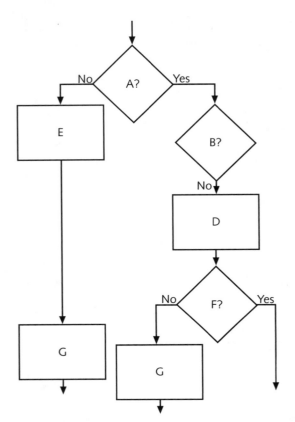

Figure A-5   Structuring Step 4

The biggest problem in structuring the original flowchart segment lies on the right side of the B decision. Pull up and get process C, as shown in Figure A-6. This looks like a loop because it doubles back on itself, up to Decision A. However, the rules of a structured loop say that it must have the appearance shown in Figure A-7: a question, followed by a structure, returning right back to the question. If the arrow coming out of C returned right to B, there would be no problem; but as it is, Question A must be repeated. The spaghetti technique says if things are tangled up, start repeating them. So bring another A decision down after C, as Figure A-6 shows.

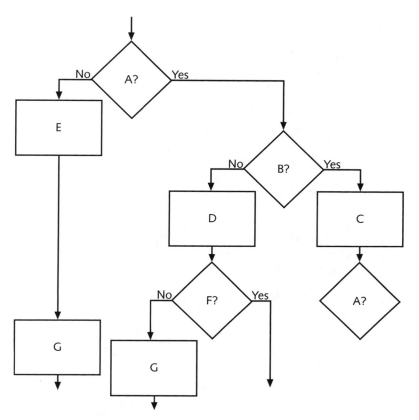

Figure A-6   Structuring Step 5

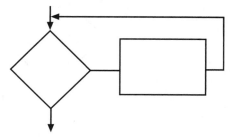

Figure A-7   A structured loop

Now, on the right side of A, B repeats. On the right side of B, C repeats. After C, A occurs. On the right side of A, B occurs. On the right side of B, C occurs. After C, A occurs again. Soon you should realize that you will repeat these same steps forever. See Figure A-8.

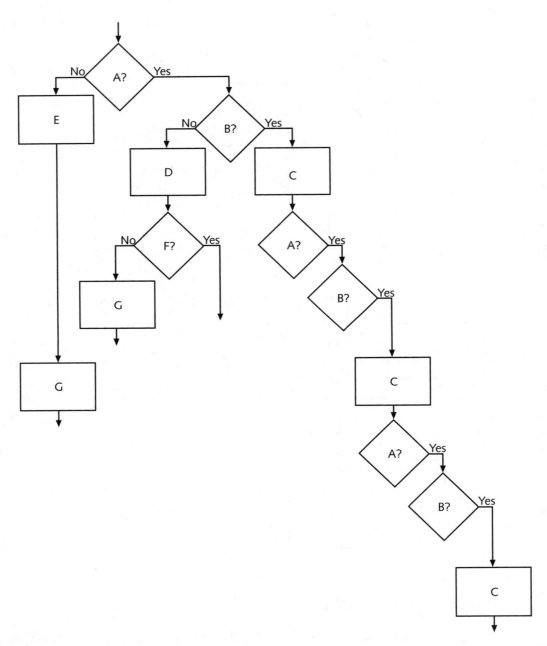

Figure A-8   Structuring Step 6

Sometimes, in order to make a program segment structured, you have to add an extra flag variable to get out of an infinite mess. A flag is a variable that you set to indicate a true or false state. Typically, a variable is called a flag when its only purpose is to tell you whether some event has occurred. You can create a flag variable named `goBackToA` and set the value of `goBackToA` to "Yes" or "No," depending on whether it is appropriate to "go back" to Step A. When A is no, the `goBackToA` flag should be set to "No" because in this situation, you never want to go back to Question A again. See Figure A-9.

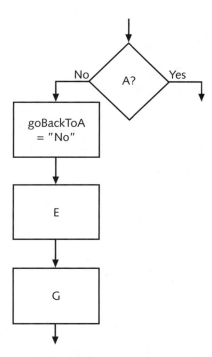

Figure A-9   Structuring Step 7

Similarly, when B is No, you never want to go back to A again, either. Figure A-10 shows that you set `goBackToA` to "No" when the answer to B is No.

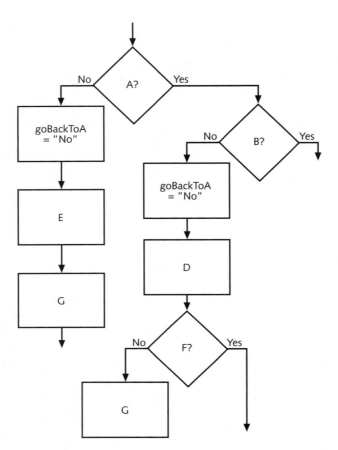

Figure A-10   Structuring Step 8

When the B decision result is Yes, however, you *do* want to go back to A. So when B is Yes, perform the process for C and set the **goBackToA** flag equal to "Yes", as shown in Figure A-11.

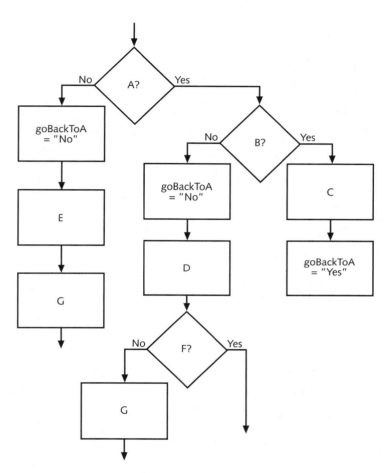

Figure A-11   Structuring Step 9

Now all paths of the flowchart can come together at the bottom with one final question: Is **goBackToA** equal to "Yes"? If it isn't, exit; but if it is, extend the flowline to go back to A. (See Figure A-12.)

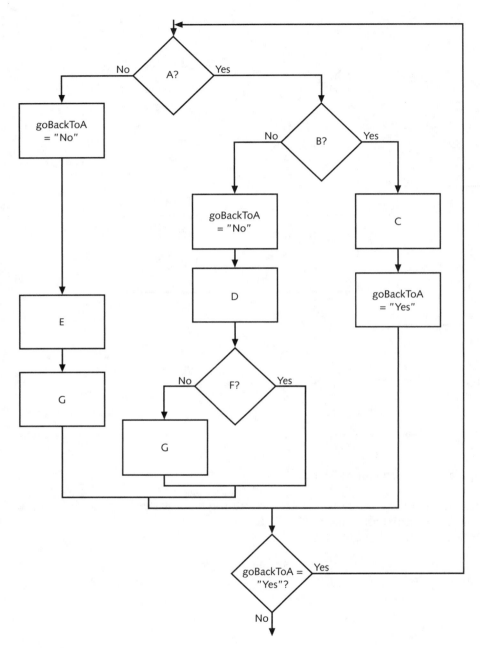

Figure A-12   Structuring Step 10

Is this flowchart segment structured now? There is so much information here that it is hard to tell. You may be able to see the structure more clearly if you create a module named `aThroughG()`. If you create the module shown in Figure A-13, then the original flowchart segment can be drawn as in Figure A-14.

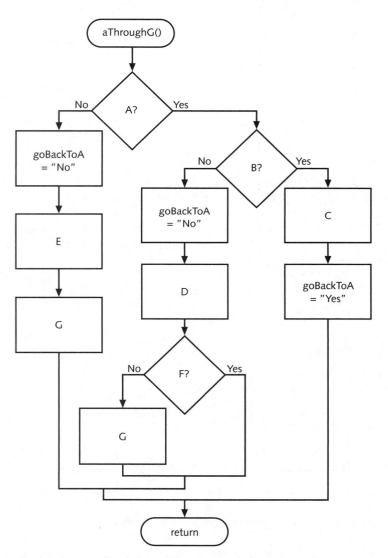

Figure A-13   The aThroughG() module

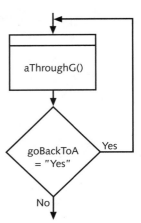

Figure A-14   Original segment using aThroughG() module and do until loop

Now you can see that the flowchart segment is a **do until** loop. If you prefer to use a **while** loop, you can redraw Figure A-14 to perform a sequence followed by a **while** loop, as shown in Figure A-15.

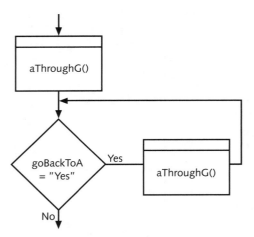

Figure A-15   Original segment using aThroughG() module and while loop

It has taken some effort, but any logical problem can be made to conform to structured rules. It may take extra steps, including using some flag variables, but every logical problem can be solved using the three structures.

B

USING A LARGE DECISION TABLE

In Chapter 5 you learned to use a simple decision table. Real-life problems often require many decisions; a complicated decision process is represented in the following situation. Suppose your employer sends you a memo outlining a year-end bonus plan with complicated rules. Appendix B will walk you through the process of solving this problem by using a large decision table.

```
To: Programming staff
From: The boss
I need a report listing every employee and the
bonus I plan to give him or her. Everybody gets
at least $100. All the employees in Department 2
get $200, unless they have more than 5 dependents.
Anybody with more than 5 dependents gets $1000
unless they're in Department 2. Nobody with an ID
number greater than 800 gets more than $100 even
if they're in Department 2 or have more than 5
dependents.
P.S. I need this by 5 o'clock.
```

Drawing the flowchart or writing the pseudocode for the `mainLoop()` for this task may seem daunting. You can use a decision table to help you manage all the decisions, and you can begin to create one by listing all the possible conditions. They are:

- empDept = 2
- empDepend > 5
- empIdNum > 800

Next, determine how many possible Boolean value combinations exist for the conditions. In this case, there are eight possible combinations, shown in Figure B-1. An employee can be in Department 2, have over five dependents, and have an ID number greater than 800. Another employee can be in Department 2, have over five dependents, but have an ID number that is 800 or less. Since each condition has two outcomes and there are three conditions, there are 2 * 2 * 2 , or eight possibilities. Four conditions would produce 16 possible outcome combinations, five would produce 32, and so on.

Condition	Outcome							
empDept = 2	T	T	T	T	F	F	F	F
empDepend > 5	T	T	F	F	T	T	F	F
empIdNum > 800	T	F	T	F	T	F	T	F

Figure B-1 Possible outcomes of bonus conditions

Next, list the possible outcome values for the bonus amounts. If you declare a numeric variable named **bonus** by placing the statement **num bonus** in your list of variables at the beginning of the program, then the possible outcomes can be expressed as:

- bonus = 100
- bonus = 200
- bonus = 1000

Finally, choose one required outcome for each possible combination of conditions, as shown in Figure B-2. Place Xs in the **bonus = 100** row each time **empIdNum > 800** is true, no matter what other conditions exist, because the memo from the boss said, "Nobody with an ID number greater than 800 gets more than $100 even if they're in Department 2 or have more than 5 dependents."

Condition	Outcome							
empDept = 2	T	T	T	T	F	F	F	F
empDepend > 5	T	T	F	F	T	T	F	F
empIdNum > 800	T	F	T	F	T	F	T	F
bonus = 100	X		X		X		X	
bonus = 200								
bonus = 1000								

Figure B-2   Decision table for bonuses, Part 1

Place an X in the **bonus = 1000** row under all remaining columns in which **empDepend > 5** is true unless the **empDept = 2** condition is true, because the memo stated, "Anybody with more than 5 dependents gets $1000 unless they're in Department 2." Only the sixth column in Figure B-3 meets these criteria.

Condition	Outcome							
empDept = 2	T	T	T	T	F	F	F	F
empDepend > 5	T	T	F	F	T	T	F	F
empIdNum > 800	T	F	T	F	T	F	T	F
bonus = 100	X		X		X		X	
bonus = 200								
bonus = 1000						X		

Figure B-3   Decision table for bonuses, Part 2

Place Xs in the **bonus** = 200 row for any remaining columns in which **empDept** = 2 is true and **empDepend** > 5 is false because "All the employees in Department 2 get $200, unless they have more than 5 dependents." Column 4 in Figure B-4 satisfies these criteria.

Condition	Outcome							
empDept = 2	T	T	T	T	F	F	F	F
empDepend > 5	T	T	F	F	T	T	F	F
empIdNum > 800	T	F	T	F	T	F	T	F
bonus = 100	X		X		X		X	
bonus = 200				X				
bonus = 1000						X		

Figure B-4   Decision table for bonuses, Part 3

Finally, fill any unmarked columns with an X in the **bonus** = 100 row because, according to the memo, "Everybody gets at least $100." The only columns remaining are the second column and the last column on the right.

Condition	Outcome							
empDept = 2	T	T	T	T	F	F	F	F
empDepend > 5	T	T	F	F	T	T	F	F
empIdNum > 800	T	F	T	F	T	F	T	F
bonus = 100	X	X	X		X		X	X
bonus = 200				X				
bonus = 1000						X		

Figure B-5   Decision table for bonuses, Part 4

The decision table is complete. When you count the Xs, you'll find there are eight possible outcomes. Take a moment and confirm that each bonus is the appropriate value based on the specifications in the original memo from the boss. Now you can start to plan the logic. If you choose to use a flowchart, you start by drawing the path to the first outcome, which occurs when **empDept** = 2, **empDepend** > 5, and **empIdNum** > 800 are all true, and which corresponds to the first column in the decision table. See Figure B-6.

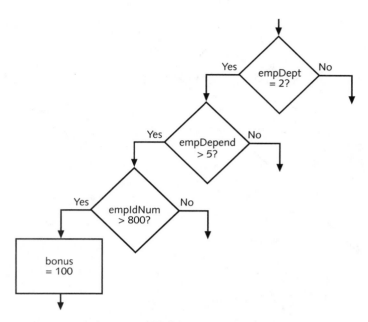

Figure B-6   Flowchart for bonus decision, Part 1

Add the "false" outcome to the **empIdNum > 800** decision, which corresponds to the second column in the decision table. See Figure B-7.

Add the "false" outcome when the **empDepend > 5** decision is No and the **empIdNum > 800** decision is Yes, which is represented by the third column in the decision table. See Figure B-8.

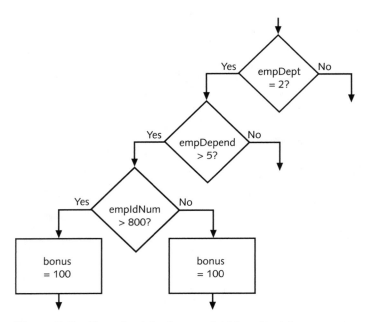

Figure B-7   Flowchart for bonus decision, Part 2

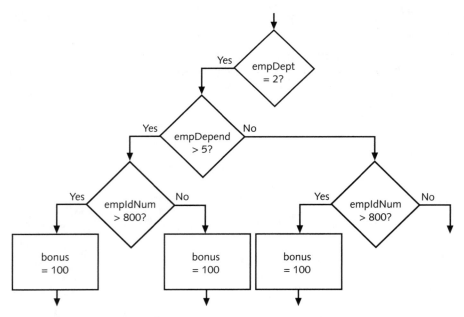

Figure B-8   Flowchart for bonus decision, Part 3

Continue until you have drawn all eight outcomes, as shown in Figure B-9.

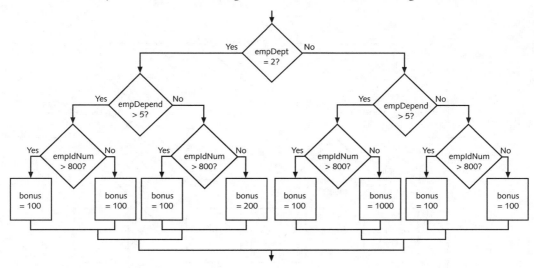

Figure B-9   Flowchart for bonus decision, Part 4

Next, eliminate any decision that doesn't make any difference. For example, if you look at the far left side of Figure B-9, you see that when `empDept` is 2 and `empDepend` is greater than 5, the outcome of `empIdNum > 800` does not matter; the `bonus` value is 100 either way. You might as well eliminate the selection. Similarly, on the far right, the question `empIdNum` makes no difference. Finally, many programmers prefer that the True or Yes side of a flowchart decision always appears on the right side. The result is Figure B-10. The pseudocode appears in Figure B-11.

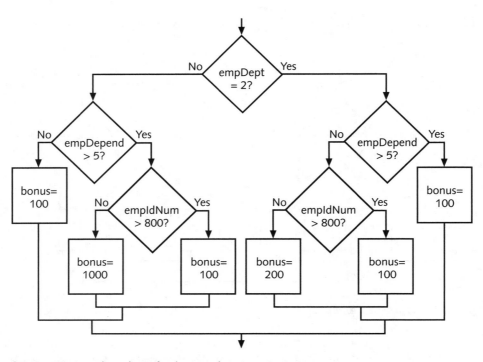

Figure B-10   Flowchart for bonus decision, Part 5

```
if empDept = 2 then
      if empDepend > 5 then
            bonus = 100
      else
            if empIdNum > 800 then
                  bonus = 100
            else
                  bonus = 200
            endif
      endif
else
      if empDepend > 5 then
            if empIdNum > 800 then
                  bonus = 100
            else
                  bonus = 1000
            endif
      else
            bonus = 100
      endif
endif
```

Figure B-11   Pseudocode for bonus decision

Index

Special Characters

& (ampersand), 126
* (asterisk), 75
$ (dollar sign), 15
" (double quotes), 23
= (equal sign), 104, 114
≠ (equal sign with a slash), 117
! (exclamation point), 117
/ (forward slash), 75
> (greater-than sign), 115, 117
- (hyphen), 15, 16
< (less-than sign), 115, 117
() (parentheses), 66
[] (square brackets), 210
_ (underscore), 15

A

abstraction
  basic description of, 62
  provision of, through modular-
    ization, 62, 65
accumulators
  accumulating totals with,
    168–172
  basic description of, 169
algebra, 21, 113
algorithms, basic description of, 6
ampersand (&), 126
AND operator, 124–127. *See also*
  AND decisions

AND decisions
  avoiding common errors and,
    125–127
  understanding, 118–122
  writing, for efficiency, 122–124
annotation
  boxes, 71, 99
  symbols, 71, 98
aNumber variable, 210
arithmetic operations, 12, 23
array(s)
  basic description of, 209–245
  bounds, remaining within, 233
  compile-time, 223–226
  declaring, 221–222
  elements of, 210
  exact matches in, searching for,
    228–230
  improving search efficiency
    and, 235–236
  initialization of, 221–222
  loading, from files, 226–228
  manipulating, to replace nested
    decisions, 211–221
  names, 210
  parallel, using, 230–231
  run-time (execution-time),
    223–226
  searching, for range matches,
    237–238
  size of, 210
ASCII (American Standard Code
  for Information Interchange), 114

assignment statements
  basic description of, 20–22
  shorthand expressions for, 20–21
asterisk (*), 75
average variable, 71
averaging program, 67–74

B

BASIC
  arrays and, 221, 222
  assignment statements and, 21
  comments and, 75
  declaring variables and, 97
  subroutines and, 61
  variable names and, 16, 71
binary operators, 115. *See also*
  comparison operators
bits, basic description of, 9
bookAuthor field, 189
bookCategory field, 189, 191,
  193, 194
bookCity field, 194, 196, 197–198
bookCity variable, 194, 195,
  197–198
bookListLoop() module, 189,
  191, 193
bookPrice field, 189, 194
bookPublisher field, 189
bookState field, 194
bookState variable, 194, 195,
  197–199

bookTitle field, 189, 194

Boole, George, 113

Boolean expressions
basic description of, 113
decision tables and, 135, 136
evaluating, 111–113
logical comparison operators and, 114
looping and, 151, 155

bounds
"out of," use of the term, 233
remaining within, 233–235

C

C (high-level language)
arrays and, 221
decisions and, 117, 126, 131
procedures and, 61

C++ (high-level language), 2, 3
arrays and, 210–211, 221
comments and, 75
data types and, 22
decisions and, 117, 126, 131
declaring variables and, 97
modules and, 66
numeric data types and, 72
procedures and, 61
variable names and, 16, 71

C# (high-level language), 2, 72
arrays and, 210–211
comments and, 75
data types and, 22
decisions and, 117, 126, 131
declaring variables and, 97
methods and, 61
modules and, 66
variable names and, 16, 71

CalculateAverage() module, 67–69

calculatedAnswer variable, 17, 20–22, 40

calculateTax() module, 74

calling (main) program, 66, 67–69

camel casing format, 16

capitalization, 16, 222

case structure, 49–51

case-sensitivity, 16, 222

categoryChange() module, 193, 194

categoryTotal variable, 191–192

CD drives. See also disk drives
categorization of, as storage devices, 3
opening files from, 99

character(s). See also symbols
basic description of, 9–10
comparing, to numbers, 114
constants, 22
data type, 22–23, 72, 83
documentation and, 83
foreign alphabet, 10
strings of, 22
variables, 22–23, 114

cityBreak() module, 196, 197, 198, 199, 201

cityCounter variable, 195

clarity, maintaining, through structures, 42

classes, basic description of, 96

cleanup() module, 226

closeDown() module, 189, 191, 193–194, 201–202

COBOL, 2, 61
arrays and, 210, 221
decisions and, 114, 115, 117, 127
declaring variables and, 95, 97
variable names and, 16, 71

code
basic description of, 7
compiling, 2, 7–8, 153
translating programming statements into, 2

comments, inserting, 75

comparison operators. See also comparisons
logical, 114–117
using equal signs in, 114

comparisons. See also comparison operators
making, 111–113
trivial, 117

compilers
basic description of, 2, 7–8
errors, 7
looping and, 153

components, understanding, 1–5

computers
micro-, 114
overview of, 1–5

conditions, 135

connector(s)
basic description of, 19
symbol, 19–20
using, 19–20

constant(s)
basic description of, 22
character, 22
creating, 22
data in reports, 77, 80–81
declaring, 97
literal, 23
names, spacing in, 77
numeric, 22

control break(s)
basic description of, 177–208
logic, understanding, 177–178

major-level, 198

minor-level, 198

modules, using control data within, 184–188

multiple-level, 194–202

performing page breaks with, 202–205

single-level, 178–184

with totals, 189–194

conversion, basic description of, 9

count1 variable, 214, 217

count2 variable, 214, 217

count3 variable, 214, 217

count4 variable, 214, 217

counters

accumulators and, comparison of, 169

basic description of, 153–154

controlling loops with, 151–156

CPUs (central processing units), 2

currentTotal variable, 114

custFirst field, 203

custLast field, 203

D

data. *See also* data types

basic description of, 2

dictionaries, 72

hierarchy, understanding, 9–11

data types

character, 22–23, 72, 83

declaring, when declaring variables, 71–73

documentation and, 83

integer, 22, 72, 222

numeric, 22–23, 71, 72, 82

testing programs with many sets of, 8–9

understanding, 22–23

databases

basic description of, 11

documentation and, 83

modularization and, 63

dayCounter variable, 167–168

decimal points, 22, 82, 220

decision(s)

AND, 118–127

avoiding common errors and, 125–127, 129

basic description of, 32

combining, 124–125, 131

double-sided, 112

making comparisons and, 111–113

nested, 117

OR, 127–131

single-sided, 112

symbols, 17

tables, 135–142

writing, for efficiency, 122–124, 130–131

declarations, 22, 71–73

decrementing, looping by, 158–159

default, use of the term, 51

detail lines, 78, 79, 105

determineDiscount() module, 239

discountRange array, 238–239

disk drives

categorization of, as storage devices, 3

data entry from, reliance on, 18–19

internal memory and, 4

opening files from, 99

do while loop. *See* do until loop

do until loop, 34, 49, 52–53, 163–166

documentation

completing, 85–86

data dictionaries in, 72

external, 75

internal, 75

input, 81–85

output, 75–81

program, 75

two categories of, 75

understanding, 75

dollar sign ($), 15

double quotes ("), 23

dummy values, 18–19

E

early exits

basic description of, 235

improving search efficiency using, 235–236

efficiency, 42, 150

search, improving, 235–236

writing AND decisions for, 122–124

writing OR decisions for, 130–131

elegant, use of the term, 211

elements, of arrays, 210

empDept variable, 132, 133, 180, 182, 183, 185, 186

empFirst variable, 180, 186

empLast variable, 180, 186

empRate variable, 127

end users

basic description of, 75

documentation and, 75, 85–86

ending programs, using sentinel values, 17–19

end-of-job routines, 92, 107

eof (end-of-file condition), 19,
39–40, 100
arrays and, 214, 219
control breaks and, 188, 204
decisions and, 120
looping and, 155
main loop and, 104, 106
equal sign (=), 104, 114
equal sign with a slash (≠), 117
equivalency, testing for, 114
errors
AND decisions and, 125–127
compiler, 7
decisions and, 125–127, 129
documentation and, 86
logical, 3, 8
exclamation point (!), 117
executing programs, basic
description of, 3
execution-time (run-time) arrays,
223–226
expressions, trivial, 114
external storage, basic description
of, 4. *See also* disk drives

F

field(s). *See also* fields (listed by
name)
basic description of, 11
choosing sentinel values for, 17
control break, 179–180
documentation and, 83
grouping, to form records, 10
in file descriptions, 84
leading zeros in, 83
looping and, 151, 153,
157–158, 167
names, 153

printing, separately, 105
updating, 183–184, 186, 202
work, 106
fields (listed by name). *See also* fields
bookAuthor field, 189
bookCategory field, 189, 191,
193, 194
bookCity field, 194, 196,
197–198
bookPrice field, 189, 194
bookPublisher field, 189
bookState field, 194
bookTitle field, 189, 194
custFirst field, 203
custLast field, 203
empMedicalIns field, 123
inlastProduction field, 157, 158,
173, 161, 165
labelsToPrint field, 157, 158,
159–160, 163, 167–168
readAddress field, 170
realPrice field, 170
rentAmt field, 228
rentFloor field, 228
figureRent() module, 225, 226
file(s)
basic description of, 10, 11
descriptions, 81–85, 91–92
grouping records to form, 10
loading arrays from, 226–228
opening, 99–100
reading, 100–103
finish() module, 179–180, 184,
187–188, 213–216, 219–220
finishUp() module, 100, 106, 107,
152–156, 163–164, 171
firstNumber variable, 71
flags, basic description of, 229

floating-point numbers, 22, 72
flowchart(s)
arrays and, 213, 224–225, 227,
239
assigning values to variables
and, 20–22
basic description of, 6, 11–15
calculating arithmetic averages
and, 67–70
control breaks and, 190–193,
199–202
decisions and, 112–115,
118–120, 124–125, 128–133,
136–141
ending programs and, 17–19
flowlines in, 12
housekeeping() module and,
98–99, 102–103
looping and, 157–158, 167, 171
mainline logic and, 93
modularization and, 66
priming read and, 38–42
representing decisions in, 17–18
spaghetti code and, 30
structures and, 30, 31–37,
43–51, 38–42
symbols, 11, 13
using connectors, 19–20
using eof markers, 19
variable names and, 16
flowlines, basic description of, 12
footers
basic description of, 185–186
writing, 186–188
for loop, 161–163
foreign alphabet characters, 10, 15
Fortran, 2
forward slash (/), 75
foundIt variable, 229–230

functionality, 65

functions, basic description of, 61–65

G

garbage
  accumulators and, 169
  basic description of, 97, 100

getFirstValue() module, 69

getInput() module, 67–69

getPrice() module, 232–236

getReady() module, 136, 203–205

grandTotal variable, 195

greater-than sign (>), 115, 117

group names, for a group of associated variables, 96

H

hard-coding, 224, 228

hardware
  basic description of, 1
  dependency of, on instructions, 2

heading(s)
  column, printing, 77
  declaring variables and, 97
  lines, 78, 79, 97–98
  printing, 100, 105

headings() module, 102–3

hierarchy charts, 73–74, 93

high-level language, basic description of, 7

hourlyWage variable, 16

housekeeping() module, 94–104, 107, 152–164, 170, 214–224
  basic description of, 92, 94–103
  arrays and, 213
  control breaks and, 179–181, 185, 188, 195
  decisions and, 119–120, 127–128
  declaring variables and, 94–99

printing headings and, 100
  reading the first input record and, 100–103

hyphen (-), 15, 16

I

IBM (International Business Machines), 4

if-then-else structure, 32–33, 112–113

inAddress variable, 153

inDailyProduction variable, 167

inDate variable, 153

indenting statements, 13, 35–36

inFirstName variable, 153, 155

initialization
  of arrays, 221–222
  of variables, 96, 151, 159–160

inLastName variable, 153

inlastProduction field, 157, 158, 173, 161, 165

inLastProduction variable, 159, 160

input operations
  basic description of, 1–3, 12
  documentation and, 85–86
  examples of, 3
  flowcharts and, 12
  object-orient programs and, 92
  opening files and, 99
  representing, with parallelograms, 12

inputNumber variable, 14–15, 17–18, 20–22, 41–52

inSalary variable, 153

inSSN variable, 153

instructions
  basic description of, 1
  logic and, 3
  writing, 5–9

integer data type, 22, 72, 222

internal storage, basic description of, 4

interpreters
  basic description of, 2, 7–8
  naming variables and, 15

invCost variable, 95, 96, 97, 99, 100, 105–6

inventoryItem variable, 23

invItemName variable, 95, 96, 97, 99, 100, 105–6

invPrice variable, 95, 96–99, 100, 105–6

invQuantity variable, 95, 96, 97, 99, 100

iterations, basic description of, 33. *See also* loop structure

J

Java, 2–3, 7
  arrays and, 210–211, 221, 222
  comments and, 75
  data types and, 22
  decisions and, 117, 114, 126, 131
  declaring variables and, 97
  methods and, 61
  modules and, 66
  numeric data types and, 72
  variable names and, 16, 71

K

keyboards, 17–19

L

labelCounter, 154–155, 158–164, 167–168

labelLine variable, 153, 155

labelsToPrint field, 157, 158, 159–160, 163, 167–168

less-than sign (<), 115, 117

line-counter variables, 203–204

logic
    connectors and, 19–20
    defined, 3
    "detangling," 45–49
    overview of, 1–5
    planning, 6
    record-reading, correct, 101
    spaghetti code and, 30
logical AND operators
    basic description of, 124
    combining decisions and,
        124–125
logical comparison operators
    basic description of, 114
    using, 114–117
logical errors. *See also* errors
    basic description of, 8
    difficulties in locating, 3
logical flow
    mainline, understanding, 91–93
    representing, with flowcharts,
        11–15
logical OR operator, 131
loop(s). *See also* loop structures
    accumulating totals with,
        168–172
    basic description of, 150
    body of, 152
    characteristics shared by all,
        165–166
    control variables, 159–160, 163
    definite, 162
    indeterminate/indefinite, 162
    infinite, 160
    main, 150
    nesting, 166–168
    unstructured, 166
loop structures, 33–34, 37, 39–42,
    44–46. *See also* loops
    advantages of, 149–150

avoiding common mistakes
    with, 159–160
basic description of, 149–176
controlling, with counters,
    152–156
with variable sentinel values,
    156–158
low-level language, basic
    description of, 7. *See also*
    machine language

M
machine language
    basic description of, 2
    modularization and, 62
    translating programs into, 7–8
Macintosh, 4
main loop
    basic description of, 104, 150
    writing, 104–6
main program, 66, 67–69
mainHeading variable, 96–99,
    102, 105
mainline logic, 91–93
mainloop() module, 100, 104–6,
    160–164, 167, 170–171, 214–221
    control breaks and, 179–182,
        187–188, 197–199
    counters and, 152–156
    how it works, 120–122
    OR decisions and, 128–131
maintenance, of structured
    programs, 42
manuals, 85–86
mathematical operations, 21–22
memory. *See also* arrays
    addresses, 21, 69
    basic description of, 4–5, 21
    declaring variables and, 94, 95
    how arrays occupy, 210–211

loading programs into, 4
main, 4
primary, 4
pseudocode and, 14
stack, 69
volatility of, 4
method(s)
    basic description of, 61–65
    names, 210
microcomputers, 114
module(s)
    advantages of, 61–65
    basic description of, 61–65
    calling other modules with,
        69–70
    creating hierarchy charts for,
        73–74
    creating, 66–69
    end of, 66
    identifying structures through,
        63–64
    naming, 66–67
    providing abstraction through, 62
    reusing your work through, 63
    structured programs and, 42–43
multiplication operation, 14
mySalary variable, 21

N
NASA (National Aeronautics and
    Space Administration), 29
nested
    decisions, 117, 122–124,
        211–221
    structures, 35, 117, 124,
        166–168
newPage() module, 182–188
NOT comparisons, 117
null case, 33

number doubling program, 11–19, 22–23, 29–31, 38–42

numeric
  constants, 22
  data type, 22–23, 71, 72, 82

O

object-oriented programming, 92, 96

oldDept variable, 180, 181, 182, 183, 184, 186

OR decisions
  avoiding common errors in, 129
  basic description of, 127–128
  combining decisions and, 131
  writing, for efficiency, 130–131

output operations
  basic description of, 1–3, 81–82
  documentation and, 85–86
  flowcharts and, 12
  representing, with parallelograms, 12

P

page
  breaks, performing, 202–205
  numbers, in reports, 79

parallelograms, 12, 99

parentheses, 66

Pascal, 2, 71
  arrays and, 211, 221
  data types and, 22
  decisions and, 117
  declaring variables and, 97
  modules and, 66
  procedures and, 61

payRate variable, 238

prep() module, 224–225, 227–228

prevCity variable, 195, 197

previousCategory variable, 191, 193

previousTotal variable, 114

prevState variable, 195, 198

priming
  read, 38–42, 101
  use of the term, 42

print charts, 76–81, 91–93, 97–98. *See also* reports
  arrays and, 211–212
  control breaks and, 178–194

printCustomerData() module, 74

printing headings, 100

printResult() module, 67–69

procedures, 45, 61–65, 92. *See also* modules

processing
  arithmetic operation statements as examples of, 12
  basic description of, 1–3, 12
  flowcharts and, 12

processRequest() module, 136, 141–142

produceReport() module, 203–204

production, putting programs into, 9

profit variable, 105, 106

programming
  basic description of, 2, 5–6
  six steps of, 5–9
  solving problems through, 5–6

programs
  ending, 17–19
  loading, into memory, 4–5
  putting, into production, 9
  running, 3

pseudocode
  arrays and, 224–225, 227, 239
  assigning values to variables and, 20–22

basic description of, 6

calculating arithmetic averages and, 67–69

control breaks and, 190–193, 199–202

decisions and, 112–113, 115, 121–122, 128, 132, 136

finishUp() module and, 107

housekeeping() module and, 102–3

inefficient, 14

looping and, 160, 167

mainline logic and, 93

mainLoop() module and, 106

statements, basic description of, 11–15

structures and, 34–37, 43, 49–53

variable names and, 16

R

range(s)
  basic description of, 237
  checks, 132–134
  matches, searching an array for, 237–238
  using selections within, 132–133

read command, 100–101

readAddress field, 170

ready() module, 231

realPrice field, 170

record(s)
  basic description of, 11
  documentation and, 83
  grouping, to form files, 10
  priming read and, 38–42
  -reading logic, correct, 101
  reading the first input, 100–103

reliability, 63

REM prefix, 75

rentAmt field, 228

rentFloor field, 228

repeat until loop, 166. *See also* do until loop

repetition, basic description of, 33. *See also* loops

report(s), 76–84, 92. *See also* print charts

  arrays and, 211–212

  control breaks and, 177–188, 202–205

  decimal points in, 82

  decisions and, 118–122

  declaring variables and, 94–99

  detail lines in, 78, 79

  footers, 185–186

  printing headings at the top of, 100

  programs, end-of-job modules for, 107

  summary, 168–169, 194–202

  total lines in, 81

reusability, 63, 65

RPG, 2, 71

  arrays and, 210–211

  comments and, 75

  decisions and, 127

  declaring variables and, 97

  subroutines and, 61

rule(s)

  for module names, 66–67

  for variable names, 15–17

run-time (execution-time) arrays, 223–226

running programs

  basic description of, 3

  documentation and, 86

S

saving programs, basic description of, 4

secondNumber variable, 71

selection structures, 36–37, 44, 48, 132–133

  basic description of, 32, 111

  dual-alternative, 112

  modularization and, 65

  single-alternative, 112

sentinel values

  basic description of, 151

  ending programs using, 17–19

  variable, looping with, 156–158

sequence structures, 37, 39, 44, 45–46

  basic description of, 32

  modularization and, 65

single-alternative ifs, 33

software

  basic description of, 1

  documentation, 75–81

  reliability of, 63

  reusable, 63

someVals array, 210

spaces

  in constant names, 77

  in files descriptions, 82

  in output, for easier reading, 225

  in variable names, 16, 71

  between words within column headings, 98

spaghetti code, 29–31, 45

square brackets ([ ]), 210

stacking structures, 34

start symbol, 13, 66

startNewPage() module, 204–205

stateBreak() module, 196, 197, 199–200

stateCounter variable, 195

statement(s)

  illegal, 21

  indenting, 13, 35–36

  priming read and, 38–42

storage operations, 1–2, 4–5, 94

string(s)

  basic description of, 22

  variables, 22, 72

structures. *See also specific types*

  basic description of, 31–37

  identifying, through modularization, 63–65

  nesting, 35, 38, 40, 43

  null case and, 33

  priming read and, 38–42

  reasons for, understanding, 42–43

  recognizing, 44–49

  spaghetti code and, 29–31

  stacking, 34, 38

  understanding, 29–59

  variable groups as, 96

stuCans variable, 213, 217

stuClass variable, 213, 214, 217–220

subroutines, 61–65, 69. *See also* modules

subscripts, basic description of, 209

summary reports, 168–169, 194–202

symbolic logic, 113

symbols. *See also* characters

  characters as, 9

  flowchart, 11

  terminal, 13

syntax
    errors, 3, 7–8
    using the correct, 7

T

tab character, 98
tables
    basic description of, 11
    decision, 135–142
tape drives. *See also* disk drives
    data entry from, reliance on,
        18–19
    opening files from, 99
taxRate variable, 22–23
tenFloor variable, 225, 226
terminals, basic description of, 13
testing
    programs, 8–9
    values by marking decisions,
        17–18
    variables, 49–51
total(s)
    accumulating totals with,
        168–172
    control breaks with, 189–194
    lines, 81
    rolling up, 193
true/false values. *See* Boolean
    expressions

U

unary selections, 112
underscore (_), 15
UNIX, 4
users
    basic description of, 75
    documentation and, 75, 85–86

V

variable(s). *See also* variables
    (listed by name)
    assigning values to, 20–22
    associated, group names for, 97
    basic description of, 15
    character, 22–23, 114
    comparing, to specific
        values, 151
    data, in report headings, 78–81
    declaring, 71–73, 94–99
    decrementing, 158–159
    distinguishing between types
        of, 22
    global, 71
    incrementing, 154
    initializing, 96, 151, 159–160
    listing, in data dictionaries, 72
    local, 71
    looping and, 151–154, 159–160
    naming, 15–17, 71–73, 233
    numeric, 22–23
    prefixes, 95, 105
    sentinel values, 156–158
    string, 22–23
    testing, 49–51
    text, 22–23
    using, 15–17
    work, 106
variables (listed by name). *See also*
    variables
    aNumber variable, 210
    average variable, 71
    bookCity variable, 194, 195,
        197–198
    bookState variable, 194, 195,
        197–199

calculatedAnswer variable, 17,
    20–22, 40
categoryTotal variable, 191–192
cityCounter variable, 195
count1 variable, 214, 217
count2 variable, 214, 217
count3 variable, 214, 217
count4 variable, 214, 217
currentTotal variable, 114
dayCounter variable, 167–168
empDept variable, 132, 133,
    180, 182, 183, 185, 186
empFirst variable, 180, 186
empLast variable, 180, 186
empRate variable, 127
firstNumber variable, 71
foundIt variable, 229–230
grandTotal variable, 195
hourlyWage variable, 16
inAddress variable, 153
inDailyProduction variable, 167
inDate variable, 153
inFirstName variable, 153, 155
inLastName variable, 153
inLastProduction variable,
    159, 160
inputNumber variable, 14–15,
    17–18, 20–22, 41–52
inSalary variable, 153
inSSN variable, 153
invCost variable, 95, 96, 97, 99,
    100, 105–6
inventoryItem variable, 23
invItemName variable, 95, 96,
    97, 99, 100, 105–6
invPrice variable, 95, 96–99,
    100, 105–6

invQuantity variable, 95, 96, 97, 99, 100

labelLine variable, 153, 155

mainHeading variable, 96–99, 102, 105

mySalary variable, 21

oldDept variable, 180, 181, 182, 183, 184, 186

payRate variable, 238

prevCity variable, 195, 197

previousCategory variable, 191, 193

previousTotal variable, 114

prevState variable, 195, 198

profit variable, 105, 106

secondNumber variable, 71

stateCounter variable, 195

stuCans variable, 213, 217

stuClass variable, 213, 214, 217–220

taxRate variable, 22–23

tenFloor variable, 225, 226

Visual Basic (Microsoft), 2, 7, 101
arrays and, 211
procedures and, 61

W

while loops, 150–152, 159–160, 165–166

word processing, 63

work
fields, 106
variables, 106

Z

zeros, leading, 82–83